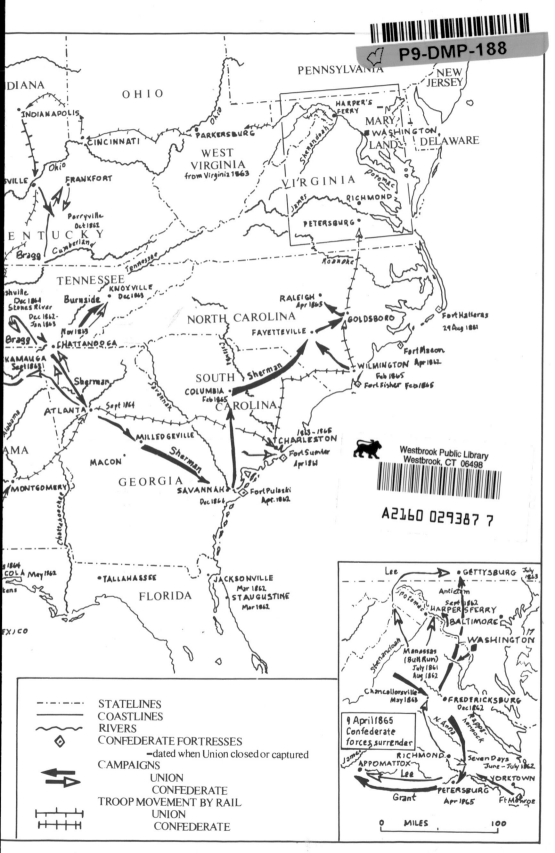

P9-DMP-188

Westbrook Public Library
Westbrook, CT 06498

A2160 029387 7

INDIANA

OHIO

PENNSYLVANIA

NEW JERSEY

INDIANAPOLIS

PARKERSBURG

CINCINNATI

HARPER'S FERRY

MARYLAND

WASHINGTON

DELAWARE

WEST VIRGINIA
from Virginia 1863

VIRGINIA

RICHMOND

*VILLE

Ohio

FRANKFORT

Perryville
Oct 1862

KENTUCKY

Bragg   Cumberland

PETERSBURG

Roanoke

Tennessee

TENNESSEE

Nashville
Dec 1864
Stones River
Dec 1862–Jan 1863

KNOXVILLE
Dec 1863

Burnside

Nov 1863

Bragg

CHATTANOOGA

RALEIGH
Apr 1865

GOLDSBORO

Fort Hatteras
29 Aug 1861

NORTH CAROLINA

FAYETTEVILLE

Fort Macon

CHICKAMAUGA
Sept 1863

Sherman

SOUTH

Sherman

WILMINGTON   Apr 1862
Feb 1865

ATLANTA   Sept 1864

COLUMBIA
Feb 1865

CAROLINA

Fort Fisher Feb 1865

ALABAMA

Savannah

MILLEDGEVILLE

1863–1865
CHARLESTON

MACON

Sherman

Fort Sumter
Apr 1861

GEORGIA

SAVANNAH
Dec 1864

Fort Pulaski
Apr. 1862

MONTGOMERY

Chattahoochee

s 1864
COLA May 1862

ens

TALLAHASSEE

JACKSONVILLE
Mar 1862
ST AUGUSTINE
Mar 1862

FLORIDA

MEXICO

Inset map

Lee   GETTYSBURG   July 1863

Antietam

Spotsylvania

Sept 1862
HARPER'S FERRY

BALTIMORE

WASHINGTON

Shenandoah

Manassas
(Bull Run)
July 1861
Aug 1862

Chancellorsville
May 1863

FREDERICKSBURG
Dec 1862

N. Anna

Rappahannock

9 April 1865
Confederate
forces surrender

RICHMOND

Seven Days
June – July 1862

James

APPOMATTOX

Lee

YORKTOWN

PETERSBURG
Apr 1865

Ft Monroe

Grant

0   MILES   100

Legend

STATELINES
COASTLINES
RIVERS
CONFEDERATE FORTRESSES
     –dated when Union closed or captured
CAMPAIGNS
     UNION
     CONFEDERATE
TROOP MOVEMENT BY RAIL
     UNION
     CONFEDERATE

SHADES OF BLUE AND GRAY

973.73   54430
HAT   Hattaway, Herman
              Shades of blue
29.95 and gray.

SEP 11 98   John Pergnton;
SEP 29 98
JUN 3 00   W8 6479
APR 17 01   Pay W8 2102
APR 17 01   W8 2102

                              54430

973.73
HAT   Hattaway, Herman
          Shades of blue and gray.

WESTBROOK PUB LIBY
GOODSPEED DR
WESTBROOK CT 06498

11/11/1997

SHADES OF BLUE AND GRAY

An Introductory Military History
of the Civil War

Herman Hattaway

UNIVERSITY OF MISSOURI PRESS

COLUMBIA AND LONDON

WESTBROOK PUBLIC LIBRARY
61 Goodspeed Drive
Westbrook, CT 06498-1998

Copyright © 1997 by
The Curators of the University of Missouri
University of Missouri Press, Columbia, Missouri 65201
Printed and bound in the United States of America
All rights reserved
5   4   3   2   1   01   00   99   98   97

Library of Congress Cataloging-in-Publication Data

Hattaway, Herman.
    Shades of blue and gray : an introductory military history of the
Civil War / Herman Hattaway.
        p.   cm.
    Includes bibliographical references (p.   ) and index.
    ISBN 0-8262-1107-0 (alk. paper)
    1. United States—History—Civil War, 1861–1865—Campaigns.
2. Military weapons—United States—History—19th century.
3. Military art and science—United States—History—19th century.
4. Strategy—History—19th century.   I. Title.
E470.H345   1997
973.7'3—DC21   97-4455
                                                                      CIP

∞ ™ This paper meets the requirements of the
American National Standard for Permanence of Paper
for Printed Library Materials, Z39.48, 1984.

Designer: Kristie Lee
Typesetter: BOOKCOMP
Printer and binder: Thomson-Shore, Inc.
Typefaces: Minion, Copperplate

TO BROOKS D. SIMPSON

In grateful appreciation for encouragement and help during an extended time when 'twas most sorely needed.

AND

to the cadets and the other military and civilian personnel with whom it was my honor and pleasure to work during that wonderful school year, 1990–1991, when it was my delight and honor to be visiting professor at the U.S. Military Academy, West Point.

CONTENTS

Preface   ix

Acknowledgments   xi

Prologue   The Dawn of Military Professionalism and an
Era of Great Technological Change   1

PART I   **Background and Opening Phases of
the American Civil War**   29

Chapter 1   Transition to Civil War   33

Chapter 2   The Fighting Begins   46

Chapter 3   The War in the West: Henry W. Halleck
and Ulysses S. Grant   61

PART II   **The War in Apparent Stalemate**   79

Chapter 4   The Peninsula Campaign   81

Chapter 5   A Rival Displaces McClellan; and a Second
Chance   91

Chapter 6   The Abortive 1862 Confederate Invasion:
Kentucky and Middle Tennessee   100

Chapter 7   The Fredericksburg Campaign: A Study in
Generalship   106

Chapter 8   The Chancellorsville Campaign   113

PART III   **The Great Turning Points**   125

Chapter 9   The Confederate "Jewels" on the Mississippi:
Vicksburg and Port Hudson   127

Chapter 10   The Gettysburg Campaign   139

Chapter 11   The "Long Pull" of the War   151

Chapter 12   Continuing Confederate Viability   164

PART IV   **Endgame Phases**   183

Chapter 13   No End in Sight: Late 1863–Early 1864   185
Chapter 14   Grant and Sherman in Grand Simultaneous
                  Advance   206
Chapter 15   The War Draws to a Conclusion   218

Epilogue   The Full Embodiment of Military
                  Professionalism   245

Glossary   265
Index   269

PREFACE

In the fall of 1960, near the end of my time as a college undergraduate, I first encountered T. Harry Williams. He changed my life. His brilliant lectures on the Civil War and his dynamic and magnetic personality drew me to him and to his field, making me want to spend my career as a historian specializing in this fascinating subject. He became my graduate major professor and directed my dissertation on the life of Confederate Gen. Stephen D. Lee.

Sometime in 1975 or 1976 I encountered Archer Jones. He changed my life almost as much as had Williams. Jones became my inspiring mentor, helping me to shape the Lee biography into the prize-winning book that it finally became, *General Stephen D. Lee* (Jackson: University of Mississippi Press, 1976), and then the two of us produced *How the North Won: A Military History of the Civil War* (Urbana: University of Illinois Press, 1983)—which I suspect is and will remain the magnum opus of my career. Subsequently, we also worked with Richard E. Beringer and William Still Jr. to write *Why the South Lost the Civil War* (Athens: University of Georgia Press, 1986; abridged as *Elements of Confederate Defeat*, 1988).

It has been a fun way to spend the past three and one-half (and still-counting) decades!

I originally envisioned this book as part of a much larger whole, a multi-authored history of the modern military art. Several of my friends, colleagues, and even a few critics, however, have persuaded me that a sufficient body of readers may find it useful, even appealing, as it is, alone. For those new to Civil War study, I hope this will be for them the "hook"—just as my relations with Williams and Jones were for me—that will give a good grounding in fundamental Civil War military history and be the guide to further reading; for those who already are my "fellow travelers," I offer this distillation of my thinking and my ideas; and for teachers and students, here is an attempt at synthesis, incorporating the important fresh work done in the past dozen or so years. I am referring to, for example, the essence of the work by Lauren Cook Burgess (on women who served as soldiers, disguised as men—over 150 specific documented cases have now been researched); Albert Castel (on the Atlanta campaign); Mark Grimsley (on "hard war"); Reid Mitchell (on the sociology of the soldiers and the nature of home-front support); and Brooks D. Simpson (on U. S. Grant.) My "suggestions for further reading" are meant to be: *stylized* by my own tastes, *limited* in scope so as not to be overwhelming for beginners (yet sufficient in scope so as not to be underwhelming, and unimpressive—as, I think, the selections all too often are in general-interest bookstores), and *varied* so as to include, for example, some good Civil War fiction. It is an unorthodox bibliography and commentary upon works all of which—for one reason or another—I have found to be instructive as well as appealing.

This book, I might dare to hope, may best be placed on the bookshelves of private libraries between Charles P. Roland's *An American Iliad: The Story of the Civil War* (New York: McGraw Hill, 1991) and Frank E. Vandiver's *Blood Brothers: A Short History of the Civil War* (College Station: Texas A&M University Press, 1992), for in many respects we three have tried to do similar things. But, as Brooks Simpson has put it, "While Roland, Vandiver, and Hattaway are in the same ballpark, perhaps even the same ball game, they definitely are playing different positions."

My main goal was to focus particularly upon certain military aspects of the American Civil War and to relate them more broadly to technological and managerial realities: to "fit" the story of the 1861–1865 conflict into the context of evolving military possibility and necessity. The nineteenth century was a time of emergent military professionalism—and the Civil War experience, perhaps paradoxically, both inhibited a normal development in this country toward incorporating that ethic within the martial structure and rendered poignant lessons that pointed to the absolute necessity of doing so thereafter.

ACKNOWLEDGMENTS

My sweet and brilliant wife, Margaret, has ever been my most precious and treasured collaborator—in all things.

Numerous persons have been kind enough to read all, or some portion, of this work in its various drafts and to give me suggestions for improvement. These folk include my previous collaborators, whose insight and judgment I value highly: Archer Jones and Richard E. Beringer. Other colleagues in the history profession who did welcome, insightful, and helpful critiques were Gary Gallagher, Richard McMurry, Richard Sommers, Dan Sutherland, Russell Weigley, and Tommy R. Young II.

Three dear friends from the Kansas City Civil War Round Table were of immense help: the late Milton Perry, who knew so much about the Civil War's "infernal machines"; retired colonel John Mahan Brooks, a collateral descendant of the famous West Point professor Dennis Hart Mahan; and my attorney, Stephen D. Treaster, who knows at least a little bit about almost everything!

Several cadets, and former cadets, of the U.S. Military Academy gave me special insights that could come from no other source. I recall with special fondness the twenty-one cadets who studied History of the Modern Military Art under my direction and the fifty-seven cadets who studied with me the Military History of the American Civil War. Detailed critiques of an earlier version of this work were prepared by Paul E. Begalka, Robert L. Bennett, Matthew Bukovac, Chris Jenks, Michael R. Spears, Anthony J. Russillio Jr., and Kevin M. Tohill.

Four students in a colloquium in military history at the University of Missouri–Kansas City suffered through a semester of agonizing work with me, during the fall of 1991, and prepared helpful formal critiques of a very early version of this book: Larry G. Gray, Travis W. Scott, James Underwood, and Rebecca Willis.

A subsequent colloquium, during the fall of 1994, did the same thing on a more mature version of the typescript. I especially thank three outstanding members of that group for tremendously insightful and helpful suggestions: Patrick Osborn, one of the best master's degree students ever; Ethan Rafuse, my outstanding doctoral student who came to me with his master's degree in hand from George Mason University and of whom I am very proud; and Dave Woodman, a devoted high school teacher for the same span of years as my university professorship and a dear friend in Boy Scouts. Other critiques, each keenly useful in one or more ways, were done by Kirk N. Brennecke, David Alan Draper, Craig B. Foster, Greg Hildreth, Joel Rhodes, Craig Smith, Robert Powl Smith, John L. Spencer III, Kimberley K. Vinalst, and Christine White. Last, Sara Lodigensky not only did an insightful critique but she also proposed what maps would be most appropriate for this book—and she drew them!

Just before the final revisions on this work were finished, a new—and obviously fine—master's degree student, Capt. Ron Machoian of the U.S. Air Force, joined my "coffle," read, and made some useful suggestions.

One more student at the University of Missouri–Kansas City, an outstanding and promising undergraduate—Diane Ferguson—who has taken several courses with me and listened attentively to many of my agonizing elaborations, suggested the title.

A number of members of the West Point History Department faculty read or discussed all or parts of the manuscript with me. I profited especially from interactions with Kenneth Hamburger, James Johnson, James Rainey, Gordon Rudd, and Dale Wilson. I should also mention my debt to Prof. Ira Gruber of Rice University—himself also a former visiting professor at West Point— who read the first three complete drafts and made many drastic suggestions. Two former faculty members of the U.S. Military Academy were also especially helpful: my first doctoral student, Mark Snell; and the most knowledgeable student of antebellum West Point, retired Col. James I. Morrison Jr. Also, I got much help, inspiration, and support from the Special Collections director at the Academy, Allan Aimone.

I owe much to Col. Robert A. Doughty, head of the U.S. Military Academy Department of History. He is indeed the gentleman and scholar that his position suggests he should be. Through his good offices I was able to become a visiting professor at West Point—one of the high points, quite possibly *the* high point, of my career.

All that remains wrong with this work, is my fault.

SHADES OF BLUE AND GRAY

The Dawn of Military Professionalism and an Era of Great Technological Change

∾

The American Civil War still, after more than a century and a quarter, elicits enormous interest from a myriad of enthusiasts—ranging from scholars to casually interested students, to hobbyists and "buffs," and to those who enjoy dressing in authentic costumes and using period equipment to "reenact." Many of the battlefields are lovingly preserved and maintained, and they attract millions of visitors year after year. The war was fought with tremendous determination and sacrifice by a great and hugely fascinating cast of characters. The mass of the participants was literate—this was the first *big* war in human history in which that was so—and therefore there is an enormous body of written records of all types. Despite the North's many obvious advantages, it was not entirely impossible that the South *might* prevail—for the weaker side does sometimes win in war.

It is useful to remember too that the nature of the Civil War was much molded and affected by its historical context— and, further, that some of what followed thereafter in military history was affected by what had happened in the Civil War. During the nineteenth century, throughout the Western world—first in Europe and subsequently in America— enormous changes occurred, and these changes had a profound impact on how warfare would be conducted. Most notable, there evolved increased division of labor. Populations also increased, continuing a trend that had commenced during the preceding century. Cities grew. Industrialism came more and more to predominate. Finally, the invention or refinement of many new machines and devices wrought a technological revolution.

Three technological developments in particular had an inestimable impact on transportation and communication—and, therefore, also on warfare. These were the steamship, the railroad, and the electric telegraph.

In 1807 the American inventor Robert Fulton produced the first commercially feasible steamboat. Subsequently, he designed seventeen other steamboats, a torpedo boat, and a ferry. He also built a steam frigate, which was launched in 1815. Later, the screw propeller—the work of a Swedish engineer, John Ericsson—provided more efficient propulsion for steamboats and also rendered war vessels less vulnerable to being disabled by damage to the large, exposed paddle wheel. Still more protection came when iron armor was added to wooden ships. The French pioneered this innovation, commencing construction in 1857 of the *Gloire*—the first of a class of vessels, wooden steam-powered warships with hulls covered by a belt of iron that was five inches thick. The British quickly followed suit, and the age of armor-clad boats had dawned.

Other inventors soon applied steam power to land transportation. In 1814 the Englishman George Stephenson developed a railway locomotive, the Rocket. Within a single generation after the Battle of Waterloo, an elaborate matrix of rail lines laced both Western Europe and the eastern United States.

On May 24, 1844, the American inventor Samuel F. B. Morse sent the first telegraphic message—"What hath God wrought?"—between Washington and Baltimore. Just sixteen years later the nation possessed transcontinental telegraphic connection.

From the military perspective, the most mind-boggling technological developments came in firepower: the variety, range, and accuracy of weapons vastly increased. The causes for these changes were the introduction of the percussion cap and the invention of a bullet that made rifle-bored shoulder weapons practicable for use by all soldiers. Early rifles were regarded as sporting or hunting firearms and not well suited to military use, except for specialty applications such as long-range sniping. The enormous and time-consuming problem of muzzle-loading a rifle with a sufficiently tight-fitting bullet was resolved during the 1840s by two French army officers. Capts. Henri-Gustave Delvigne and Claude Etienne Minié developed the hollow-base cylindro-conoidally shaped lead minié bullet (often misnomered the "minié ball"). The rifle would still be loaded from the muzzle, but the projectile could be slightly smaller than the rifle bore, hence easily rammed down the barrel. Upon firing, the bullet would expand, and the lead would grip tightly against the spiraled rifling grooves. Thus, a spin would be placed on the elongated bullet, and it would leave the muzzle at a higher velocity and follow a truer trajectory, traveling from three to four times farther than when fired from a smoothbored musket.

Warfare, like everything else in society, became much more complex. Quite suddenly it had become possible to convey armies rapidly to battlefields, to have them arrive less fatigued and better able to commence operations immediately, and to communicate with them easily, efficiently, and quickly. Very large forces, now with more lethal weaponry, could be maintained and kept concentrated for long periods of time, because they could be supplied rather than have to rely on foraging. The need for management, of a higher order, forced its way into the military equation; in response, a new form of revitalized military professionalism emerged. This professionalism evolved slowly, sometimes haltingly. It took new directions usually only after painful lessons were learned by experience.

The Emergence of Revitalized Military Professionalism

Three factors further contributed to the development of military professionalism. These were the growth of the nation-state, the rise of democratic ideals and parties, and the existence of a single recognized source of legitimate authority over the nation-state's military forces. Putting emphasis on and rewarding good performances within the officer corps, in the countries where it came—and, to be sure, this occurred in various countries at vastly different moments in time—made it possible for individual merit, rather than social or political position, to be the prime prerequisite for commissioning and for promotion.

Modern Military Professionalism Defined

Modern military professionalism came into being when military officers became professional men, distinguished from warriors of previous ages. Pioneering students of the topic, such as the renowned Samuel P. Huntington, suggest that it was a phenomenon that commenced early, and discretely, in the nineteenth century in Prussia. More recent scholarship, especially that of Russell F. Weigley, sheds light on an emerging military professionalism throughout the modern period of history. Similarly, students of American military professionalism previously focused almost exclusively on its full-blown manifestation late in the nineteenth and early in the twentieth century, while the historians Roy P. Roberts and William R. Skelton have illustrated a gradual development with deep historical roots.

The distinguishing characteristics of a profession are its knowledge, ability, responsibility, and corporateness. Professional knowledge, being intellectual in nature, can be preserved in writing. To possess it requires some knowledge of its history. It transcends a skill or craft, because it embraces a distinguishing dimension of breadth.

Military officers possess the peculiar skill of directing, operating, and controlling a human organization whose primary function is the application of violence. By definition, the military professional strives to perfect mastery in the management of violence. An individual's professional competence is measured by the size and complexity of the organizations of violence that he is capable of directing and the number of different situations and conditions with which he can cope.

The emergence of a newer form of modern military professionalism is among the most significant institutional creations of the nineteenth century. The development came forth with the evolution of five key constituent elements within the military vocation: prerequisites for becoming an officer, advancement in rank, the nature of the military educational system, the military staff system, and esprit and competence within the officer corps.

The Emergence of Modern Military Professionalism

One prominent manifestation of evolving modern military professionalism occurred in Prussia. A disaster in 1806, cataclysmic and thoroughly jolting, rendered the Prussians suddenly willing to experiment with military reform. Napoleon's well-led combat veterans scored twin victories on October 14, 1806, in the Battles of Jena and Auerstadt, and the main Prussian army disintegrated. In response, there followed a period from 1806 to 1812 of significant Prussian military reforms.

The conduct of all the higher officers during the recent war was scrutinized; some eight hundred of them were disciplined, many were dismissed, and others were demoted. Universal liability for military service became the norm. Cadet schools were established. Harsh corporal and other demeaning punishments were ameliorated; thenceforth troops would be disciplined by education and persuasion. Class preference was abolished, education declared essential, and merit proclaimed to be the main measurement of worth for retention or promotion.

Chief of Staff Gerhard Johann von Scharnhorst, assisted by August Wilhelm von Gneisenau, undertook reorganization of the army. Their institutions and ideals dominated in Prussia for the rest of the century, and their achievements furnished the model upon which all other officer corps of modern Western nations ultimately would be patterned. Insisting that ongoing education, not just at the entry level, be required, in 1810 Scharnhorst established the Kriegsakademie in Berlin, the world's first military university dedicated to the higher study of warfare.

The most revolutionary aspect of the Prussian system was its denigration of genius as an essential attribute: average men could become capable officers through superior education, organization, and experience. Most conspicuously visible, however, was the overhaul of the general staff. The new general staff of the army would have four sections. One was for strategy and tactics, one was for matters of internal administration, one was for reinforcements, and one was for artillery and munitions.

The culmination of the Prussian reforms soon became manifest in a dramatic reversal of Prussia's previous humiliation by France. In 1812 Napoleon invaded Russia. The Prussians joined the Russians in 1813, and soon the Austrians also commenced a war against France. Prussia managed to send 280,000 men into the field—some 6 percent of its total population. To support so ambitious a mobilization would have been impossible without the prior managerial achievements of the reformers. The most notable feature of the ensuing campaign was excellence in staff work. The resulting conclusion came on October 16, 1813, with Napoleon's spectacular defeat at Leipzig.

During the aftermath of the Napoleonic Wars, most Western nations established military schools and, at least to some extent, democratized their officer corps. Another Prussian, Karl von Clausewitz—in his lectures at the Kriegsakademie and in his posthumous 1833 publication of the three-volume book *On War* (Vom Kriege)—provided the theoretical rationale for the new profession. Clausewitz was unique in his grasp and articulation of the essence of how warfare had been transformed.

Not until much later in the century, however, would the English-speaking peoples appreciate the Prussian achievement, for *On War* was not translated into English until 1873. The Americans long continued to look to France for military example. Thus, Antoine Henri, Baron de Jomini, and not Clausewitz, became the principal interpreter of Napoleonic strategy to Americans. As the military scholar Archer Jones has shown, however, this was not as bad as has been implied by numerous military historians, because Clausewitz and Jomini were not as diametrically different as had been assumed. The earlier historians, unlike Jones, had not actually read very much of the writings either by Clausewitz or by Jomini!

The real problem was that rather few American officers read much either, and worse, the relatively few American officers who did read any of Jomini's work tended to misunderstand it, because they wrongly concluded that he advocated a place-oriented strategy. Too, as the brilliant young historian Mark Grimsley recently pointed out: "Many American officers . . . missed one critical element of Napoleonic warfare. . . . [T]he success of Napoleonic armies ultimately depended on their ability to derive sustenance from the countryside through which they passed. Hence the burden they placed on civilians in their path was far from light." The will of a populace to sustain a war is crucial in modern times.

Military education continued to grow in significance. The French founded the Ecole Polytechnique in 1794. The British established the Royal Military College in 1799. In 1802 the United States founded the U.S. Military Academy at West Point. Even more important was the later implementation of institutions for advanced study of warfare.

A few Americans early in the nineteenth century inclined toward military professionalism, most notably Alexander Hamilton and John C. Calhoun, whose ideas were implemented only in minor part. West Point, for example, as established at its outset, was only one-fifth of the military university that Hamilton had envisioned; he had hoped that it would also include a matrix of postgraduate and professional schools to which officers would return for more advanced studies at various intervals in their careers. Later, when Calhoun tried to restructure the military along Hamiltonian lines, he was stymied. Calhoun did, however, establish the U.S. General Staff—not a true general staff on the Prussian model but at least a rudimentary beginning of bureau management, staff planning, and facilitation in logistics.

Significant Improvements at the U.S. Military Academy

The poor performance of the army in the War of 1812 sobered the thinking of President James Madison, and in 1815—for the first time—he separated the positions of chief of engineers and superintendent of the Academy, thus making it possible for the superintendent to truly and fully concentrate on his tasks at the Academy. Thirty-year-old Capt. Alden Partridge became the first superintendent.

During his tenure, from 1815 to 1817, Partridge effected some crucial improvements. He imposed discipline and order. Believing that music would improve drill and raise morale, he induced the War Department to station a band at West Point. He was keenly interested in the history of past campaigns, and he captivated cadets with his stories. He designed the "Cadet Gray" uniforms, the color still worn today (a color later alleged to have been selected to honor Winfield Scott's men at the Battle of Chippewa; actually it probably was a happy accident: George S. Pappas in *To the Point,* offers evidence that the reason was simply that gray cloth was cheap). Partridge also established the first set of specific requirements for graduation.

On July 17, 1817, President James Monroe named a new superintendent, thirty-two-year-old Bvt. Maj. Sylvanus Thayer. The greatest changes of all at the Academy were to come under Thayer's direction, and during his sixteen-year tenure as superintendent, from 1817 to 1833, he earned the title "Father of West Point." Thayer had been fascinated with things military since his childhood, and he practically worshiped Napoleon. In 1807 Thayer graduated with highest honors from Dartmouth and then matriculated at West Point, where in one year he qualified for graduation and a commission. He performed well in field assignments during the War of 1812. In 1815 the government dispatched him to Europe, where he spent nearly a year in study and in purchasing European books on the art of war for the Academy. Early in 1816 he was given the opportunity to observe the operation of France's Ecole Polytechnique for several months.

Singularly dedicated to the soldierly life, so serious that many people thought him humorless, always neat and orderly in his person, Thayer's unfailing punctuality became legendary. He came to know every cadet personally. He worked sensitively with his faculty, probed deeply about all that they did, and sought their suggestions for improvements. Thayer prescribed stringent changes. In short order he dismissed hopelessly deficient cadets. He forbade cadets to leave the post without his permission, as theretofore they had done freely. He forbade them to bring or receive any money from home so that all had to live on the same amount, the standard government pay scale for cadets. He instituted a summer training encampment, organized the corps structure and created the cadet ranks, carefully laid out the prescribed four-year curriculum, and established the system of merit and demerit rating. The hallmark of the

Thayer academic system became thoroughly practical instruction, in small classes, with every cadet being required to recite every day. Thayer created the position of commandant of cadets, the officer in charge of tactical training and discipline. Soon Thayer added assistants to the commandant, junior officers who lived in the cadet barracks to provide continual close supervision.

West Point became the nation's foremost engineering school, indeed its only one of any note, until the introduction of engineering at Rensselaer Polytechnic Institute in 1828. Graduates made tremendous and varied contributions in supervising all manner of engineering projects, including canals, railroads, public buildings, and elaborate seacoast fortifications. Engineering remained preeminent, and purely military subjects were taught only as a brief afterthought. Not until 1858 did Congress create a Department of Tactics at the Academy.

Nevertheless, Dennis Hart Mahan (an 1824 graduate who returned in 1830 to commence a forty-year teaching career at West Point) infused a concept of military science into the engineering-oriented course work. His greatest contribution was his stress on the lessons to be learned from history. Most crucial, Mahan perceived that strategy involved certain fundamental and unvarying principles, while tactics did not. He taught that history was *essential* to mastering strategy, but it had no relevance at all to tactics.

One of Mahan's best students was Henry Wager Halleck, who in 1846 published the brilliant lecture series *Elements of Military Art and Science,* a virtually complete exposition of the professional military construct. Halleck had a somewhat caricatural persona, and many persons either disliked him or held him in ridicule. He was, however, truly what his nickname, "Old Brains," implied: *quite* brainy! His contributions to the American military establishment were enormous.

Thus "Thayer's men," the 606 who graduated during his tenure as superintendent, and "the Long Gray Line" that followed, reflected creditably in their careers upon the positive benefits produced by the Thayer system. Many Americans nevertheless continued to assert that professional military training was not really necessary. In the United States many political elements feared and distrusted military professionals, and a majority of American statesmen were determined to put *primary* reliance on a militia system.

Good performances by the West Point men in the Second Seminole War, and more spectacularly in the Mexican War, shielded the Academy from an extended series of political attacks that were unleashed upon it. The Academy came under severe attack during the period when Andrew Jackson was president, from 1829 to 1837, and subsequently while members of the political party he nurtured continued in prominence and power. It is a complicated story. Jackson himself once called West Point "the best school in the world," but he came to intensely dislike John C. Calhoun, who was a friend of Thayer, which had much to do with Jackson ordering the replacement of Thayer as superintendent. The deeper problem sprang from the contempt displayed by Academy men for the militia, an institution that Jacksonians loved, they being outspoken proponents of the "common man."

The Pre–Civil War Era

Two wars provided combat experience for many of the American soldiers who would later find themselves involved in the Civil War: the Second Seminole War (1835–1842) and the Mexican War (1846–1848). A third conflict, the Crimean War (1853–1855), which was of more interest globally, offered significant examples concerning the realities of new approaches to warfare that modernity and evolving technology would necessitate. Few Americans, however, perceived these at the time.

The Second Seminole War

The United States fought three wars against the Seminole Indians (the first, from 1817 to 1818; the second, from 1835 to 1842; and the third, from 1857 to 1858), with the primary aim of forcing the Seminoles to move to new homes away from white settlement. Only the second war—a dreary, long, ongoing series of nondescript clashes—is of serious military interest. Climate, geography, and a difficult supply situation made things hard for the American soldiers. Men sometimes remained wet for months at a time, sleeping in their clothes and boots. While none of the American generals were graduates of West Point, the vast majority of the company-grade and field-grade Regular Army officers had attended the U.S. Military Academy.

When the Seminoles could be brought to pitched battle, the Americans tended to prevail. Interestingly, almost all the Seminoles were armed with rifles, modern small-bore Spanish weapons manufactured in Cuba. While rapidity of fire for the Seminoles was impossible, their weapons offered much greater accuracy. However, the Seminoles tended, in their haste when reloading after a first volley, to use insufficient powder. So, following what might be a prodigious opening salvo, their fire was impotent: once, a soldier was hit in the forehead but only knocked out. On another occasion, when Gen. Edmund P. Gaines was hit in the mouth, he just spat out a couple of teeth and was otherwise unhurt. One participant claimed that Seminole fire was not dangerous beyond twenty yards, and he had seen it miss at four.

The Seminoles never fared well under prolonged siege operations, and they tended to ignore night security; but they were quite elusive and relied heavily on terror tactics, which proved effective. As John K. Mahon, the eminent master of the topic, concluded, "to have subdued them in one campaign would have required tactics totally different from any then-standard American technique: small parties of rangers, living off the land, operating separately yet in touch with each other."

Innovation was required. It came, but only to a scanty extent. One regiment experimented with using rifles; another dabbled with deception and surprise. Bloodhounds were briefly used to help track the Seminoles, but the experiment proved too controversial to continue. The most noteworthy achievement was that of Bvt. Maj. Gen. Thomas S. Jesup, who oversaw the development of a new and lighter field ration: a day's allowance of food that weighed no more than three-quarters of a pound. It was Jesup, too, who brought about the war's end, for all practical purposes. But he resorted to the unethical technique of treachery by violating truces and taking Seminoles captive who had come in to talk. The lid was at last placed on the war by Col. William Jenkins Worth's relentless employment of troops as partisan combatants, campaigning even through the sickly season. Worth proclaimed the war to be over on August 14, 1842, after the capture and incarceration of the Seminole chief, Osceola.

Most of the Seminoles were forcibly removed to Arkansas and subsequently to Oklahoma (3,824 total by the end of 1843), but a remnant eluded capture and remained in Florida, withdrawing into the Everglades after the war. The number of that remnant was reduced to fewer than one hundred as a result of the Third Seminole War in the 1850s. They refrained from contact with whites until the 1880s when their isolation at last began to erode.

The impact of the Second Seminole War on the Regular Army was significant. Seventy-four commissioned officers were killed. Those who survived gained important experience, which they would apply in future conflicts. Most notable of these included the two top American commanders in the Mexican War, Winfield Scott and Zachary Taylor. Virtually all of the officer veterans who were still alive served in the Mexican War when it commenced four years later. And when the Civil War started, numerous Second Seminole War veterans would attain appointments to high command: William S. Harney, Samuel P.

Heintzelman, Joseph Hooker, George Gordon Meade, Edward O. C. Ord, William T. Sherman, and George H. Thomas for the Union; Braxton Bragg, Joseph E. Johnston, and John C. Pemberton for the Confederacy (as well as Gabriel J. Rains, who invented the antipersonnel mine).

The Second Seminole War illustrated several lessons. These included the importance of mobility and supply—sometimes troops needed to be able to carry everything they needed on their backs. And the conflict amply showed much about guerrilla—that is to say, partisan-style—warfare. The army was forced to allow a handful of unconquered Seminoles to remain in Florida—a clear example of the potency of this kind of combat, if an enemy is sufficiently determined and dedicated.

The casualties were high. But less than one-quarter of the Regular Army's losses were due to wounds sustained in battle; disease was the greatest killer. Disease, too, was by far the principal cause for losses among the approximately 30,000 citizen soldiers who mustered at one time or another for short periods of duty. Only 55 militiamen were killed in action (contrasting with the 328 Regular Army deaths from combat wounds), though this illustrates neither their better luck nor their superior ability but rather their tendency to quail in the face of danger, to break and run. Regular Army officers were quite correct in their critical assessments that militia units were undisciplined and unreliable.

The Condition and Structure of the U.S. Army

During these years, pursuing a career as an officer in the U.S. Army brought much disappointment and frustration. The army was small, occasionally varying from a total strength of fewer than seven thousand to as many as twelve thousand, with more than one hundred different posts being manned; therefore it was necessarily an institution of small, widely dispersed units. Because in essence there was no retirement system, officers tended to stay on active duty until they died, and promotions for younger officers might be excruciatingly slow in coming. In 1835 the adjutant general estimated that the average twenty-one-year-old West Point graduate after eight years as a brevet second lieutenant and second lieutenant, ten years as a first lieutenant, twenty years as a captain, ten years as a major, and ten years as a lieutenant colonel, if he managed to live, would finally reach the grade of colonel and the command of a regiment at the age of seventy-nine.

In an attempt to remedy the problem of inadequate career incentives, as well as to make the nation's military forces more efficiently and effectively able to transform a small peacetime establishment into a much larger wartime one, John C. Calhoun when he was secretary of war (from 1817 to 1825) propounded a concept called "the expansible Army." According to this idea, large numbers of units would be organized, though maintained at low levels of strength. The commissioned and noncommissioned slots would be filled, while many of the lower enlisted positions remained vacant until some emergency called for numbers of additional recruits to fill up the ranks. The plan offered obvious advantages, but because it would make peacetime military expenditures rise significantly it was never possible to pass it in Congress.

As late as 1846 the majority of the Regular Army forces continued to be armed with smoothbored, muzzle-loading flintlock muskets, though over time design was improved. The arsenal at Harpers Ferry turned out new models in 1816 and 1822, and in 1840 the U.S. Army Ordnance Department commenced production of still another type of flintlock musket. In 1842 the army adopted a new standard shoulder weapon: the U.S. Model 1842 Springfield Percussion Musket. Although still a muzzle-loading smoothbore musket that fired a spherical projectile, it offered tremendous improvement in reliability. Only a limited number of them, however, were produced and put into service during the Mexican War.

In 1841, just prior to the appearance of the minié bullet, a company owned by Eli Whitney Jr., son of the famous inventor, began production of a percussion rifle. Whitney coped with the loading problem by using spherical bullets smaller than the bore, with the shooter wrapping each round with a poplin patch.

At the outset of the Mexican War, a number of the West Pointers who had previously resigned their commissions returned to the army. One of them, Jefferson Davis, who left a seat in the U.S. House of Representatives to serve as colonel of a regiment of Mississippi Mounted Volunteers, managed to arrange for his unit to have the new "Whitney Percussion Rifles."

In use, these rifles proved to be superior in every way to smoothbore pieces, so the army adopted them, the last of its round ball–firing shoulder weapons, and officially designated them the U.S. Model 1841 Mississippi Rifle. The Mississippi Rifle still had a rather short range and had very poor accuracy at four hundred yards, but at one hundred yards it offered vastly superior performance over smoothbore pieces, consistently shooting groups of rounds into ten-inch target patterns.

The Mexican War

The Mexican War presented challenges of unprecedented proportions to American military men. It was a bigger and more complicated affair than any they had previously experienced. The general officers, as before, were men of long service but had no formal professional training. The total number of volunteers mustered for duty slightly surpassed 75,500; they were invariably in all-volunteer units that selected their own officers, usually by election. After twelve months in service each volunteer could choose to be discharged; most did.

The major campaigns of the war would be, as it turned out, commanded by two very interesting and contrasting individuals: Zachary Taylor and Winfield Scott. Scott believed, much more than Taylor, in the value of formal military schooling and relied heavily on the services provided by the talented West Pointers (many of them by now in field-grade ranks) with whom he liked to surround himself. Taylor, "Old Rough and Ready," was a more simplistic man and had a disdain for West Pointers and little interest in training or staff work. In many respects Scott transcended into a military professional (at least a budding one), while Taylor did not.

Many thousands of short-term volunteers joined Taylor's army for his ultimately successful Monterrey campaign. Huge numbers of the men fell sick, and nearly all of them displayed a lack of discipline and inadequacy of training. Logistic deficiencies continually vexed the American staff officers. Another difficulty was exacerbated by the militantly Protestant religious attitudes espoused by the mass of volunteers. Thinly veiled and thoroughly hostile manifestations of anti-Catholicism—which was rampant in America at that time—sorely upset the inhabitants of so starkly a Roman Catholic country as Mexico and nearly turned the conflict into a holy war. The most notable of the measures taken to counteract this hostility included the securing of Roman Catholic chaplains to accompany the American columns.

President James K. Polk's administration had no clear strategy beyond supporting Taylor and spurring rebellious events in California. Polk gradually crystallized his thinking. Wishing to acquire greater New Mexico as well as Texas and California, he decided to send expeditions to seize the principal settlements in the desired area and then whatever Taylor held below the Rio Grande could be used as a lever at the peace table to induce Mexico to capitulate. All of this was accomplished, but without bringing the expected results. Worse, as far as the Democratic Polk administration was concerned, Taylor—a Whig—was becoming not only a war hero but also a future candidate for president. Hence, the decision was made to reduce Taylor's army in favor of a large expedition to take the capital city and force Mexico into submission. Unhappily for Polk, there was no suitable Democratic general available to command the expedition, so the job fell to the general in chief, Winfield Scott. He too was a Whig, but he was not believed to have presidential ambitions nor serious chances even if he did.

General Scott did not attach any further significance to Taylor retaining the territory he had occupied, but Taylor had other cravings, and his acting upon them resulted in the Battle of Buena Vista on February 23, 1847. Mexican Gen. Antonio Lopez de Santa Anna's men unleashed an all-out attack on the American left. The defenders reeled backward. The left wing was smashed. Many Indiana volunteers began to flee in terror toward Buena Vista. At 9:00 A.M. Taylor's whole army was threatened with disaster. At this critical moment Taylor himself rushed to the scene, accompanied by his reserves, and he ordered the Mississippi Mounted Volunteers to advance. Col. Jefferson Davis conducted them forward in column, and then they redeployed into line, holding their fire until the foe came well within range of their Whitney Rifles. Davis's men then opened a terrifically accurate and devastating fire. It was a supreme moment of glory for Davis (who received a painful wound in his right foot but refused to retire from the field).

Shortly after noon Santa Anna attempted another grand assault on the American left. This time he hoped to get around to the rear and seize the Saltillo Road and perhaps then be able to snatch the wagon train parked at Buena Vista. This led to some of the bloodiest fighting of the day. Again Jefferson Davis played a key role: gathering all the Indianans who remained, and a couple of artillery pieces, he formed them with his regiment into a V-shaped line. The Mexicans were allowed to advance into this open-faced triangular-shaped position— some as close as sixty yards. At this range the Whitney Percussion Rifles proved to be deadly accurate. The fire withered the Mexican charge.

One more memorable episode at Buena Vista, an American attack followed by a Mexican countercharge, produced a moment that became legendary. About 4:00 P.M., Taylor attempted to seize the initiative and ordered a forward thrust. Three American regiments were quickly cut up. Santa Anna then tried a last and desperate assault, this time against the American center. Massed American artillery tore gaping holes in the Mexican lines. At a critical moment Capt. Braxton Bragg arrived at a threatened sector with his battery. Bragg's guns were loaded with canister, and Taylor shouted to him: "Double-shot your guns and give 'em hell, Bragg!" (Melodrama altered the truth; it came later to be recounted as "A little more grape, Captain Bragg.") Bragg's first salvo ripped into and slowed the Mexican line. The second and third drove it back, ending the fighting. In late October, Taylor departed to await political developments and his nomination to run for the presidency.

As for Davis, he returned home from the Mexican War a wounded hero. His combat record, West Point education, and seven-year career in the Regular Army all combined with his political prominence to propel him into the position of secretary of war during Franklin Pierce's 1853–1857 administration. Davis subsequently assumed the chairmanship of the Senate Committee on Military Affairs and membership on the Board of Visitors at West Point. In truth Davis did know a great deal about things military, but later his Civil War–time critics—led by the bitter and acerbic Richmond newspaper editor and historian Edward A. Pollard—asserted that he had learned enough about war in a few minutes at Buena Vista to defeat the Confederacy and that perhaps the epitaph of the would-be Southern nation should be "died of a V."

The final great extended phase of the war was Scott's campaign to Mexico City. Scott derived much benefit from his brilliant array of young professionally trained subordinates—especially Capt. Robert E. Lee and Lt. Pierre G. T. Beauregard. Thus, at the first notable battle, Cerro Gordo on April 18, 1847, Lieutenant Beauregard provided useful reconnaissance; and in the battle, to the tremendous surprise of the Mexicans, Scott's men attacked from both front and rear. Thousands of Mexicans fled in confusion, with 199 officers and 2,837 enlisted men falling prisoner, and huge amounts of material, including Santa Anna's personal effects—even his wooden leg—were taken. The Illinois troops who found the artificial leg took it home with them and for years thereafter it was on display at their state capitol.

The American army moved to Jalapa, and there Scott wrestled with a grave problem: the term of enlistment for his twelve-month volunteers was due to expire in six weeks. In vain, Scott passionately attempted to persuade them to remain in service. Fewer than 10 percent agreed to continue; Scott dispatched the rest home. By the end of May, Scott relocated his headquarters to Puebla, and there he spent ten dismal weeks during which morale plummeted. But through it all the army persevered, Scott and the Regulars rigorously trained the remaining volunteers, and at last reinforcements arrived. On August 7 Scott's army set out on the final part of its march; their destination was Mexico City, seventy-five miles west.

Time after time Santa Anna mistakenly assumed that the Americans would assault his force frontally; but Scott consistently managed to do the unexpected.

First, Santa Anna felt sure that the Americans would assault at El Penon, a hill commanding the National Road. The American engineers, however, discovered a muddy route south of Lakes Chalco and Xichimilco along the base of the mountains that would lead them to San Augustin. On August 17, making a flanking movement, one of the most important maneuvers of the entire war, William J. Worth's division swung around and took San Augustin easily.

Again the American engineers made reconnaissances, this time west toward Contreras, across a lava bed called the Pedregal. They returned, assuring the troops that it was possible to cut a road through the rocky field. Five hundred men, superintended by Capt. R. E. Lee, worked to create a road, even while harassed by enemy fire. When the commander at Contreras was informed what was happening, he replied, "No! No! You're dreaming, man. The birds couldn't cross that Pedregal." The Americans attacked first from the front and then from behind. Within five minutes the Mexicans broke and ran in utmost confusion. In this Battle of Contreras, one of the most decisive of the campaign, the Americans lost only 60 men killed or wounded, while they inflicted a toll of about 700 enemy killed, took 843 men prisoner, and captured twenty-two pieces of artillery. And so, onward to the end of the campaign, the Americans always prevailed.

The Castle of Chapultepec became the next major objective. Guns at that castle, where a Mexican military school was located, swept both routes that led into Mexico City. From the early morning on September 12, a daylong bombardment pounded the castle. At 5:30 A.M. on September 13 the bombardment recommenced, and at 8:00 A.M. the Americans assaulted. During the bitter struggle, the Americans made a number of appalling blunders, such as failing to have scaling ladders in the proper place at the proper time, but the battle concluded ninety minutes later, with the Americans victorious. When Santa Anna saw the American flag that soon fluttered over the castle, he exclaimed, "I believe if we were to plant our batteries in Hell the damned Yankees would take them from us." Another officer shook his head and sighed, "God is a Yankee."

The city surrendered on September 14. Although guerrilla and irregular warfare long persisted, in essence the war was over. The Treaty of Guadalupe Hidalgo was signed on February 2, 1848, and ratified by the U.S. Senate on March 10, 1848, wherein the United States gained ownership of the vast Mexican Cession territory and in turn compensated Mexico somewhat for her financial losses.

Scott's campaign to Mexico City stands as a brilliant accomplishment. In 1860 Scott asserted in congressional testimony that the services of the young officers who had learned the techniques of war at the U.S. Military Academy had been crucial: "I give it as my fixed opinion, that but for our graduated cadets, the war between the United States and Mexico might have lasted some four or five years, with, in its first half, more defeats than victories falling to our share." It was a fine testimonial to emergent professionalism. In the broader world, too, events soon heralded the necessity for a higher level of military professionalism.

The Crimean War

The war in the Crimea was the first big war waged by mostly rifle-armed combatants on both sides. It was also the first major conflict covered by newspaper correspondents, including William Howard Russell, whose dispatches to the *Times* (London) are classic. They went instantaneously, via the Mediterranean underwater cable, to London. Too, it was the first much photographed war. And this war was the first one in which women established their position as army nurses. The English nurse, hospital reformer, and philanthropist Florence Nightingale took thirty-eight nurses to Scutari in 1854 and organized a barrack hospital, where they introduced sanitation and lessened the severity of countless cases of typhus, cholera, and dysentery.

The war, which initially pitched Russia against Turkey, was officially declared by the sultan on October 4, 1853, but on March 28, 1854, France and Britain also declared war on Russia. Setting sail on September 7, 1854, the allied armies invaded Russia, landing unopposed on September 14 at Eupatoria, on the Crimean peninsula, the scene of all the important fighting.

The allies achieved victory in the first big clash, which culminated in the Battle of the Alma on September 20, 1854, but not without the troops suffering considerable hardship. From the outset things went awry when no tents were disembarked for the British landing forces, who were not at all ready for the harsh realities they now faced.

Furthermore, the British officers were not well prepared, and there was no service corps or any full-time staff. Fitzroy James Henry Somerset, First Baron Raglan, was in command. Sixty-seven years old, he had never commanded even a company of troops. He was thoroughly inadequate for his job, as were most of his principal subordinates, who, like him, were superannuated.

The celebrated Minié Rifle had for several years been manufactured by license in England, but it had only recently been issued to the combat troops. Only a scant few of the men had them by the start of the war; and for almost four months after the landing a good many of the British soldiers had nothing better than a Brown Bess—a truly antiquated weapon that one soldier said was "about as useless as a broom stick."

The allies—twenty-seven thousand British, twenty-five thousand French, and some eight thousand Turks—did rather little at first, except to drink and wish that unveiled women might be found nearer than Bucharest, though one anxious pasha complained that "the veils of our women fall lower every day." The British looked at their friends in amazement and perhaps envy, for initially the Frenchmen and the Turks were in better shape equipment-wise. Each Frenchman landed with a third section of the famous *tentes à abri* (Civil War–era Americans—who eventually used similar versions of these tents—called this type of shelter "dog tents," and smaller versions [made up of halves rather than thirds] were used by succeeding generations who called them "pup tents"). The Turks had large bell-shaped tents, and all possessed plenty of equipage.

The allied commanders learned that the Russians were established on the heights above the Alma River, and rather slapdash plans were soon made to assault. Fortunately for the allies, the Russian leaders proved even more inept. The Russians were best prepared to face an enemy that fought in column as the Russians themselves did—not a rifle-armed foe that deployed in line formation. Nearly all the Russian regular infantry were armed with smoothbore muzzle-loading muskets that had only recently been converted from flintlocks to percussion firing mechanisms. (Much effort was soon made to procure and issue rifles, and many—but not all—of the Russian smoothbores were replaced.)

In the battle, the French rifle fire proved murderous. The Russian troops were then withdrawn to the formidable defensive emplacements around Sevastopol, and the allies laid siege. The first bombardments occurred October 17–19, 1854. The Russian entrenchments and fortifications were under the general direction of Col. E. I. Totleben, one of the most insightful and able military engineers of the day, then in his fullest vigor of body and mind. In an attempt to break the initial investment, the Russians fought two spectacular offensive battles: Balaklava (on October 25, 1854) and Inkerman (on November 5, 1854).

The Battle of Balaklava is interesting primarily because of the epic quality imparted to it, by its actual reality, and by the unreality injected into its mythic image by Alfred, Lord Tennyson's famous poem "The Charge of the Light Brigade." The battle was fought, not as Tennyson described it, in a "valley of death," but rather on a plain above the city of Balaklava. The battle is also interesting because of the long-range accuracy achieved by some shooters on both sides.

The famous charge occurred because of a confusion in orders and because of misunderstood command-intent. The Russians had captured a British fort and were engaged in hauling away the fort's guns. Raglan wanted to prevent the guns from being taken. But he had not meant for the Light Brigade of Cavalry— between six and seven hundred horsemen—to assault, as they did, headlong into an obviously formidable twelve-piece enemy artillery emplacement.

Fire came from both sides of the plain, from massed Russian infantry recently armed with Minié Rifles, and frontally from the twelve guns as the attackers approached. But the important thing to note, and perhaps too-often unnoticed, is that the guns *were* taken! Unsupported, or not closely defended, artillery *is* ultimately vulnerable to attack.

After the Battle of Balaklava, the primary task of besieging Sevastopol was entrusted to a siege corps comprised of 18,500 French and 16,500 British soldiers. Other allied troops, some 23,000 men, formed a corps of observation facing east to guard the long allied right flank. The investment was not absolute, however, so the Russians could still move troops in and out by boat. Menshikov, a Russian general, had a total of 107,000 men, many of them freshly arrived, allowing him to enjoy a 30 percent numerical superiority, and he was stronger than the allies in artillery.

The Russians tried to dislodge the besiegers with a series of attacks, collectively known as "Little Inkerman" and "Inkerman," on November 5, 1854. When the big battle erupted, it came suddenly—quite unlike most great battles in modern fluid campaigns—with no warning at all and with little or no advance preparation. Not a single British staff officer recognized anything unusual, despite the obvious much increased activity within the Russian camps.

In the first phase of the battle, between 5:45 and 7:50 A.M., the Russians pressed hard, enjoying an initial advantage in firepower, not only because they were more numerous but also because they had been issued plugs to keep the night rain out of their gun barrels. The British had no plugs, and many of their pieces could not be fired until after a time-consuming drying. Then the fog lifted, making it easier for the Russians to advance on the very unfamiliar ground. The British riflemen, their pieces activated at last, well exploited the terrain—not only the elevation but also the brushwood that many of them found cover behind.

Overall, some fifteen thousand assaulting Russians were repulsed by less than one-fourth of their number. How could this happen? It was caused first by the Russians attacking in the open and moving uphill, against a rifle-armed enemy that enjoyed relative cover and concealment, and second by the density of the formations the Russians inflexibly employed. The mass of these Russians *still* lacked rifles, while the British riflemen not only poured forth a murderous fire from much longer range but also, owing to the density of the attack formations, many British bullets passed through more than one Russian's body!

All of the ensuing periods of the battle were sanguinary, some rather more so than others, and occasionally there was intense hand-to-hand fighting and horrifying massacre. But, always, the end results affirmed and reaffirmed the utter stalemate. The deadlock continued for many more months.

The winter of 1854–1855 was especially hard on all the combatants. The season commenced rather precipitously with a violent hurricane on November 14. At the close of the storm, the evening brought snow. During the ensuing weeks and months, the grossly ill-equipped British, ill-served by incompetent logisticians, chronically suffered from scanty diet and even shortages of fuel for cooking—despite the well-stocked stores at Balaklava, which could not now be accessed because of inadequate transportation. Scurvy and other diseases became rife. The British troops ultimately owed their very survival to the work of the newspaper correspondent William H. Russell. Keenly observant, gracefully articulate, sometimes blunt, his candid dispatches aroused public awareness and probably saved the British army from annihilation, which had nearly been caused by sheer neglect.

The allies were ultimately able to enhance their supplies of ordnance and commissariat stores via the Grand Crimean Railway, a branch of which the British constructed to connect their siege emplacement with the rear of the British camp at Kadikoy. The rails—the first in history that were laid for a purely military purpose—eliminated several miles of animal transport. "If war is a great destroyer, it is also a great creator," Russell wrote. Too, an electric telegraph linkage was eventually established between the British headquarters and Kadikoy.

In March 1855, the allies intensified the bombardment, employing newly arrived rocketry. From April through June, violent attacks were hurled in desperate and vain attempts to break the Russian resistance. The allied commanders remained resolute: "If it costs ten or ten millions," so went a popular French expression, "we will take it." And on June 18, 1855, a joint allied assault was launched. On June 17 eight hundred allied guns had preceded the attack with a daylong cannonade. It was, thought one observer, like none the world had seen or heard before. Embrasures crumbled, and guns and parapets disappeared. Surely, the allied commanders thought, success would come on the morrow. Many of the attackers were now armed with the notably superior, newly issued Enfield Rifle in place of their Miniés. But when the ground troops advanced, the Russians were quite ready to deal with and repulse the attack.

Springtime faded into summer, and summer wore on, and the two sides remained locked in an ever more disheartening stalemate. "Not a woman left, not a restaurant," the later-famous author Tolstoy (who was there) wrote of the spreading gloom and despair in Sevastopol. "No music; the last brothel went yesterday. It's melancholy."

The siege finally ground to its bitter end. At long last, after 322 days, came the conclusion of the Sevastopol siege. On September 5 the allies commenced the final bombardment: a three-day-long pounding by 800 guns firing 13,000 shells and 90,000 round shot. The French fired in synchronized volley, 250 guns at a time. The French, aided by a movable bridge on rollers that was run across the ditch, succeeded in taking the Malakov Tower, a key position. On September 11, 1855, the Russians evacuated Sevastopol; they blocked the harbor by sinking their ships not needed for troop transport and blew up their forts as they left. A peace treaty was signed on March 30, 1856.

The Crimean War illustrated several lessons. One obvious truth: it was the height of folly to commit non-rifle-armed troops against foes who did have rifles; all future wars would be fought with troops on both sides armed with rifled shoulder weaponry. The United States adopted a standard rifle in 1855, a Springfield .58-caliber minié. The United States also adopted a new tactical system, embodied in *Hardee's Rifle and Light Infantry Tactics*. Prescient observers also could have seen that entrenchments and field fortifications would be necessary and commonplace in the future. (But were there any prescient observers of this war? More specific, were there any prescient *American* observers? A three-man American commission of officers—which included George B. McClellan—went not only to look at the ongoing siege of Sevastopol but also to visit and observe the other European military establishments. The career marine later turned historian J. D. Hittle opined that these men wasted most of their time in frivolities such as studying how best to hang hammocks!)

Another lesson of the Crimean War was that sieges of well-constructed and strongly defended places—unless raised by outside force (as had been the case since the days of Sébastien Le Prestre de Vauban, from 1633 to 1707)—

would succeed eventually, but only at *great* costs in time, resources, and lives. Moreover, disease and exposure had produced four-fifths of the Crimean War casualties; this would continue to be a principal problem in future modern conflicts.

Conclusion

The rapid revolution in technology made warfare a more complex enterprise. With the advent of the rifle, the tactical defense had been rendered much stronger, and the problem of overcoming modern defenses emerged as an even more serious problem than it already long had been. If one rule had not become obvious, it should have: find a way to avoid frontal assaults, and instead make flanking attacks or turning movements.

Long-concentrated mass armies also became possible because of the enhanced ability to supply them. Along with this possibility came enormous problems in planning, managing, and caring for such hosts. A big question, and it was a critical one from the American perspective, was whether a small extant core of professional soldiers could adequately and effectively train *masses* of newly recruited citizen-soldiers raised to meet an emergency.

════════ SUGGESTED READINGS ════════

General Works on War and Warfare

The Age of Battles: The Quest for Decisive Battle from Breitenfeld to Waterloo, by Russell F. Weigley (Bloomington: Indiana University Press, 1991). Weigley is the top scholar in military history.

The Art of War in the Western World, by Archer Jones (Urbana: University of Illinois Press, 1987). Jones's masterful insight is the result of a lifetime of dedicated reading.

The German General Staff, 1657–1945, by Walter Goerlitz (New York: Praeger, 1953), is an important classic in translation.

On War, by Karl von Clausewitz, edited and translated by Michael Howard and Peter Paret (Princeton: Princeton University Press, 1976), has a new edition with an index published in 1984. It is also available on cassette tape through Blackstone Audio Books, P.O. Box 969, Ashland, OR 97520. The reader is female—a bit grating in *this* case; but it still is pleasant to hear such a book as this read aloud.

The Politics of the Prussian Army, 1640–1945, by Gordon A. Craig (Oxford: Clarendon Press, 1955), is a hard book to read but very useful in understanding the Prussian reform process.

The Soldier and the State, by Samuel P. Huntington (Cambridge: Harvard University Press, 1957), is incomparably important! It dates professionalism later than Russell Weigley.

The American Experience

An American Profession of Arms: The Army Officer Corps, 1784–1861, by William B. Skelton (Lawrence: University Press of Kansas, 1992), is absolutely essential on the topic and shows much embryonic professionalism in antebellum America, perhaps inhibited somewhat by the coming of the Civil War.

"The Best School in the World": West Point, the Pre-Civil War Years, 1833–1866, by James L. Morrison Jr. (Kent: Kent State University Press, 1986), is the best of several revised doctoral dissertations on the history of West Point.

Blacks and the Military in American History, by Jack D. Foner (New York: Praeger, 1974), is a pioneering work on this topic.

Duty, Honor, Country: A History of West Point, by Stephen E. Ambrose (Baltimore: Johns Hopkins University Press, 1966), is classic and readable, although perhaps faulty in parts—owing much to Ambrose's occasional tendency to rush into print before completing as exhaustive a research effort as he might have.

"John C. Calhoun as Secretary of War, 1817–1825," an unpublished Ph.D. dissertation by Roger J. Spiller (Louisiana State University, 1977), is available from University Microfilms, 300 North Zeeb Road, Ann Arbor, MI 48106. Spiller—who, like myself, is one of thirty-six "wee Harrys" (students who completed doctoral work under T. Harry Williams)—has achieved career eminence that has been excelled among us perhaps only by Otis A. Singletary.

The Old Army: A Portrait of the American Army in Peacetime, 1784–1898, by Edward M. Coffman (New York: Oxford University Press, 1986), is a masterful military history in an unorthodox vein—Coffman is one of the "greats" in the field.

School for Soldiers: West Point and the Profession of Arms, by Joseph Ellis and Robert Moore (New York: Oxford University Press, 1974), is a sometimes caustic but insightful analysis—Ellis and Moore imply much criticism of the West Point system.

Soldiers and Civilians: The Martial Spirit in America, 1775–1865, by Marcus Cunliffe, 2d ed. (New York: Free Press, 1973), offers a unique insight from the perspective of a British writer.

To the Point, by George Pappas (New York: Praeger, 1993), is the newest history of West Point and debunks some old legends.

"The United States Army in the South, 1789–1835," an unpublished, two-volume Ph.D. dissertation by Tommy R. Young II (Louisiana State University, 1973), is available from University Microfilms, 300 North Zeeb Road, Ann Arbor, MI 48106, and is considered essential.

"Young Fuss and Feathers: Winfield Scott's Early Career, 1808–1841," an unpublished Ph.D. dissertation by Timothy D. Johnson (University of Alabama, 1989), is available from University Microfilms, 300 North Zeeb Road, Ann Arbor, MI 48106. This is a brilliant work by a young scholar, destined to become, when it is completed, the standard modern Scott biography.

Zachary Taylor: Soldier of the Republic, by Holman Hamilton (Hamden, Conn.: Archon Books, 1966), is the first of two volumes and is by far the best biography of Taylor.

The Second Seminole War

History of the Second Seminole War, 1835–1842, by John K. Mahon, rev. ed. (Gainesville: University Press of Florida, 1985). Mahon is the unsurpassed expert on this subject.

The Mexican War

Eyewitness to War: Prints and Daguerreotypes of the Mexican War, 1846–1848, by Martha A. Sandweiss, Rick Steward, and Ben W. Huseman (Fort Worth: Amon Carter Museum of Western Art, 1989), is a superb meld of art, art history, and military history—I recommend it very highly.

The Mexican War, by Otis A. Singletary (Chicago: University of Chicago Press, 1960), is short, readable, and generally reliable.

The Mexican War, 1846–1848, by K. Jack Bauer (New York: Macmillan, 1974), is the best modern one-volume account.

Personal Memoirs of U. S. Grant, by Ulysses S. Grant, edited by E. B. Long (New York: Grossett and Dunlap, 1952), is superior.

To Mexico with Taylor and Scott, 1845–1847, edited by Grady McWhiney and Sue McWhiney (Waltham, Mass.: Blaisdell, 1969), is a marvelous anthology.

With Beauregard in Mexico: The Mexican War Reminiscences of P. G. T. Beauregard, edited by T. Harry Williams (New York: Da Capo Press, 1969), sheds a lot of good light on the staff work that the young engineers performed.

The Crimean War

Cadogan's Crimea, text by Lt. Col. Somerset J. Gough Calthorpe (New York: Atheneum, 1980), was originally published in 1856 as *"Letters from Headquarters" by a Staff Officer.* The 1980 edition is magnificently illustrated with the superb contemporary watercolors by Gen. the Hon. Sir George Cadogan.

The Crimean War, by Alan Palmer (New York: Dorset Press, 1992), was originally published in 1987 as *The Banner of Battle* and is the single best one-volume scholarly history of the war.

Russell's Dispatches from the Crimea, 1854–1856, edited by Nicholas Bentley (New York: Hill and Wang, 1966), is very readable—an absolutely delightful book, and I highly recommend it.

The War in the Crimea, by Gen. Sir Edward Hamley (London: Seeley, 1894), is the best work by a participant.

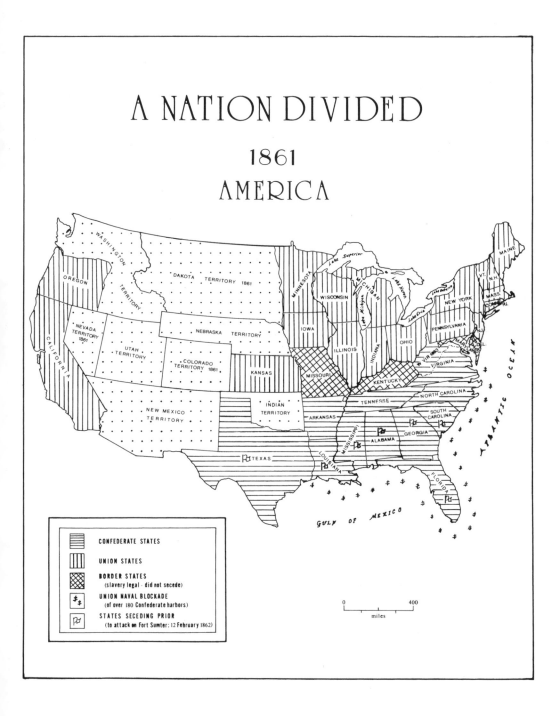

A NATION DIVIDED

1861

AMERICA

CONFEDERATE STATES

UNION STATES

BORDER STATES
(slavery legal - did not secede)

UNION NAVAL BLOCKADE
(of over 180 Confederate harbors)

STATES SECEDING PRIOR
(to attack on Fort Sumter; 12 February 1862)

0   400
miles

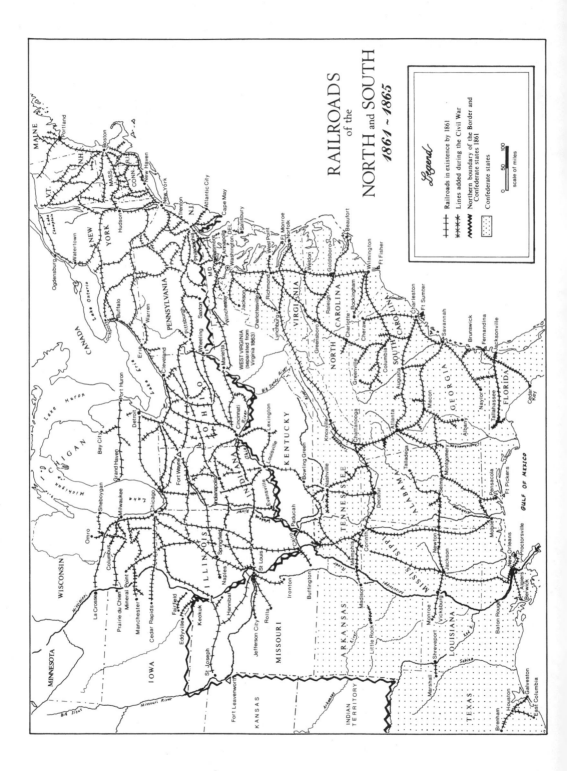

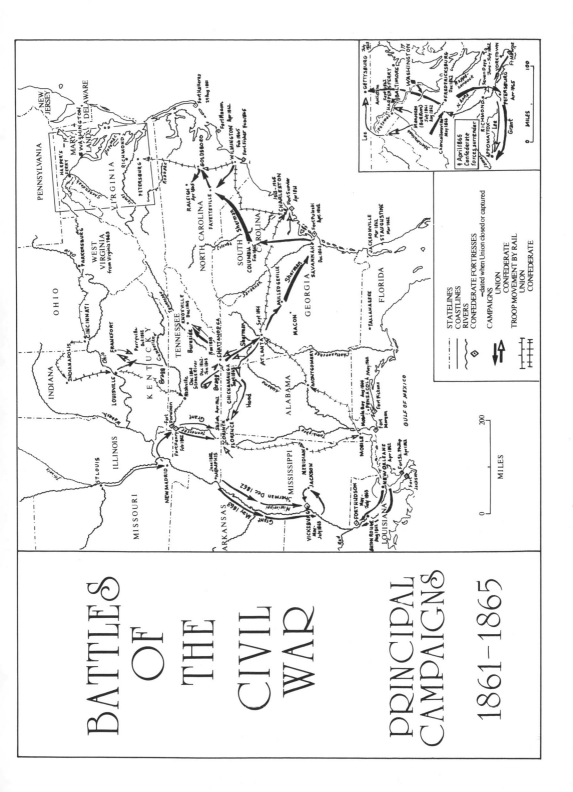

BATTLES OF THE CIVIL WAR

PRINCIPAL CAMPAIGNS 1861–1865

PART I

Background and Opening Phases of the American Civil War

ॐ

W hat caused the American Civil War is an enormously complex and sometimes controversial subject (or matrix of subjects); much has been written on the matter. The final three-step process that brought the war about was this: (1) Beginning late in 1860 and continuing in early 1861, seven Southern states left the Union, soon to form a new national government—the Confederate States of America—and on April 12–14, 1861, they bombarded and seized a U.S. Army post, Fort Sumter, in Charleston Harbor, South Carolina. (2) Under the potent leadership of the great nationalist, President Abraham Lincoln, the Union proved determined to fight a war to force the seven seceded states to return. (3) Led by the Confederate president, Jefferson Davis, the seven seceded states (which were joined, soon after Lincoln's virtual presidential declaration of war, by an additional four states) elected to fight in order to try to maintain their new allegiance.

Slavery, not the sole divisive issue to be sure, nor even the primary initial motivating factor for a great many of the war's participants, was nevertheless the ultimate essential cause of the war. If that unfortunate institution had not existed, compromises on the other matters could have been fashioned. It is ironic, though, that the burning and divisive issue in the years immediately preceding the war was not slavery itself but, rather, the question of whether or not the institution should be allowed to expand into new territory. Southerners believed that freedom to expand was an essential right; Northerners had come to feel more and more that it was absolutely crucial to prevent slavery's further spread.

Abraham Lincoln was not an abolitionist, but he was dedicated to the ultimate destruction of slavery because he adamantly opposed its further spread, and he (like many others) believed that stopping it from spreading would eventually bring its demise. Southerners regarded Lincoln and his ilk as "Black Republicans" and believed that his having captured the presidency in 1860 was a slap in the face that demanded retribution. For some years previous the so-called fire-eaters, Southern radicals, had urged disunion as the only viable way to protect Southern rights. But now the radicals' arguments made more sense to a wider audience, because Black Republican ascendancy had dishonored a people who made honor an essential part of their way of life.

The people of the eleven states that consummated the secession process (a process that they themselves asserted to be legal), and other combatants who supported their cause (some persons from the four slave states that remained in the Union—Delaware, Maryland, Kentucky, and Missouri), fought in order to preserve the existing social and economic systems, as they perceived them, and they believed that state rights were essential to that preservation. But whether there were or were not distinct cultures, large enough segments of the population in each section deeply believed that theirs was indeed a distinct and superior way of life and that their way of life was profoundly shaped by the presence or the absence of slavery.

Sentiments espoused by persons in the so-called border states and upper South were sorely divided. Tennessee, North Carolina, Arkansas, and Virginia would secede in the second wave. But western Virginia broke away, and in 1863 was admitted as a new state in the Union (a process made possible by the reality that Northern military control of the area had been established early in the war and continued to be maintained). Tennessee quite probably would have divided as Virginia had, but there the situation was reversed: in the eastern portion, where Unionist sentiment was strong, the Confederacy maintained control; in the western portion the Union gained early control, but the populace remained rabidly pro-Southern. Both the North and the South claimed Kentucky and Missouri, states in which the secession process began but was not completed. The Confederacy even had stars in its flag and representatives in its Congress from those two states.

Some historians have asserted that there existed very distinctly different Northern and Southern cultures. Grady McWhiney, sometimes in collaboration with Forest McDonald or Perry D. Jamieson, argues that Southerners by and large were Celtic while Northerners in essential part were Anglo-Saxon. Historians of religion, notably Samuel S. Hill Jr. and James H. Moorhead, have presented much evidence to show that differences between Northern and Southern religious denominations were sufficiently stark as to render the respective populace in each section fundamentally different—as well as to have some impact on the conduct of the war. Furthermore, C. C. Goen has shown the potent impact that the antebellum divisions in mainline Protestant Christian denominations had in paving the way for dividing the nation. And it is important to note that the American people of the mid-nineteenth century, Northerners *and* Southerners, were an intensely patriotic and fervently religious people. The Civil War ultimately became something of a holy struggle.

Whether or not there continues to exist enough will among a populace to protract an armed struggle is especially crucial in any civil war. And the South *did* try harder than the North; it made greater sacrifices. Ultimately, the Confederacy put at least 80 percent of its white men of military age into uniform, while the North mobilized roughly only about 50 percent of its potential soldiery. While both sides eventually resorted to conscription—the South did so a year earlier than the North—the majority of the troops were volunteers as a result of appeals to patriotism and pride as well as financial inducement. Some 80 percent of the Rebel soldiers were volunteers, and nearly 94 percent of the Yankees were volunteers.

In terms of population, and by almost any material measure, the North was vastly richer. But the Crimean War had illustrated to those with enough insight to perceive it that modern ordnance had rendered fighting forces relatively invulnerable to annihilation: they could hurt each other mightily, but the defense was too potent to be totally demolished. The weaker side could win in war—it merely had to hold out long enough; an uneven contest might gradually grind to an indecisive conclusion. Too, foreign intervention was a possibility (much expected by the South and much feared by the North). For the first year and a half of the war Southern hopes burned bright that England and perhaps France also would help them, but in the fall of 1862 those hopes began to fade, and—while they lingered long—they continued to diminish steadily.

Confederate President Jefferson Davis seemed to have understood clearly what the Confederacy's best course for ensuring its survival was when he indicated that the strategy of his government would be, as he put it, "defensive-offensive." That is, they would primarily lie on the defensive and await whatever challenge the Union might put forward, but they would also take advantage of any propitious moment to strike offensively. (Perhaps as the war progressed they misread propitiousness. The Confederates attacked in fully one-half of the major battles, but when they did they suffered nearly twice as many casualties as when they defended.)

The first major formulation of Union strategy was proposed by the general in chief, Winfield Scott. Critics who were derisive of the strategy called it "the Anaconda Plan," after the serpent that squeezes its prey slowly to death, but the name was apt and so it stuck. Scott proposed to put pressure on the entire periphery of the South and to use naval power to cut contact and support from the outside world. Next, Scott's plan called for dividing the Confederacy by seizing the Mississippi River. Then, he expected, pro-Union elements within the South would be induced to depose the revolutionary government. President Lincoln did not much like the plan, because he felt it would take too long to achieve desired results—if indeed such a plan as this could ever produce them at all. In the meantime, both the North and the South moved tentatively and uncertainly toward preparing for a war that, events would prove, leaders on both sides ill-perceived how unready they were to wage.

CHAPTER 1

Transition to Civil War

Procurement of Officers

Scholars who study the history of the U.S. Military Academy call the two decades prior to the Civil War the "Golden Age" of West Point. It was the time when the officer corps of the army changed from being composed primarily of men who had been commissioned directly from civilian life or who had risen from the ranks to one wherein professionally trained men predominated. Not one of the thirty-seven men who became general officers between 1802 and 1861 was an alumnus of the Academy, but even as early as 1833 more than half of the active officers were graduates, and their numbers had increased to more than 75 percent by 1860 on the eve of the Civil War.

When the country divided, 9,103,332 persons among the nation's total population of 31,443,321 lived in seceded states. So, too, did the cadet corps and the officer corps divide into similarly proportionally sized groups. At the war's outset, seventy-four Southern cadets resigned their appointments or suffered dismissal for refusing to take a required oath of allegiance, and all of those subsequently served in the Confederate army. A few Northerners chose to side with the South; and a few Southerners remained loyal to the North. Of the 266 Southern-born West Point alumni who fought in the Civil War, 39 (14.7 percent) served the Union.

For a variety of reasons, the South had a keener appreciation of military professionalism than the North did. Early in the Civil War the South did a better job than the North in identifying its more able officers and getting them sooner into high levels of command. More to the point is that the South— from the outset—was much more welcoming to its military professionals and capitalized upon their talents. Among the Regular Army officers who went to fight for the South, 64 percent became generals, while less than 30 percent of those Regulars who stayed with the Union did so.

Virtually none of the nonbrevet general-grade officers in the rather small pre–Civil War army could be expected to take the field. Winfield Scott, the general in chief, a Regular Army major general and brevet lieutenant general, was seventy-five years of age and physically unfit. Brig. Gen. John E. Wool, who was seventy-seven years old, ably handled an administrative command for a time and was promoted to major general on May 17, 1862, but diminished vigor forced him to retire on August 1, 1863. Seventy-two-year-old Brig. Gen. David E. Twiggs sided with the Confederacy.

Huge numbers of general- and field-grade officers had to be appointed from sources other than West Point; the importance and role played by the volunteer officers cannot be discounted. To be sure it was politics—and not their military capacity—that motivated some of their appointments. But some volunteer officers possessed genuine merit, and many of them productively strove to improve. Too, West Point had some meaningful competition as a source of sound formal military education, most notably from the Virginia Military Institute and the military college in Charleston, South Carolina, known as the Citadel.

Nevertheless, West Pointers—many of them still very young—dominated the key positions; the Civil War was a "West Pointers War." Some of the Academy men performed poorly; only a very few proved adequate to the tasks of top command positions. It was in the lower-level commands and in staff positions that West Pointers—augmented by the best of the volunteer officers—truly excelled. Most significant, they succeeded in molding huge numbers of raw, unmilitary, young Americans into formidable soldiers, integrating them into well-functioning armies. The reality was demonstrated: modern wars can be conducted satisfactorily by armies that are largely nonprofessional if there exists an adequate professional core and if there is at least minimally sufficient time to mobilize and train.

Both sides started off with relative parity in administrative apparatus for command and control. Both had little technical information and few military maps. (A major western campaign in 1862 was conducted by a Confederate general who had bought his maps in a bookstore.) There was no staff school and no general-staff system. The Union had long used a regional military department system, and (with necessary modifications) this continued in existence throughout the Civil War. The Confederacy copied the idea; but, with the passage of time, the Confederate military department system came to have more impact on strategy than did the North's geographic arrangement, which remained more administrative in nature.

Enlisted Personnel

At the outbreak of the Civil War, the U.S. Army mustered just 16,367 men. On April 15, 1861, President Lincoln called up 75,000 militiamen for three months. Three weeks later by executive fiat he increased the Regular Army by 22,714 men and the navy by 18,000. Over the next four years, the Union ultimately mobilized 2.6 million men.

The Confederacy, meanwhile, also mobilizing, had even farther to go. (It was long believed, due to a misstatement by Emory Upton in his postwar writings, that only twenty-six enlisted men from the U.S. Army joined the Confederate forces. Actually, at least seventy enlisted individuals changed from North to South early in the war, and the full number of such deserters eventually approached four hundred.) The Confederate Congress had authorized the muster for a period of one year of as many volunteers as President Davis desired, and on March 6 he called for 100,000. The Confederacy ultimately mobilized close to 1 million men.

Initially, many recruits flocked to the training camps of both sides; but two particularly critical periods eventually rendered reenlistment a vital problem for both sides. First, early in the war, even before any real fighting had taken place, because many of the initial enlistments were for very short periods—usually for three months—the necessity arose to institute drastic change. Troops thereafter were typically enlisted for three years or for the war's duration, whichever came first. Thus, if the war was still dragging on, sometime in 1864 there would come a crucial period when vast numbers of soldiers' terms of service were due to expire. For example, of the 956 Union infantry regiments on duty at the outset of 1864, 455 were scheduled to disband during the spring and summer. But both sides proved able in 1864 to effect a significantly large, though not total, reenlistment of its veterans.

While every individual, to be sure, is unique, it is nevertheless possible to do some "collective personality profiling" of the Civil War soldiers. In such a process it becomes starkly evident that—at least in terms of human propensity—the people of the North and the South were much more alike than different. But if there existed any difference at all, what was the nature of this difference? The answer seems to be complicated. It well may be true, as the brilliant young scholar Reid Mitchell has concluded, that "the North had a superior will to fight the war it had to fight than the South had to fight its war"; and Yankees and Rebels were like *mirror images*—not truly different, yet quite thoroughly opposites.

But why did the Civil War soldiers fight, and why did they continue to do so? It is an intriguing question, one that Reid Mitchell and James McPherson, separately, have done good work in probing—and into which McPherson is continuing to inquire.

To fight, and to continue to fight, required some prodigious motivation, for the war became quite early a hard thing to endure. Mitchell found documentation that "a preacher's sermon on 'the dear ones at home' could start veterans crying." "I must say I have had enough of the glory of war," one trooper wrote in August 1862. "I am sick of seeing dead men and men's limbs torn from their bodies." Another would write in the following December, "I did not have to go into the battle because I am so near bare-footed . . . [and] I can tell you I was glad that my shoes did not come, because I would rather lose a hundred dollars than go into battle."

Yet, save for a truly negligible proportion of slackers and deserters, the soldiers usually did go into battle. Soldiers cared what the folks back home thought of them and, more important, they wanted to be regarded as truly having done their duty. But Mitchell perceives a different quality of motivation, North and South—and ultimately over time the North's cohesion grew tighter while the South's gradually deteriorated. The reality was that the Confederate experiment was in trouble from the outset: quite simply and starkly Confederate nationalism was weak while Northern nationalism was strong. This issue has been thoroughly discussed by many scholars: most notable are Paul D. Escott in *After Secession;* Richard E. Beringer, Herman Hattaway, Archer Jones, and William Still in *Why the South Lost the Civil War;* and most recently (in a newly insightful context) Mark Grimsley in *The Hard Hand of War.*

As the conflict unfolded in an intensifying, stunning, and escalating process, it became very violent. If *hatred* for the enemy did not exist at the outset—and in some cases it *did* initially exist—it assuredly developed as the conflict wore on. Soldiers projected stark differences upon the individuals, *and the culture,* of the other side. This helped them not only to nurture their inner feelings of hate but also to become agents of depravity and destruction. "Americans surprised themselves with the extent of violence they could attain," concluded Charles Royster, a recent student of the subject, "and the surprise consisted, in part, of getting what they had asked for."

It was not, however, as tempting as it might seem on the surface to assume, that Northerners were motivated by a fight for universal freedom or that Southerners uniformly and consciously fought to maintain slavery. Racism, in one form or another, permeated the attitudes of nearly all the soldiers, North and South. Most white Southerners—directly or indirectly—did have some stake in the ongoing oppression of blacks, because their collective "way of life" depended on that. But in the minds of a great many Southerners, slavery was far from being among their concerns of the moment. More to the point, white Southerners dreadfully feared abolition and its inevitable (both the fancied and the real) aftermath, for few of them could imagine abolition unaccompanied by insurrection. On the other hand, while Northerners typically—to varying degrees—might dislike slavery, that did not necessarily mean that they loved, or even empathized with, black people. Indeed, many of them did not feel comfortable with the *thought* that blacks might be equals or deserving of respect. The war itself would prove to be the catalyst for much change.

In the case of the common soldiers, over time they grew harder but also closer in their mutual feelings about war and their regard for each other. Brave deeds, and above all a shared military experience, tended to breed a potent brotherly affinity. More than anything else the war welded the loyalties of the combatants to one another and also somewhat alienated them from the society at large. More than for country, or home, or any abstraction . . . soldiers in combat *fought for each other.* The men who endured the taste of hell that the Civil War proved to be tended to internalize a certain indifference to brutality and savagery—in contrast to the evil cruelty (real or not) of those on the other side—and it became every individual's own virtue and courage, and collectively that of his fellows, that provided a sustaining element.

While there occurred countless instances of fraternization across the lines— the myriad stories are poignant and emotionally stirring—this phenomenon was *not* as prevalent as postwar myth has asserted. Yet, Civil War soldiers were usually willing to give quarter, to take prisoners, and to not wantonly abuse or callously kill their captives. But manifestations of brutality increased toward the war's end (especially when Southerners faced black Union troops during the war's second half, as well as in the military prisons). The fighting men, purely and simply, grew harder over time.

Weaponry

The nominal standard U.S. rifle at the outbreak of the Civil War was the .58-caliber muzzle-loaded Model 1855 Percussion Rifle, manufactured at Harpers Ferry Arsenal between 1857 and 1861. Just slightly more than 7,000 were made,

Clinch rifles (Company A, Fifth Georgia Infantry). Sometimes, and especially early in the war, Rebel troops looked a lot like Yankees. (courtesy Leib Image Archives, York, Penn.)

however, and a large portion of that number were lost, destroyed in a purposely set fire to prevent their capture by Confederates who raided the arsenal in April 1861. Also in 1861, the Springfield Armory began manufacturing the .58-caliber Model 1861 U.S. Percussion Rifle Musket. The armory turned out more than 250,000 of them, and other contractors produced more than 450,000. A variation of this design, known as the "Special Model 1861," was also made, some 100,000 of them by the Colt Firearms Company and about 80,000 by other companies.

Both sides used several other makes of rifles, some of them manufactured in the United States, but the majority were foreign-made—by far the most popular being the British Enfield. Each side imported roughly 400,000 of them, made by various private contractors in London and in Birmingham, England. Most of these pieces conformed to an 1853 pattern, with occasional modifications. They fired a .577-caliber smooth-sided minié bullet. Their greatest shortcoming was that their parts were not interchangeable. Otherwise, they were equal or superior to the American Springfield, and just as accurate.

The two most notable innovative features offered by several other lesser-used pieces were breech-loading and repeating firing capability. The best-known breech loader was the repeating Spencer carbine, some 11,400 of which were acquired by the Union army, and the Sharps single-shot carbine, of which about 9,000 were purchased by the Federals. (Carbines are smaller versions of prototype rifles, although sometimes the rifle itself might not exist. Carbines were more convenient for the cavalry to use but were less powerful and therefore shorter in range and too lightweight for the heavy and rough use of shoulder weapons made for infantrymen.) The most technically advanced of the Civil War rifles was the Henry lever-action repeater, of which 1,731 were purchased for the Union army. Its magazine held fifteen shots, and an additional round could be loaded in the chamber.

The Confederacy obtained many of its arms from stores of military weapons already in the region before the war commenced; the Southerners seized about 190,000 small arms from former Federal arsenals. Later, Confederate weaponry came via capture from Union troops, or manufacture in the South, or foreign importation. The Fayetteville Armory in North Carolina, for example, made several thousand copies of the U.S. Model 1861, at first using parts captured at Harpers Ferry and later fabricating its own parts. Other important Confederate factories were the Richmond Armory in Virginia and the Palmetto Armory in Columbia, South Carolina. The Southerners engaged in much successful blockade running. Although frivolous items sometimes took up precious cargo space, blockade running did meet the Confederacy's essential needs. The standard Southern weapon was either the U.S. Rifle Musket models of 1842 or 1855, or the Rifle Model 1842 with the bore reamed out to .577 caliber.

Both sides experimented. Various special rifles were devised for use by sharpshooters and snipers. Shotguns were also fairly commonly used, typically cut down in length. And some early versions of machine guns were introduced: the twenty-five-barreled Billinghurst-Requa Volley Gun, the .58-caliber Ager "Coffee Mill" machine gun, and the Gatling gun—considered the great missed opportunity of the Civil War because not until 1866 did the army choose to order any versions of this weapon, which had been demonstrated as effective in 1862. Twelve Gatlings were purchased personally by Maj. Gen. Benjamin F. Butler (the Union general most interested in and supportive of new weaponry concepts), and, late in the war, his troops made good use of them. These guns were little used in the Civil War primarily because few persons in authority were interested in them, there being scant understanding of how they could be integrated into the prevailing tactical theories.

The basic Civil War artillery piece was the "Napoleon," or Model 1857 gun howitzer, a twelve-pounder smoothbore named for the then French emperor, Napoleon III. Despite its name, the piece was not a true howitzer, for it had no chambered interior and did not arc its shells. A smoothbore cannon of earlier design, which was also much used in the Civil War because large numbers existed before the conflict commenced and because they were highly mobile, was the six-pounder. Smoothbore pieces, when charged with case (a hollow shell packed with lead balls and gun powder) or canister (essentially a very large shotgun shell), were very effective against infantry at short and medium range.

Despite that, a number of types of rifled artillery pieces were gradually introduced; infantrymen rightly feared smoothbores more because rifled artillery had smaller bores and could not fire large rounds of case or canister—the special, and deadly, antipersonnel types of short-range ammunition. Early results with rifled artillery were poor because bronze guns could not stand the added strain. Beginning in 1860 a large number of smoothbore pieces were rendered into rifles by the "James Conversion"—that is, by cutting spiral grooves into the inside of smoothbore barrels. This seriously weakened the guns, however, so while range and accuracy were increased, they tended to burst. The Union rapidly phased out the use of James Rifles, while necessity forced the Confederacy to employ them for a longer time.

Noteworthy and potent new artillery pieces were designed for the Union by Capt. Thomas J. Rodman and by former captain Robert P. Parrott. The Rodman gun was a smoothbore, the Model 1861 Columbiad, cast using a special cooling process. The Parrott was rifled, the second-most widely used rifled artillery piece of the Civil War (the most common piece being the three-inch ordnance rifle). The Parrott was distinguished by its single wide reinforcing band at the breech, attached by using a particular metallurgical method devised by Parrott, an 1824 graduate of West Point. Parrott guns ranged in caliber from ten-pounders to three hundred–pounders, and although many problems were encountered with them, they were regarded as tough, versatile, practical, and relatively cheap and easy to produce. While the Confederacy did manage to produce some of its own artillery—they even cast a couple of Rodmans late in the war—the bulk of Southern artillery was obtained either through seizure at the outset or later through capture.

The Civil War would prove to be one that had its share of sieges, and special types of weapons for siege warfare were employed. Both sides made much use of mortars. The "Coehorn Mortar" had long existed, having been developed by the Dutch soldier and military engineer Baron Menno van Coehoorn (1641–1704). The standard version was a small bronze muzzle-loading smoothbore with a caliber of 4⅗ inches, mounted on an oak block to which carrying handles were attached; but, in addition, during the Civil War much larger versions of siege mortars were devised—typically mounted on boats or railroad flatcars.

In the production of what became a newly standard weapon of war, hand grenades, the North far outdid the South. Handheld bombs were an old invention, but their use had died out by the time of the Civil War. Earlier versions had been too heavy, hence clumsy to throw, and their detonation was egregiously unreliable. Several grenade designs were used in the Civil War: the best known was a Northern-produced device, known as "Ketcham's grenade." These grenades were made by packing a gunpowder charge into a cast-iron egg-shaped head to which a wooden tail rod fitted with pasteboard fins was attached. The front end had a hole bored into it, terminating with a cap nipple, similar to those on percussion rifles. While grenades were being stored or carried, a short metal rod was kept in the hole. When one was ready to arm the grenade, the rod was pulled out, a percussion cap put over the nipple, and the rod replaced. A total of 93,200 of these remarkably reliable grenades were produced for the Union army. There were several weights, ranging from one to five pounds— troops much preferred the lighter ones. A good number of crude grenades were produced within the Confederacy, but the South was obliged to obtain the bulk of its supply of grenades by occasionally capturing quantities of them. (Grenades were used only in static or prolonged operations and sieges.)

Some viable, and some ultimately *not* so viable, innovations were introduced into armament during the Civil War. Both sides—the Confederates more tenaciously—tried to use double-barreled cannon. Two cannonballs were linked together by chain and the two barrels fired simultaneously, but the concept proved impracticable, as it was impossible to always get the necessary simultaneous explosions.

The South's Greater Propensity to Experiment

The materially weaker side in war often tends to be more experimental, more inclined to resort to expedients, and more likely to develop ideas for new machines or new ways to use old ones. Within the Confederacy a number of

Double-barreled cannon. The Confederates were very innovative and willing to experiment. This interesting gun proved unsatisfactory: it was impossible to get the necessary *simultaneous* firing of the two barrels. (photo by Henry M. Troth)

brilliant, inventive men conceived, built, and employed a number of remarkable devices. The most widely used of these implements was an improved fuse for artillery shells, perfected by Capt. Ambrose McEvoy. Millions of the fuses were produced. McEvoy also worked on several types of "torpedoes," which later became known as "mines."

The idea for explosive mines was not new. A primitive one had been used by the colonists against the British during the American Revolution, and methods for improving them were subsequently toyed with by Robert Fulton of steamboat fame and Samuel Colt, the firearms developer. Just prior to the Civil War, floating mines were employed at Canton, China, during the Anglo-French seizure of that place, and by the Russians in the Crimean War, but only the men who developed them seemed to take them seriously. Some technically inclined Americans noted them, however, and individuals within the Confederacy—following the lead of Gabriel J. Rains—developed them to a surprisingly sophisticated level. The South successfully used floating mines to kill hundreds of men, both soldiers in the field and sailors aboard ship, and to sink twenty-nine Federal vessels, seriously damage five more, and inflict minor damage on several others.

The South also developed two ingenious new kinds of hand-delivered bombs. They were designed and built by members of the small but extremely innovative and quite active Confederate Secret Service Corps, organized and led by Capt. Thomas E. Courtney. The group worked on explosives that were fitted into sticks of wood, and one of the members designed a clock-activated torpedo. Their crowning achievement was conceived by Courtney himself: highly explosive, small cast-iron torpedoes that were irregularly notched or toothed on the edges and painted so that they looked like pieces of coal. These became the principal weapon of the Confederate Secret Service Corps.

Rather little is known about the disguised coal-lump torpedoes, because scrupulous secrecy was maintained by the South's secret service, and its files were deliberately destroyed when the Confederate capital fell. One sample of the device was secured by the occupying Union troops: it had been presented to President Jefferson Davis, and in fleeing he had left it behind in a cabinet of personal possessions. The idea for their use was to somehow sneak them into supplies of Union coal, and the Southerners hoped the lumps would eventually wind up in the boiler of a Federal ship (or maybe even in some Union officer's potbellied stove) where they would explode. Precisely how many of the devices were used is not known and can probably never be ascertained, but a number of mysterious explosions, their cause never proved, did occur. The most notorious one was at City Point, Virginia, on August 9, 1864.

Nearly all of the impressive innovative devices developed and used by the South were too primitive, too unreliable, were never available in sufficient numbers, or could not be used in conjunction with other orchestrated endeavors to bring more than relatively momentary impact. But, in addition to their obvious promise for use in future wars, the new weapons did render the South some benefit. They often induced fear, intimidating men and eliciting wary caution.

Tactics

Because the Americans had successfully attacked fieldworks at Monterrey, Cerro Gordo, and elsewhere during the Mexican War, many of the Civil War commanders began the new conflict with only scant regard for entrenchments.

Some officers even believed that the use of entrenchments was detrimental to morale. Hardee's *Tactics* remained the standard for both armies, although a recapitulation appeared in 1862, Gen. Silas Casey's *Infantry Tactics,* which was used by Northerners thereafter so that they would not have to employ a book authored by a Rebel. Casey's work did in one respect, however, go beyond Hardee's in that it attempted to prescribe brigade and larger-unit tactics—formations that were larger than any American had led before the Civil War.

Most Civil War commanders exhibited a preference for the tactical offensive, which proved costly, because the new firepower gave the defense so much more potency. The defense was further strengthened because as the war progressed, field entrenchments became commonplace. To be sure, commanders quickly perceived the strength offered by the entrenched tactical defensive, but they long clung to false hopes that élan would make a sufficient difference. The famous Rebel yell—a loud, shrill animal-like shriek—was consciously intended to induce élan, as were other yells and cheers used on both sides.

Successive rushes sometimes came about, largely by accident. It has been asserted that Southerners, because of their laxer discipline, tended to fight in more irregular formations and patterns. This, however, is easy to overstate, because, in truth, once fighting commenced it always tended to degenerate into irregularity. No commander, save a very few only late in the war, seems to have perceived much potential in successive rushes.

It was intended that attacking troops would close quickly with defenders and fight hand-to-hand, using bayonets. In actuality, this proved rare. Assaults most typically were stopped with firepower alone, and even if a charge succeeded, the defenders tended to give way and retreat before any bayoneting occurred. Even in instances when troops did come close to each other, the fighting was more likely to be characterized by using the weapons as clubs. At Gettysburg on July 3, 1863, for example, when some of the charging Rebels did manage to come into close proximity with their enemy, an officer of the Eightieth New York recalled: "A curious thing about this fighting was that, although all the men were armed with bayonets, no one seemed to be using them. Those nearest clubbed their muskets and beat each other over the head, while those not so close kept loading and firing as fast as they could." The fighting around Spotsylvania, Virginia, in 1864 also featured some close-in combat, but Grady McWhiney and Perry Jamieson point out in *Attack and Die* that medical records show only thirty-seven bayonet wounds were treated by army surgeons during the quite violent period of May 1 through July 31.

Attacks most commonly were made in a two-line formation, the distance between the two lines depending on terrain or other particular circumstances. The alternative formation was the column. This was not normally thought to be a wise choice, but as the war unfolded there did come occasions when storm tactics using columns, in some particular or special manner, were attempted. Sometimes they produced success, most times not. A lot depended on quickness of execution and surprise, which was rarely achieved. No tactical formation—line, column, or combination—ever overcame the power of determined, rifle-armed troops who were well arrayed in an entrenched tactical defensive.

The use of skirmishers and loose-order formations became ever more popular. Later in the war, whole regiments might be so employed, partly because it had become evident through experience that loose order would lessen losses. Too, there was an added cause for this in the Union army, wherein some regiments were not reinforced and new ones simply were created, while the ranks of the old ones remained badly depleted. Such units were too small to be used in a line, but could always array as skirmishers. Ever increased use of skirmishers and loose order, however, intensified problems of command and control.

The vast array of battles were fought in locales where, at least to some extent, terrain or other natural features obscured wide or far visibility. It was most typical that any given battle site comprised much wooded area; but if the woods were missing, then there tended to be cornfields or sunken roads or densely overgrown depressions in the ground. Thus, terrain conditions typically compelled troops to be fairly close to each other before they could effectively shoot. These conditions were coupled with the reality that—owing to the scarcity of ammunition and opportune time—almost no Civil War soldiers got much meaningful target practice; most of them were *not* in truth very good marksmen. And that tended to lessen the impact that the long-range shooting capability of the weaponry might have produced and compelled more dependence upon massed firepower.

CHAPTER 2

The Fighting Begins

A potentially confusing disparity in nomenclature was employed by the two sides: the North and the South tended to name armies and battles according to a different rule of thumb. The North often named its armies after rivers: hence, Army of the Potomac, Army of the Tennessee, Army of the Ohio, Army of the Cumberland, Army of the James, and so on. The South either named its armies after states, or portions thereof: hence, Army of Northern Virginia, or Army of Tennessee; or it named them the same as the military department in which they served, as in Army of the Department of Alabama, Mississippi, and East Louisiana. The North often named battles after the nearest stream or body of water, while the South tended to name them after the nearest town or physical feature: hence, Bull Run and Manassas, Antietam and Sharpsburg, Wilson's Creek and Oak Hills, Pittsburg Landing and Shiloh, Stones River and Murfreesboro, and so on.

The war officially opened with the Confederate bombardment of Fort Sumter, in Charleston Harbor, South Carolina. The fort was a state-of-the-art masonry structure, but it had been designed to defend against an attack from outside the harbor—not one supported from inside the city it was supposed to shield. Maj. Robert Anderson held the place with a garrison of eighty-four U.S. soldiers.

Irate and impatient South Carolinians clamored for the fort to be taken. President Lincoln sent a naval expedition to resupply the garrison. Initially, the so-called Army of South Carolina, bolstered by volunteers from the militia and cadets from the Citadel, invested the fort. Soon the Provisional Government of the Confederacy took charge of the operation and sent Brig. Gen. Pierre Gustave Toutant Beauregard—the Creole thought by many to look like Napoleon Bonaparte in a gray uniform—to command. "I find a great deal in the way of

Pierre Gustave Toutant Beauregard. Not only, as T. Harry Williams asserted, "the most colorful of all the Confederate generals" but also, as Thomas L. Connelly and Archer Jones suggested, the one man in the South who most nearly could have forged a successful Rebel strategy had his unfortunately foul relationship with Jefferson Davis not prevented him from even having a chance. (courtesy Leib Image Archives, York, Penn.)

zeal and energy around me, but little professional knowledge and experience," Beauregard soon reported.

The Provisional Government of the Confederacy decided to open fire at daylight on April 12, 1861. During the ensuing thirty-three hours, five thousand artillery rounds were fired (only one-fifth of them from the undermanned fort). The wooden barracks caught fire, and on April 13 Anderson prudently capitulated.

During the bombardment there had been several visits to the fort by various Confederate aides and officials, essentially to try to prod Anderson. During one of these visits, the "fire-eater" Roger Pryor of Virginia (interesting that he would have been there, for his state had not yet seceded) helped himself to a drink that he thought was whiskey but was actually iodide of potassium, a medicine that was extremely poisonous in anything but very small doses. Pryor had to have his stomach pumped out by his enemy, assuredly ending his warlike feelings for the moment. Some of the Union soldiers objected to their doctor helping Pryor, but the good-natured doctor replied that he was responsible to the United States for all the medicine in his hospital and therefore could not allow a Rebel to carry any of it away.

No one had been killed on either side, and one of Beauregard's aides noted that mutual "congratulations were exchanged on so happy a result." War had come, but many of the officers and men on each side still liked each other. The first Federal casualty of the war, however, did occur the next day. Yankee Private Daniel Hough was killed as a result of an accidental explosion during the flag-lowering ceremony. Several other soldiers were badly injured, and the women who helped care for them became the Civil War's first female nurses.

The elated South had found its initial military hero, the commander of the operation, Brigadier General Beauregard. The North was enraged. The bulk of the populace was brought together, in sympathy for the war effort, in much the same process that would result eighty years later from the Japanese attack on Pearl Harbor. The historian Richard N. Current plausibly surmises that Lincoln perceived this would happen and consciously planned and maneuvered so that the first shot would be fired by the South. Of course, the benefit that Jefferson Davis derived from the Sumter episode was to force Lincoln's action, and that brought four more states into the Confederacy—Tennessee, Arkansas, North Carolina, and Virginia—and this was quite crucial for the Confederacy's hopes to survive because it much needed the manpower, resources, and wealth that were within those states.

First Battles

The first land battle of the war occurred on June 3, 1861, at Philippi, (now West) Virginia. It was small. No one was killed, and very few were wounded. It had relatively little significance, save to provide good early publicity for Union Maj. Gen. George B. McClellan and to help establish permanent Federal control in the already largely pro-Union western portion of the state, as well as to help shield the Baltimore and Ohio Railroad.

Bull Run

The first significant land battle was Bull Run, on July 21, 1861. Neither side was ready for a big engagement, but President Lincoln was hopeful that somehow an early victory might be achieved and perhaps prevent the Rebel legislature from meeting at Richmond, the newly relocated Confederate capital, so he urged his army commander, Brig. Gen. Irvin McDowell, to put the main army in motion.

Further, enlistments of the three-month men were beginning to expire: it was a matter of having action right away or enduring much unwelcome delay. On the morning of the battle, Federal troops moving forward passed an infantry regiment and an artillery battery whose enlistments had expired. They were returning to Washington to muster out!

The battle would be distinguished by the bizarre presence of large numbers of civilians. McDowell invited newspaper correspondents to accompany the army. Large numbers of other citizens and assorted dignitaries also helped themselves to what they considered an open invitation. William Howard Russell (the English journalist of Crimean War fame now visiting in the United States) prepared perhaps typically for the adventure: "I swallowed a cup of tea and a morsel of bread, put the remainder of the tea into a bottle, got a flask of light Bordeaux, a bottle of water, a paper of sandwiches, and having replenished my small flask with brandy, stowed them all away in the bottom of the gig." The Civil War at this early moment struck many people as something of a picnic.

Four main forces became involved: for the Union, an army of thirty thousand men based in Washington, D.C., under McDowell and an army of fourteen thousand men in the lower Shenandoah valley under Bvt. Maj. Gen. Robert Patterson; for the Confederates, a "corps" of twenty thousand men based at Manassas, Virginia, under General Beauregard and a force of eleven thousand men in the upper Shenandoah under Gen. Joseph E. Johnston. (Beauregard's was the first body of troops to be officially designated a corps in the Civil War, on June 20, 1861. But this was because Beauregard himself so designated it, stretching—if not outright exceeding—his authority.) While Johnston and Patterson faced each other in the valley, McDowell began a march toward Manassas, planning to cross Bull Run and attack Beauregard's left. The ill-functioning Federal army awkwardly used two and one-half days to march some twenty miles. Beauregard planned to attack the Union left, but the Federals gained the initiative, forcing the Confederates to refocus their attention on defense.

At nearly the last feasible moment, Johnston was able to deceive Patterson, disengage, and move the bulk of his force—some six thousand men—via the Manassas Gap Railroad, to unite with Beauregard's army. Col. James E. B. Stuart's Confederate cavalry so well screened Johnston's movement that two days passed before Patterson learned what had happened. This strategic use of railroads was a spectacular harbinger of things to come: to rapidly and effectively redeploy masses of troops, who could arrive unexpectedly and fresh— ready for battle. Roadbeds and rolling stock thenceforth were vital possessions;

rail junctions soon became as significant and possibly more significant than road junctions.

Both commanders had planned attacks toward their right, so much depended upon which side moved first or, more precise, which was able to make any significant forward progress across Bull Run. Neither battle plan was adequately understood by the second echelon of command. On the Confederate right, some of the Rebel brigades crossed the stream, while others remained in confusion awaiting further orders. When the Union main force got across Bull Run, Southern observers atop a high hill behind the Confederate lines noted this and sent a warning message via "wigwag" signaling (which was a mode of communicating, with code signals sent by distantly visible flags).

Hot and heavy fighting erupted, and for some hours the contest remained relatively close. A Union breakthrough almost occurred. One portion of the Confederate line was smashed: Col. William Tecumseh Sherman managed to maneuver his brigade so that it could assault from a flank rather than frontally. But the advance was blunted, and then contained, by a Rebel rally. Brig. Gen. Thomas J. Jackson brought up fresh troops to a critical area in the nick of time; there he was nicknamed "Stonewall" because of his men's tenacious stand. Charges and countercharges swirled. Ill-trained soldiers on both sides fought as best they could. Some of them showed great bravery, but egregious mistakes were made. Often troops were confused by mistaken uniforms; some Confederate units were dressed in blue, others were in civilian clothes. The absence of battle flags and unit ensigns added to the problem; the first national flag of the Confederacy, especially if hanging limp, looked much like the United States flag.

A critical turning point came when two Union artillery batteries pushed too far forward, and the guns were captured by the Southerners. During the midafternoon a desperate struggle surged over Henry House Hill, but by late afternoon the Confederates prevailed. The exhausted Federals were compelled to retreat. Some Union units had broken and run as rumors spread that the Rebels were preparing to unleash the "Black Horse Cavalry." Fear of the unknown paled for volunteers with scant experience. Some Rebel cavalry units did make a few sallies, but the Confederates had but small numbers of mounted men in this battle. Still, their psychological impact was significant: "I talked with those on all sides of me," the English newspaperman Russell wrote. "Some uttered prodigious nonsense, describing batteries tier over tier, and ambuscades, and blood running knee deep."

An artillery shell hit a wagon on Cub Run Bridge, blocking the road to Centreville—the main avenue of retreat, already congested with civilian buggies and carriages—and some of the Federal soldiers and most of the civilians began to panic. The withdrawal quickly turned into a rout. Describing the scene humorously, one pundit later remarked, "These are the times that try men's soles." One Ohio congressman, himself out for the expected festivities, described the spectacle that followed:

> There was never anything like it for causeless, sheer, absolute, absurd cowardice, or rather panic, on this miserable earth before. Off they went, . . . anywhere, everywhere, to escape. . . . The further they ran the more frightened they grew. . . . To enable them better to run, they threw away their blankets, knapsacks, canteens, and finally muskets, cartridge-boxes, and everything else. . . . A cruel, crazy, mad, hopeless panic possessed them.

But this particular observer saw only a small portion of the total Federal army; much of the remainder withdrew in fairly commendable order. And the Confederates were too spent and too disorganized to mount an effective pursuit—despite the frenzied hopes expressed by Jefferson Davis and Stonewall Jackson.

Bull Run jolted the thinking of a good many persons on both sides. Contrasted with what would follow, which no one could imagine, the losses were modest, but at this time they seemed enormous. The battle cost the Southerners 387 killed, 1,582 wounded, and 13 missing, for a total of 1,982 out of the some 32,000 men present. The Federals had managed to actually engage only some 18,500 of the 35,000 men available, and they lost 2,896–460 killed, 1,124 wounded, and 1,312 missing.

The battle's outcome elated Southerners, some to a deceptive degree of delusion. Still, according to the historian Michael C. C. Adams, Bull Run gave the Rebels a genuine psychological upper hand. While it induced huge numbers of new Federal volunteers to come forth, and many of the ninety-day men to reenlist, it "spooked" many Northerners. The U.S. Congress was startled into action and authorized the muster of a half million men to serve for three years or the war's duration.

From the day of this battle onward, President Lincoln took a firm grip on management of the conflict. Soon he drafted his Memorandum of Military Policy Suggested by the Bull Run Defeat, which contained his first proposal for simultaneous advances as a way to maximize the North's numerical advantage and to minimize the South's ability to respond to challenge and military threat. Lincoln's early plan was a modest one, but the concept of simultaneous advances would later be much refined and ultimately applied with decisive effect. As yet

Lincoln possessed no military competencies, but as a strategist and commander in chief he would grow a great deal during the ensuing four years.

Wilson's Creek

The next battle of note, and of considerably greater significance, occurred far to the west, in southwestern Missouri at Wilson's Creek on August 10, 1861. It was important to the Union war effort to retain control in Missouri, because if the Confederates got that state they would enjoy easy access into Kansas or, more crucial, Illinois. A newly formed Union army of some fifty-four hundred men under Brig. Gen. Nathaniel Lyon had concentrated in the town of Springfield. A Confederate army of some eleven thousand effectives under Brig. Gen. Ben McCulloch advanced toward Springfield, planning to attack Lyon's force. On the night of August 9 McCulloch encamped fifteen miles from the town, along Wilson's Creek.

The Union army delivered a surprise attack at 5:00 A.M. on August 10. Lyon acquiesced in the unwise plan insisted upon by his subordinate, Brig. Gen. Franz Sigel, which was to divide the numerically inferior Federal force and attack both ends of the Confederate camp simultaneously. The fighting escalated into a very bitter and close struggle, lasting four or five hours, said by one officer to be "the severest battle since Waterloo." Lyon's initial assault nearly achieved spectacular success, but the thrust was blunted. The situation stabilized when Confederate infantry rushed to the front under the commander of the Missouri State Guard, Maj. Gen. Sterling Price (who squabbled with McCulloch over rank and status, both before and during the battle). Sigel's attack also achieved some initial success, but eventually his force was defeated and driven from the field in disorder.

While trying to mount a fresh assault, Lyon was killed, becoming the first Union general to lose his life in the war. The battle concluded about 11:00 A.M., when the exhausted Confederates withdrew. The remaining Federals also subsequently fell back, to reunite with Sigel's men at Springfield. The Confederates had lost about twelve hundred men and the Federals thirteen hundred. The battle was a tactical victory for the Confederates, and it considerably buoyed Southern morale while further depressing that of the North; but nearly all of the strategic benefit accrued to Lyon's men, who had been able to inflict enough damage to force the Confederates to halt rather than move farther into Missouri as they had planned. Even so, the Confederates retained domination in the southwestern section and presented a continuing and serious threat to Union control.

George B. McClellan: The Union's Great Hope

After McDowell's failure at Bull Run he was demoted to a division command. George B. McClellan, who had attracted favorable attention for the early success achieved by the Union forces in western Virginia, now took over the army. McClellan has been called by T. Harry Williams "the problem child of the Civil War," because interpreting his career has been difficult and controversial; McClellan had many obvious qualifications, yet he failed as a field general. Why was he a failure? The scholarly arguments range from assertions that President Abraham Lincoln did not allow McClellan an adequate chance to fulfill his great promise—that McClellan was simply unlucky in rising to a high level of command and responsibility *before* Lincoln had learned sufficient forbearance with generals—to assertions that McClellan himself was tragically flawed in character.

Born on December 3, 1826, McClellan rose to be the commanding general of the U.S. Army before his thirty-fifth birthday. His admirers call him "the Young Napoleon," but he has a host of critics, and they deride him as a "Young *Mc*Napoleon." He had a brilliant mind, and he worked hard. Because of his outstanding early record of scholarship, he was granted permission to enter West Point at the age of fifteen, and there he excelled, graduating second in the class of 1846. McClellan saw action in the Mexican War, serving as the third-ranking commissioned officer in an elite company of engineer soldiers. He keenly observed Winfield Scott and was especially impressed with the value of avoiding costly head-on assaults. Deeply moved by the Battle of Cerro Gordo, McClellan dreamed of someday repeating the achievement, the grand turning movement that he regarded as "a tactical master-stroke." Perhaps the sharpest impression that McClellan perceived from observing the Mexican War was that civilian management of the conflict had been grotesque and warped. Additionally, he was struck with how difficult it was to manage woefully inexperienced soldiers.

McClellan had enjoyed a rich and varied pre–Civil War military career. After the Mexican War he spent time at West Point as a member of the engineering faculty. He used some of his time to write a manual, *Bayonet Exercise,* which was based on a similar French work. In 1852 as second-in-command, he embarked on an expedition to discover and map the sources of the Red River of the North; and subsequently he commanded a unit engaged in mapping and making a survey of rivers and harbors on the Texas coast. (But on those trips he demonstrated a certain contentiousness with higher authority, and this trait

George B. McClellan. The commanding general of the U.S. Army at the age of thirty-six, either his own shortcomings or the impossibility of his position and circumstance kept him from succeeding—but he was undeniably keenly able, and therefore explaining him is something of an enigma; T. Harry Williams called him "the problem child of the Civil War." (courtesy Leib Image Archives, York, Penn.)

would again be manifest during the Civil War.) In 1853 McClellan commanded one-half of the expedition that explored one of four proposed routes for a new transcontinental railroad, this one the northernmost: from St. Paul, Minnesota, westward through the Cascades to Fort Vancouver.

McClellan caught the eye of President Franklin Pierce's secretary of war, Jefferson Davis, who embraced McClellan as a young protégé. In 1854 McClellan was sent on a secret mission to the Dominican Republic to select and survey a suitable location for a planned U.S. Naval coaling station. But the choicest plum of McClellan's relationship with Davis came the next year, 1855, when McClellan was promoted to captain and was selected to accompany Majs. Richard Delafield and Alfred Mordecai on an observation tour to visit and observe the military establishments of various European nations and to see some of the war then being fought in the Crimea.

It was an extremely heady experience. On his return McClellan wrote an extensive report, including a cavalry manual that he had interpolated from Russian cavalry regulations. The army adopted his manual and also adopted a design that McClellan drew up for a new type of saddle. The famous McClellan saddle, standard issue for as long as the United States continued to have any horse cavalry, was a derivation from the Hungarian plan as applied in the Prussian service with some further modifications from other European plans that McClellan perceived as valuable.

As was the case with many officers in this era of growth and expansion, economic opportunity in civilian life beckoned to McClellan. In 1857 he left the service to spend the ensuing years before the Civil War working as a railroad executive. When the conflict was less than one month old, on May 14, 1861, the thirty-four-year-old civilian was elevated to the rank of major general in the Regular Army. Immediately after the debacle at Bull Run, McClellan was called to Washington, D.C., to assume command of the Division of the Potomac—the principal army and the fortified defensive emplacements in and around Washington. Several weeks later the army officially took the name he chose for it: the Army of the Potomac.

Against the preferences of President Abraham Lincoln, McClellan wisely counseled patience. The general and his small cadre of professionals undertook the task of converting the thousands of untrained civilian volunteers into something resembling able soldiers. Too, a great many essential items of supply still needed to be procured and issued. McClellan quickly imposed order and efficiency. He possessed considerable ability as a military administrator and had an inspiring manner. He was magnetic, well liked, and admired by his subordinates. Most important, he could instill confidence; he could make new troops believe in themselves. He appointed a provost marshal and employed a squadron of Regular Army cavalry to clear out the stragglers and empty the barrooms and other popular gathering places and spirited the men away to training camps outside the city. He held daily staff conferences, and each afternoon he rode out for inspections and reviews. He displayed an uncanny ability to remember people's names, and he strove to be so frequently visible to the troops that he would be as familiar to them as were their company commanders.

McClellan literally infused his personality into the Army of the Potomac; and this brought both positive benefits *and* negative, limiting qualities. Above all else, McClellan was conservative, indeed to a fault. Having taken General Scott as his beau ideal, McClellan could emulate the older man's caution but not his boldness or his relentlessness. And if McClellan garnered much deserved credit for his observations made while a member of the Delafield commission, he failed to profit from having seen staff structures far superior to any the United States then had. Worst of all, McClellan tended toward self-deception and fatalism, and he always exaggerated the odds against which he contended. Thus, all of his limiting qualities combined to keep him from ever taking full meaningful advantage of the innovative weaponry and equipment that was becoming available.

An Era of Significant Technological Impact on Warfare

On at least two occasions McClellan made aerial observations from Prof. Thaddeus S. C. Lowe's coal gas–filled balloon. Professor Lowe became the Civil War's best-known aeronaut. Involved prominently in ballooning since 1856, soon after the war's outbreak Lowe was asked by the U.S. secretary of war to report on possible military uses for balloons. On June 17, 1861, Lowe and two telegraphers ascended near the White House with telegraph lines dangling to the earth. Lowe sent President Lincoln a message: "Abe: All is Well." Impressed, Lincoln named Lowe the chief aeronaut of the Army of the Potomac. Lowe subsequently recruited and managed the North's balloon squadron—the nation's first air arm.

Both the North and the South on various occasions employed balloons, primarily for observation. Nevertheless, despite its inherent value, the Union's air squadron languished. Many administrative problems remained unsolved, and Lowe encountered much difficulty in persuading officers of the value of aerial observations.

The Confederacy had far fewer resources for making balloons, or anything else for that matter, than the North did, but the Rebels often made up for physical deficiencies with superior ingenuity. The first Confederate balloons were made of varnished cotton and were inflated with air heated by burning pine knots and turpentine. Rebel balloons were tethered by a half-mile of rope, one end secured to a windlass. Haul-downs through danger zones could be hastened by hitching teams of artillery horses to the windlass and sending the animals galloping down a nearby road. The Confederacy's cotton balloons proved unsatisfactory, as they were unstable and had inadequate lift. But, using cloth from donated dresses, the South later constructed two silk balloons, which were inflated with coal gas. Aerial developments, however, were not destined to make nearly so enormous an impact on the Civil War as naval innovations were.

Both the North and the South made dramatic, and nearly simultaneous, entrances into the era of ironclad war vessels. In a sense, both of the original American ironclads, the USS *Monitor* and the CSS *Virginia,* owed their development to the same man, the Swedish inventor John Ericsson, who had perfected the screw propeller. Ericsson's other ideas were not new: iron armor, light draft, steam power, ventilation systems, and the concept of a gun turret. While a gun turret allowed the use of only two guns, those guns could be of extremely large caliber, and, more important, could turn through 360 degrees easily and quickly. What Ericsson did was to incorporate for the first time all the above-listed features into one superbly conceived vessel. Both ships represented early examples of a class of ship destined to be long employed as coast-defense vessels. By sacrificing speed and seaworthiness, relatively small ships could incorporate heavy armor and powerful guns.

The Union eventually built sixty more ships like the *Monitor*, which sank late in 1862 in a storm off Cape Hatteras. Much more cumbersome and hopelessly underpowered, the *Virginia* remained permanently near her first port until the Rebels destroyed her in May 1862 to prevent her capture. Nevertheless, the Confederacy entered into an ambitious ironclad-building program and began or planned perhaps another fifty warships with the *Virginia* casemate design and actually commissioned twenty-two.

The first two of the ironclads collided in a dramatic engagement at Hampton Roads. It was purely a matter of luck that the two ships became operational at the same time. On March 8, 1862, the *Virginia* steamed down the Elizabeth River into Hampton Roads and attacked the wooden boats of the Union blockading squadron. With astonishing ease she withstood heavy fire from the thirty-gun USS *Cumberland* and the fifty-gun USS *Congress*. Soon the *Virginia* belched out hot shot and set the *Congress* afire. To do this, cannonballs were heated to red-hot temperatures in the ship's furnaces and hauled up in iron buckets and placed in a gun muzzle by means of tongs that gripped "tugs," special holes in the ball. A water-soaked wad separated the glowing hot shot from the powder charge to prevent premature explosion. The *Virginia* then rammed the *Cumberland* and sank her. Then she withdrew, intending to return the next day to finish off the grounded *Minnesota*, which had been trapped by the receding tide, and to destroy the other nearby wooden vessels.

But at dawn the Confederates got their first view of the *Monitor*, then lying between their ship and the *Minnesota*. The crews of the two iron vessels watched each other intently until 9:00 A.M. on March 9, 1862, when they commenced a historic two-hour duel. The *Monitor* outmaneuvered the *Virginia*, but neither vessel could do serious damage to the other. Shot after shot ricocheted away. As the ships closed, one of the *Monitor*'s officers believed the two ships actually touched at least five times. The battle waned when the Federals withdrew to resupply the turret with ammunition, but it was renewed a half-hour later. At one point the *Virginia* ran aground. The crews managed to pull her free at the last moment before the *Monitor* could place a shot into a vulnerable spot. The *Virginia* eventually concentrated her fire on the *Monitor*'s pilothouse and, at about noon, struck the sight hole, blinding the Union commanding officer and compelling the vessel to disengage, ending the stalemated battle.

Both sides claimed that they had won the great ironclad engagement, although that mattered not at all: each contestant now possessed a form of the new iron ship, and neither had gained the possibly overwhelming advantage that even temporary singular possession might have conferred. Actually, both sides could have claimed both a victory and a defeat. The Union wooden ships were now safe, but the James River was closed for Union naval operations, and this had a major impact upon the ensuing Peninsula campaign.

Robert E. Lee and the Early Confederate Military Establishment

The Confederacy tended to adopt the same military form and structure as the United States, but with the early difference that President Jefferson Davis appointed no general in chief. Davis, however, strengthened the post of adjutant and inspector general and was able to fill that position with the same man who had held it in the U.S. Army for the nine years preceding, the now sixty-three-year-old Samuel Cooper. Cooper failed, however, to ascend to his newly enlarged responsibilities and continued to function mainly as a coordinator. Cooper assisted Davis to some degree, and the two, together with the series of men who held the post of Confederate secretary of war, collectively performed the duties of general in chief.

In some administrative respects, the South bolted ahead of the North. This was manifested first in establishing an effective conscription system. Both sides were eventually compelled by necessity to resort to a draft, because adequate volunteering did not long continue and the one-year enlistments began to expire, but for a critical time the Union limped along without a national conscription, while during April, May, and June 1862, healthy musters filled the Confederate training camps and bolstered the ranks for the early summer campaigns.

Davis made other changes in the spring of 1862. Most significant, he called Gen. Robert E. Lee from obscure coastal defense duty in South Carolina, to which Lee had been relegated late in 1861 after a rather lackluster performance in western Virginia. Lee's position is distortingly described in many accounts as "military assistant to the President"; in truth, Davis assigned him to "the seat of government . . . under the direction of the President" in charge of "the conduct of military operations in the armies of the Confederacy." The position significantly departed from the prewar U.S. organization; Lee's new powers resembled those of the present-day U.S. Army chief of staff.

Many observers at the time, and many students since, failed to appreciate Davis's revolutionary step toward modernity. It was a giant step, which the Confederate Congress soon bolstered by enacting a law that provided Lee with a staff of one colonel and four majors, plus up to four clerks. While this staff did not divide into separate sections, G-1 though G-4, as would be the case on a modern general staff, it performed collectively as the operations staff of the Confederate high command. With no formal division of labor between himself and the war secretary, Lee primarily supervised operations while the secretary devoted much of his time to coordinating logistics and to implementing the new conscription act, effectively allocating the flow of recruits. Davis and Lee made an admirable team. West Point graduates of the same era and combat veterans of the Mexican War, they understood warfare in the same way. Davis trusted Lee, and Lee in turn kept the president fully informed, sought counsel, made recommendations, and referred major strategic decisions to him. The relationship between Lee and the secretary of war worked out smoothly also, thanks to the particular personalities and temperaments of the men involved.

There is no question that Lee was an extremely able general. His mind was brilliant, and his temperament was one well suited to high command. He had been a stellar student, graduating second in his class at West Point (though it is worth noting that he was one of the few graduates of West Point who became key generals in the Civil War who had not studied under Mahan). Lee had rich and profitable experience in the Mexican War, where he learned firsthand from Winfield Scott the potency of the offensive and the efficacy of the turning movement. Lee was, however, narrowly concerned with Virginia, perhaps not adequately caring about the war as a whole. Resplendent and majestic in appearance, after he became the commander of a field army (although his becoming one was the result of something of an unplanned accident) he elicited an obviously manifest love from his troops. Strangely, although a full general, he wore the insignia of a Confederate colonel—three stars. Why? Was it modesty? Or was it, *perhaps,* an act of *extreme* egotism: could it be that he was identifying with George Washington? While the regulations did not explicitly stipulate that they do so, colonels typically wore a larger star in the middle of the array of three; Lee wore stars of a uniform size—the same as Washington's historic

One of the best photos of R. E. Lee, taken by Matthew Brady just after the war's end. Lee is holding one of the AK47s that enabled his beloved South to prevail—that is, in the imaginations of countless unreconstructed Rebels, Lost Cause adherents, and in the mind of Harry Turtledove, who fancied how Lee got these weapons in the novel *The Guns of the South.* (original artwork by Tom Stimpson)

insignia. Assuredly, the "mind of Robert E. Lee" is an intriguing subject, a "main strength" *and* a "weakness" for the South's chances of achieving ultimate success in its war effort.

CHAPTER 3

The War in the West

Henry W. Halleck and Ulysses S. Grant

The western theater, delineated by the Appalachian Mountains on the east and the Mississippi River on the west (and sometimes also including an expanse of land along the river's west bank), was the scene of fighting more crucial and significant than that which occurred in the eastern theater. Further, it was there that the war's greatest general, Ulysses S. Grant, enjoyed all the successes that eventually led to his promotion to lieutenant general. This was the only appointment to that rank made by the Union and the first such elevation since George Washington. Grant was thirty-nine years old at the beginning of the war. In 1854 he had resigned his captaincy in the U.S. Army, because his military career had gone sour. Peacetime service and routine duties depressed Grant terribly. Inactivity and separation from his wife and children made life at the frontier posts unbearable, and he resorted to heavy drinking. He had trouble obtaining his first Civil War command, because almost no one sensed his real worth. His career had never surpassed the modest future forecast by his graduating from West Point in 1843 only twenty-first in a class of thirty-nine.

Beginning on April 22, 1861, Union troops occupied Cairo, Illinois, and from there on November 7, 1861, soldiers under Grant raided Belmont, Missouri. Several subsequent operations continued the thrust of Union forces down the Mississippi River. On April 6, 1862, the fall of Island No. 10 (in the river about sixty miles below Columbus, Kentucky) and the June 6, 1862, seizure of Memphis, Tennessee, were major steps toward the Union's goal of gaining control of the Mississippi River.

✺

Meanwhile, to the very far west, two violent episodes of some import unfolded. The first was the engagement at Valverde, New Mexico Territory, on February 21, 1862. Hoping to seal the legitimacy of the South's claim to western territory, Brig. Gen. Henry Hopkins Sibley had departed in November 1861 from San Antonio, Texas, leading the 3,700 men of the Army of New Mexico that he planned to conduct subsequently through Arizona to California, gathering supplies and recruits. They secured several positions in New Mexico, leaving small garrisons. Sibley led 2,600 of his men across the Rio Grande hoping to cut off a Union garrison from its headquarters at Santa Fe. Union Col. Edward R. S. Canby led 3,810 Yankees against this Rebel force.

The first shooting was exchanged with the two forces on opposite sides of the river, an artillery and small-arms duel at fairly long range. But the Confederates found the fire rather too hot and began to slip rearward, so the Union cavalry splashed across the river in pursuit. The Rebels fell back to better positions, in front of the old channel of the Rio Grande. Canby led the rest of his army and the artillery up to continue the fighting, and some hotly contested moments followed. The Confederates tried a cavalry charge and subsequently attempted storming frontally. A melee of hand-to-hand fighting ensued, punctuated with shooting from double-barreled shotguns, muskets, and revolvers. Canby's men at last broke, and he ordered a retreat. The Confederates allowed them under truce to secure the dead and wounded and to move away. So, technically, Sibley was the winner, but he was stung by his losses and sobered by the intensity of the resistance he had encountered.

The Confederate invasion of the western territory reached its peak on March 4 when Sibley occupied Santa Fe, which the Federals had abandoned following Canby's defeat at Valverde. But another pyrrhic Confederate victory followed on March 26–28 at La Glorieta Pass (sometimes called Apache Canyon). Although the Rebels emerged again the winners, during the night the Yankees managed to snatch most of the Rebel's supplies. Desperate for food and other material, the Rebels went north to Albuquerque only to discover that the Federals had destroyed a large store of goods that had been there. Sibley concluded he had lost too many men and was now too destitute to continue his mission. Fearing defeat if he chanced any more engagements, and fretting the possibility of starvation, he retreated into Texas and was harassed most of the way by Canby's force. The seventeen hundred Confederate survivors of this abysmally failed expedition reached safety in El Paso on May 4, 1862. The Confederate presence in the Far Western territory had come to naught.

Henry Wager Halleck. *Much* more one of the key architects of the
Northern victory than very many writers and students credit him
with having been; probably the reason he is so often downgraded is
because people, wrongly, feel they have to do so in order to further
build up U. S. Grant. (courtesy the Library of Congress)

The Western Departmental Commands

Destined to be one of the war's key figures, the forty-six-year-old Henry W.
Halleck had already demonstrated brilliant potential. He compiled an outstanding record at West Point, graduating third in the class of 1839, and thereafter

taught French at the Academy before going to France to inspect harbors. Upon his return he wrote *Report on the Means of National Defense,* a congressional publication that brought him an invitation to deliver a lecture series that soon appeared in print as his famous book *Elements of Military Art and Science.* He well merited his nickname "Old Brains," though it may have been pinned on him at least as much because of his huge forehead as for his scholarliness. Strangely, considering his capabilities, many persons either disliked or felt uncomfortable about Halleck because he lacked charisma and had an occasionally abrasive personality. His physique also belied his reputation, for, unlike the handsome McClellan, nothing of the classic soldierly image appeared in this paunchy, balding general. Still, it is revealing that Scott had wanted Halleck, and not McClellan, to succeed him as general in chief in November 1861.

Early in the war Halleck was placed in command of a department that stretched westward from the Cumberland River and included the part of Missouri that was then held by Union troops. The other major western department, centered in Unionist Kentucky east of the Cumberland, was under the command of Brig. Gen. Don Carlos Buell, who was something of a martinet—which antagonized his soldiers. A respected and competent Regular Army officer, the austere, methodical, and painfully conscientious Buell possessed the character and ability to make hard decisions. This led his superiors to expect him to become a good commander, but he lacked brilliance—and worse, he argued better than he fought.

On the Confederate side, the West was a unified command under Gen. Albert Sidney Johnston. This department—sometimes referred to as "Department No. 2" and at other times as "the Western Department"—stretched from the Appalachian Mountains west to include forces in Arkansas under Maj. Gen. Earl Van Dorn. General Johnston, fifty-eight years old, was an old chum of Jefferson Davis's. When the war began Johnston was in the Far West, and it took some time for him to get to Richmond. Davis was ill and in bed when he heard someone coming up the stairway. "That is Sidney Johnston's step!" exclaimed the gleeful Davis. Davis's feelings for him notwithstanding, Johnston was also the darling of Confederate luminaries who devoutly believed that he could bring victory. He possessed sound credentials, having graduated from West Point in 1826 eighth in the class. He had seen action in the Black Hawk War, the Texas Revolution, and the Mormon War of 1858. He was the second-ranking full general in the Confederate army and its senior field commander, junior only to Samuel Cooper, the adjutant and inspector general.

But if the Confederates achieved good organizational structure in the West, they failed abysmally to allocate adequate resources and leadership to that significant theater. True, Johnston had an able assistant in the person of Brig. Gen. Simon Bolivar Buckner; but Johnston had two not-very-able political brigadier generals as principal subordinates, Gideon J. Pillow and John B. Floyd, and he also had Maj. Gen. Leonidas Polk, whose precipitate and unauthorized invasion of self-declared neutral Kentucky had lost that state for the Confederacy.

Now Polk had command of a crucial district that included two defensive works that protected the line of the Tennessee and Cumberland Rivers, Fort Henry on the former and Fort Donelson on the latter. Although he was a West Pointer, and a close friend of President Davis, Polk had not served in the military after graduation. He went instead into the ministry and became a missionary bishop of the Episcopal Church. He doubtless had some managerial and organizational skills, but whatever warlike abilities and related insight he may once have possessed had hopelessly atrophied long ago. As the historian Grady McWhiney observed, Polk had been a bishop too long to be a good general.

On Johnston's order, Buckner scrounged some four thousand armed men, all he could find, and moved with them from Nashville to Bowling Green, Kentucky. Eventually, Maj. Gen. William J. Hardee reinforced this position to a total of twenty-five thousand men, blocking an invasion along the Louisville and Nashville Railroad. Brig. Gen. Felix K. Zollicoffer, a valiant, magnetic, and patriotic journalist and politician, otherwise quite unfit for command, took another four thousand men to Cumberland Gap, a relatively secure position in the absence of any rail or water approach from Kentucky. This "cordon" defensive line had been necessarily bowed southward to include Forts Henry and Donelson, which had been built in Tennessee because of the early effort to woo Kentucky by respecting its proclaimed neutrality. Of course, they *should* have been constructed nearer the mouths of the rivers that they protected.

The Cordon Ruptured: The Fort
Henry and Fort Donelson Campaigns

Brigadier General Buell concentrated fourteen thousand men in southeastern Kentucky, giving the field command to a capable Regular Army officer, Brig. Gen. George H. Thomas. On January 19, 1862, Thomas's force met the enemy along the north bank of the Cumberland River. Having advanced his four thousand troops some seventy miles northwest of his original mountain position, the Confederate commander, Zollicoffer, dug in near Beech Grove.

Zollicoffer's immediate superior, Maj. Gen. George B. Crittenden, had ordered that the Confederate force withdraw south of the river, but Zollicoffer delayed, and Crittenden went out to take personal command. Upon arrival he discovered Thomas's advancing army of equal size, four thousand, and decided to defend the position. But then spurning the advantage of a static emplacement, he sallied out in a driving rain to assault his attackers. At the height of the battle, Zollicoffer, brave to the point of rashness and conspicuous in a white rubber raincoat, rode far ahead of his troops and right up to the enemy. So nearsighted that he mistook a mounted Federal officer for one of his own men, he proceeded to give him an order when the man fired at him point-blank and put a fatal bullet though his chest. The Southerners withdrew, yielding the first break in the Kentucky defense. Both sides sustained only slight losses in this small battle, variously called Fishing Creek, Mill Springs, Somerset, Logan's Cross Roads, and Beech Grove, but it was a significant Union action that presaged things to come in the West.

Halleck correctly assessed his enemy's weakness on the Tennessee and Cumberland Rivers, and he formulated a grand plan to penetrate the Confederate cordon. Halleck intended to use the superior mobility conferred by water transportation, capture Forts Henry and Donelson before the Rebels could reinforce them, and break the Memphis and Ohio Railroad where it crossed the rivers, thus paralyzing Confederate mobility and depriving them of their interior lines. He instructed General Grant to move by steamer up the river, land near Fort Henry, occupy the road to Dover, and fully invest the fort, cutting off the retreat of the garrison.

Seven gunboats (four armored and three timber-clad) under the capable flag officer Andrew H. Foote would support the waterborne move. The four metal-sheathed vessels, with two and one-half inches of iron protection, had been constructed by the Eads Shipbuilding Company of St. Louis. They were formidable 175-foot-long craft that drew only six feet of water and mounted thirteen guns. Eads eventually completed seven of them, and they later proved of much value in the ongoing Union riverine war effort, on the Mississippi and on the Ohio.

In Grant, Halleck had chosen a good executor for his enterprise and equipped him well. Commanding so large a force, fifteen thousand men, reinforced Grant's natural confidence. He landed and immediately sent half of his force to the rear of Fort Henry, interrupted its communications, and confronted the garrison of twenty-five hundred men backed against the Tennessee River, where his seven gunboats lay. The fort was not a very formidable obstacle, much owing to its ill-conceived site: by now parts of the fort were hopelessly flooded. Of the fort's nine riverside guns, only two, a rifled piece and a Columbiad, could damage the gunboats' armor. On February 6, 1862, the Confederate commander prudently withdrew his garrison and sent the bulk of the men overland ten miles to Fort Donelson. The commander remained in the flooded Fort Henry to surrender it to the Union navy.

Grant promptly broke the Memphis and Ohio Railroad bridge over the Tennessee and prepared to move his army swiftly eastward. Brigadier General Floyd commanded the Donelson forces—twelve thousand men. A former governor of Virginia, Floyd's ignorance of military affairs had been little remedied by lackluster service as U.S. secretary of war in the late 1850s. While Grant was outnumbered at the outset, his force was gradually bolstered, ultimately to twenty-three thousand, so eventually he would outnumber Floyd by almost two-to-one. Grant was much hampered by floods and bad roads, but showing both energy and competence he cut enemy communications while reestablishing his own direct link with the river system.

The Confederate commanders at last realized their perilous situation. Their delay and failure to meet Grant west of the fort deprived them of their previous advantage of the tactical defensive. The Confederates continued to possess a line of retreat to the south, but the vacillating and indecisive Pillow and Floyd failed to take advantage of this opportunity. Not willing to accept the generals' decision to surrender, during the night of February 15–16, Col. Nathan Bedford Forrest's cavalry regiment and as many infantrymen as the horsemen could carry riding double managed to get away. Grant retained his composure, ordered a counterattack, again closed his lines around the fort, and soon forced the garrison's surrender on the morning of February 16, 1862.

In the correspondence concerning surrender terms, Grant acquired the most memorable of his several nicknames. Floyd, fearing reprisal after capture because of his previous position in the U.S. government, fled the fort and left the negotiations to Brigadier General Buckner, who then proposed "the appointment of commissioners to agree upon terms of capitulation." Grant replied: "No terms except unconditional and immediate surrender can be accepted. I propose to move immediately upon your works." Approximately 11,500 men and forty guns were surrendered. When news of this, and of what had been said, spread across the country, Northerners went wild with enthusiasm for "Unconditional Surrender" Grant. The government rewarded him with promotion to the rank of major general of volunteers. Ironically, while gaining

Ulysses S. Grant. William B. Hesseltine, only thirty-nine years old when the war began, and something of a ne'er-do-well, titled the first chapter in a short biography "Forty Years of Failure"; then, suddenly, and splendidly, Grant became *great*. Directing warfare at its highest levels was his true forte. (courtesy Leib Image Archives, York, Penn.)

both in rank and in the acquisition of an immortal appellation, Grant also during this campaign first took up smoking cigars, which grateful Unionists lavished upon him. Smoking them, however, was the probable ultimate cause of his eventual death due to throat cancer.

Shiloh

In order to reunite their divided and scattered forces, the Confederates had to retreat all the way to the northeastern Mississippi town of Corinth, an important railroad junction. Middle Tennessee was now open to invasion by Union troops; Buell's army occupied Nashville, while Grant's force pushed southward along the Tennessee River. About twenty-three miles northeast of Corinth, where the Confederates had managed to redeploy some forty-four thousand troops by the end of March, was Pittsburg Landing on the west bank of the Tennessee. Grant assembled his thirty-nine thousand men in that vicinity to await Buell, who was coming from Nashville with another thirty-six thousand men. Grant expected that the Confederates would do nothing until he was ready to attack them. The

Confederates, who were now under the direct command of General Johnston, seconded by Beauregard, and who had been organized into four tentatively conceived corps, had other plans.

The Southerners left Corinth on April 3, intending to make a one-day march and then a quick strike. Poor organization and faulty management at all levels caused delay, and the force did not clear Corinth until the afternoon. The troops had only two dirt roads that they could use; otherwise the movement was through heavily wooded countryside. Hard rains rendered the roads muddy and difficult, the creeks overflowed, and night marching became nearly impossible. These factors and the men's raw inexperience resulted in the twenty-mile march requiring three days. During that time, in addition to lapses of fire security as men shot at scurrying rabbits and deer, there was even sporadic skirmishing between enemy troops. Sherman, however, discounted the gravity of reports that reached him about this skirmishing, and Grant trusted him.

Beauregard, who had formulated the attack plan, despaired of all hope for surprise, which he thought vital, and he urged that the Rebels go back to Corinth. Johnston nevertheless insisted that the attack be made, saying, "I would fight them if they were a million." Much simply depended on luck. Legend holds that if the Confederates could have been allowed to inspect the Union campsites and rearrange the Federal units to better suit their intended assault, they would have requested no changes. No entrenchments at all had been dug (Grant having come to discount their usefulness owing to his Mexican War experiences). But the more doleful neglect was the total failure of most Union commanders to have required adequate reconnaissance and security; many astonished men were caught unexpecting and unready.

At 8:00 A.M. on Sunday, April 6, 1862, the first wave of gray-clad attackers slammed into Brigadier General Sherman's division, on the Union right flank, near a small log church named Shiloh. Sherman's inexperienced troops, supported by Maj. Gen. John A. McClernand's veterans of the Donelson campaign, were methodically driven back. Subsequently, the Union left flank was also enveloped. But when the Rebels struck the center they encountered a different situation. Located there was a dense wood with open fields on either side and an old sunken road that provided a ready-made entrenchment. The Federal division of Brig. Gen. Benjamin M. Prentiss, supported by portions of the divisions under Brig. Gens. Stephen A. Hurlbut and William H. L. Wallace, offered stiff resistance. Sherman's scattered troops reformed and joined in the bitter and costly defense. Both sides suffered many casualties; but the much more numerous Confederates at last prevailed, and the positions were overrun, save for Prentiss and his men in what came to be called "the Hornet's Nest." Grant maintained his cool manner and managed well in stabilizing his position, ordering that the Hornet's Nest be held at all cost.

By midday the Confederate organizational array began to unravel. The several corps had attacked following directly after one another, the first assault wave being reinforced by a different corps behind. Top commanders experienced difficulty maintaining control. Disorganization and loss of unit integrity resulted, and the Confederate offensive lost much of its momentum. More modern military doctrine would call for the Confederates to leave a containing force at the Hornet's Nest and continue the advance. Instead, charge after charge, a dozen or more of them, stormed into this seemingly impregnable stronghold.

About 2:30 P.M., General Johnston, directing the attacks against the Union left, was fatally wounded. A stray bullet struck his leg and severed the femoral artery. He quickly bled to death. Beauregard, who was ill, assumed command and directed maximal attention to the Hornet's Nest, eventually bringing sixty-two artillery pieces to fire en masse on the place. For two hours the Southern guns pounded the thicket, and at last, about 5:30 P.M., Prentiss and his force of twenty-two hundred men could endure no more, and they surrendered. The episode illustrated lessons for those who could perceive them: the strength of the defense when under cover and the potency of massed artillery.

The long defense of the Hornet's Nest gave Grant needed time, which he knew should redound to his benefit because he would be able to gather reinforcements. He fashioned a formidable perimeter on the ridge overlooking Pittsburg Landing, bolstered by artillery and two gunboats in supporting range. As dusk began to fall, Beauregard suspended the assault, hoping to reorganize and rest. But during the night Grant's force was bolstered by Maj. Gen. Lew Wallace's division (which had lost its way and not made it to the battlefield on the first day) and by four divisions of Buell's army that had arrived in the nick of time. Sufficiently reinforced, Grant decided to assume the offensive.

About 7:30 A.M. on April 7, 1862, the Union forces rolled forward. The now outnumbered and haggard Confederates (for it had rained unmercifully during the night, while Union gunboats lobbed shells into the Southern campsites) fought doggedly throughout most of the day. Again the combat was very bloody, but the progress achieved on this day was in the opposite direction as that which had occurred on the preceding day. Although the Union advance began to falter when it reached beyond the supporting fire of the gunboats on the river, Southerners still continued to be pushed back, and late in the afternoon

Beauregard ordered a full withdrawal to Corinth. Why did Grant not vigorously pursue? Because his men were also tired, battered, and disorganized as was always the result of major battle during the Civil War.

Shiloh offered any number of lessons. The nightfall that had induced the Confederates to terminate fighting on the first day and the timely arrival of the Union reinforcements are the principal obvious factors that allowed the Union forces to prevail. It has often been asserted, however, that the Confederates were doomed to lose the battle because of their intricate plan coupled with their extremely faulty corps organization. Too, and quite profound, was what happened with respect to artillery. On the first day many Union guns fell, captured by the Confederates; the reverse was true on the second day. In no other Civil War battle did so many pieces change hands. The Southerners came out probably only four guns ahead, but now a great many Confederate batteries were armed with Yankee guns and vice versa—and the quality of the Northerners' pieces was superior. It should have been a jolt to those persons who still clung to the once prevailing axiom that artillery was essentially defensive in nature to note both that artillery had not created the Hornet's Nest and that it was artillery that at last reduced the stronghold.

Shiloh was the first great bloody battle of the war. Each side lost about one-quarter of the troops engaged, and the casualty lists appalled a horrified citizenry. The costs far outweighed those of Bull Run. Union losses at Shiloh were 1,754 killed, 8,408 wounded, and 2,885 captured, for a total of 13,047; Confederate casualties reached 10,694—1,723 killed, 8,012 wounded, and 959 missing. Northerners severely castigated Grant; many critics called for his dismissal, citing alleged drunkenness. Nonetheless, Lincoln stood by and defended him. The president supposedly said, in reaction to his own frustrated dissatisfaction with the failures and the delays thus far produced by his eastern generals in the war's more politically sensitive theater, "I can't spare this man; he fights."

Almost immediately after Shiloh, Major General Halleck arrived from St. Louis and assumed personal command. Soon the remainder of his troops from the Mississippi area joined him, and with more than one hundred thousand men he faced Beauregard's force of barely half that strength. Halleck commenced a cautious and slow advance toward Corinth, while the capable Beauregard, rapidly gaining in experience, protected well against any major disaster. Halleck's careful tactics, constant entrenching, and major road-building held his progress to a snail's pace: this advance continued for seven weeks, at the rate of less than one mile per day. Commencing the night of May 29,

Beauregard, with great skill and efficiency, pulled his army out of besieged Corinth and headed south toward Tupelo. Halleck thus attained an objective he had pursued for months—breaking the Memphis and Charleston Railway, a road so important that one of the Rebel secretaries of war had called it "the vertebrae of the Confederacy."

Conclusion

The first full year of the Civil War, from Sumter to Shiloh, ended with the Union having achieved a good deal more than seemed apparent. True, President Lincoln was somewhat justified in his dissatisfaction with matters in the eastern theater, and he was to be much more dissatisfied with them during the year that followed. But no devastating disaster had occurred. The long-term effects of Bull Run accrued more to the Union's benefit than to the Confederacy's. That battle had bolstered Southern pride and given false assurance, while it had induced greater Northern efforts to mobilize and to gear up.

As 1861 wore on, with both sides attempting to prepare for a bigger struggle than either had anticipated, other achievements of note were scored by the Union navy. The Capture of Hatteras Inlet in August 1861 and the Union seizure of Port Royal on the Atlantic coast (and, even more crucial, the Union success in taking Roanoke Island the following February) had long-term significance, giving the Union potential staging and jumping-off areas for inland invasions. Most important, they provided coaling stations for what gradually became an ever more powerful blockading squadron. Early in 1862 Union forces also seized and occupied St. Augustine, Florida, and New Bern, North Carolina. The late 1861 occupation of Ship Island, off the Mississippi coast, set the stage for an early 1862 operation against New Orleans, which fell into Federal hands on April 27–29, 1862. Earlier, on March 7–8, 1862, the bitter but inconclusive Battle of Pea Ridge or Elkhorn Tavern was fought. A frontier-type struggle, marked by much rough close-quarter fighting and personal courage, it proved to be the biggest battle west of the Mississippi River during the entire war. Because the Rebel force was augmented by Indians from Oklahoma, there were widespread, but mostly untrue, charges of Confederates scalping fallen Federals.

It was now quite obviously going to be a big and probably long war. Very large armies had been created, although much still needed to be accomplished in organizing, training, and equipping them. The poor functioning of the Confederacy's corps organizations at Shiloh starkly illustrated that the South had taken only the most primitive and initial steps. In November 1862 the thirty-eight thousand men of the Army of Tennessee would be restructured into two corps of about equal size, under Lieutenant Generals Polk and Hardee. But, in truth, both sides still had far to go in needed restructure.

The war was also going to be more costly, more bloody, and more expensive in terms of life and limb than had seemed possible to imagine at the outset or possibly that very many persons had yet perceived: U. S. Grant wrote shortly after the battle that he expected "a speedy move, one more fight and then the end of the war." His thinking on this topic changed somewhat slower than he liked to recall in later years; in his memoirs he asserted that "up to the battle of Shiloh I, as well as thousands of other citizens, believed that the rebellion against the Government would collapse suddenly and soon, if a decisive victory could be gained over any of its armies." But Forts Henry and Donelson had been just such victories, and they were followed by a massive and impressive Confederate redeployment, making notable use of both the railroads and the telegraph in the process. Shiloh was a rather sobering episode. After that, Grant wrote, "I gave up all idea of saving the Union except by complete conquest."

What Grant *did* do in the immediate aftermath of Shiloh was to write one of his friends a letter that revealed his attitude concerning what it would take to extinguish the Confederacy: "The iron gauntlet must be used more than the silken glove to crush this serpent." Despite the essentially stalemated engagement at Shiloh, the North had turned the South's western concentration into a strategic victory; the South had hoped to destroy Grant's force and thereafter to recapture western Tennessee, but Grant had now extinguished those hopes.

SUGGESTED READINGS

Thoughtful Commentary by Modern Historians

After Secession: Jefferson Davis and the Failure of Confederate Nationalism, by Paul D. Escott (Baton Rouge: Louisiana State University Press, 1979).

The American Civil War and the Origins of Modern Warfare, by Edward Hagerman (Bloomington: Indiana University Press, 1988).

Americans Interpret Their Civil War, by Thomas J. Pressly, 2d ed. (New York: Free Press, 1962), is an essential classic but an update is sorely needed.

Attack and Die: Civil War Military Tactics and the Southern Heritage, by Grady McWhiney and Perry D. Jamieson (Tuscaloosa: University of Alabama Press, 1982), is highly controversial but includes the best description of Civil War tactics ever.

The Battle of Belmont, by Nathaniel Cheairs Hughes Jr. (Chapel Hill: University of North Carolina Press, 1991).

Battle Tactics of the Civil War, by Paddy Griffith (New Haven: Yale University Press, 1989), contains important and sometimes provacative insights by a non-American.

"The Best School in the World": West Point, the Pre–Civil War Years, 1833–1866, by James L. Morrison Jr. (Kent: Kent State University Press, 1986).

The Civil War in the American West, by Alvin M. Josephy Jr. (New York: Knopf, 1991), is about the Far West, beyond that which is called the "western theater." Josephy is a good writer, and the story is important, but the book is a little disappointing because of its jumpy organization and unchronological arrangement. Further, it focuses on military events alone (and thus is lacking in analysis and commentary), and it is based only on secondary and published primary sources.

Civil War Soldiers: Their Expectations and Their Experiences, by Reid Mitchell (New York: Viking, 1988), is a worthy and very readable supplement to the classic and pioneering works of Bell I. Wiley on the subject of the Civil War common soldiers.

Civil War Sutlers and Their Wares, by Francis A. Lord (New York: Thomas Yoseloff, 1969), is a classic.

The Confederate Regular Army, by Richard P. Weinert (Shippensburg, Pa.: White Mane, 1991), is an underappreciated, essential work.

Drawn with the Sword: Reflections on the American Civil War, by James M. McPherson (New York: Oxford University Press, 1996). I and my various collaborators are in fundamental disagreement with some of McPherson's conclusions, but he is a prolific and very successful scholar, widely acclaimed as "the dean of living Civil War historians." His work merits attention.

Duel between the First Ironclads, by William C. Davis (New York: Doubleday, 1975), is very readable.

Embattled Courage: The Experience of Combat in the American Civil War, by Gerald E. Linderman (New York: Free Press, 1987).

The First Battle of Manassas: An End to Innocence, by John Hennessy (Lynchburg, Va.: H. E. Howard, 1989).

Forts Henry and Donelson: The Key to the Confederate Heartland, by Benjamin Franklin Cooling (Knoxville: University of Tennessee Press, 1987). Cooling is too underappreciated.

The Hard Hand of War: Union Military Policy toward Southern Civilians, 1861–1865, by Mark Grimsley (Cambridge: Cambridge University Press, 1995), is one of the best works, by one of the best scholars, produced by the younger and rising generation of historians.

History of Military Mobilization in the United States Army, 1775–1945, by Marvin A. Kreidberg and Merton G. Henry (Washington, D.C.: Department of the Army, Pamphlet 20–212, November 1955), is essential for full understanding of mobilization.

A House Divided: Sectionalism and Civil War, 1848–1865, by Richard H. Sewell (Baltimore and London: Johns Hopkins University Press, 1988), is a fine short survey of the

period. It almost, but not quite, deserves to be equated with Roland's *American Iliad.*
This book's strongest suit is its clear delineation of the interrelationship between
slavery and the process of the war.

The Politics of Command, by Thomas Lawrence Connelly and Archer Jones (Baton
Rouge: Louisiana State University Press, 1973), is important and provocative. It is
perhaps not well suited for beginners, as the authors demand much hard thought
from readers.

The Private Civil War: Popular Thought during the Sectional Conflict, by Randall C.
Jimerson (Baton Rouge: Louisiana State University Press, 1988), is something of an
artful tour de force, probing the mind-sets of civilians *and* soldiers.

Symbol, Sword, and Shield: Defending Washington during the Civil War, by Benjamin
Franklin Cooling (Hamden, Conn.: Archon Books, 1975). Cooling's work is far too
underappreciated; and this is one of his best.

The Training of an Army: Camp Curtain and the North's Civil War, by William J. Miller
(Shippensburg, Pa.: White Mane, 1990), presents important information on an
egregiously neglected topic.

The Vacant Chair: The Northern Soldier Leaves Home, by Reid Mitchell (New York and
Oxford: Oxford University Press, 1993), is very readable, thought-provoking, and
provocative.

What They Fought For, 1861–1865, by James M. McPherson (Baton Rouge: Louisiana
State University Press, 1994). Presented as the Walter Lynwood Fleming Lectures,
these three essays are a foretaste of McPherson's larger work-in-progress about "why
they fought."

Campaign Study

Pea Ridge: Civil War Campaign in the West, by William L. Shea and Earl J. Hess (Chapel
Hill: University of North Carolina Press, 1992), sets a new modern standard for this
type of work.

Memoir

Hardtack and Coffee, by John D. Billings (Boston: G. M. Smith, 1887). Numerous
subsequent editions were published. By far the best memoir by a Union veteran,
this work contains marvelous, entertaining, and informative accounts of army life
and the recalled feelings of a common soldier. It is also available on cassette tape
from Blackstone Audio Books, P.O. Box 969, Ashland, OR 97520.

Diary

My Diary North and South, by William Howard Russell, 2 vols. (London: Bradbury
and Evans, 1863). Several republished later editions exist. Enormously amusing

writing, but not as good as his dispatches from the Crimea, this book earned him the nickname "Bull Run" Russell. It treats only the first nine months of the war in the East.

Abraham Lincoln

Lincoln, by David Herbert Donald (New York: Simon and Schuster, 1995), is now the best one-volume biography.

Lincoln and the First Shot, by Richard N. Current (Philadelphia and New York: Lippincott, 1963).

Lincoln and the Tools of War, by Robert V. Bruce, new ed. (Urbana: University of Illinois Press, 1989), is a great book.

Lincoln in American Memory, by Merrill D. Peterson (New York: Oxford University Press, 1994), is quite interesting.

Lincoln's Loyalists: Union Soldiers from the Confederacy, by Richard N. Current (Boston: Northeastern University Press, 1992), is a delightful little book that sheds fresh light on a little studied topic. The literary crafting is enhanced by the obvious touch of an accomplished master: my "Uncle Richard."

Robert E. Lee

"The Fabric of Command: R. E. Lee, Confederate Insignia, and the Perception of Rank," by Edward D. C. Campbell (*Virginia Magazine of History and Biography* 98 [April 1990]: 261–90), sheds light on Lee's possible egotism.

Other Biographies

Beauregard: Napoleon in Gray, by T. Harry Williams (Baton Rouge: Louisiana State University Press, 1955), is a biography of "the most colorful of all the Confederate generals."

Confederate General of the West: Henry Hopkins Sibley, by Henry Thompson (1987; College Station: Texas A&M University Press, 1996). While Thompson, as well as Frank Vandiver who wrote the foreword, argues that Sibley just might have been the Confederacy's *worst* general, the man was capable, he had bad luck, and he *did* accomplish some things. This is a very readable and interesting biography of an out-of-the-way figure.

Damned Yankee: The Life of General Nathaniel Lyon, by Christopher Phillips (Columbia: University of Missouri Press, 1990).

Quartermaster General of the Union Army: A Biography of M. C. Meigs, by Russell F. Weigley (New York: Columbia University Press, 1959), is a fine biography, the early work of an accomplished and much loved master in military history.

That Man Haupt, by James A. Ward (Baton Rouge: Louisiana State University Press, 1973), is a biography of Brig. Gen. Herman Haupt, who was a West Pointer and a major figure in the development of nineteenth-century American railroads; Ward is one of the "wee Harrys."

The Zollie Tree, by Raymond E. Myers (Louisville: Filson Club, 1964), is a good biography of Brig. Gen. Felix K. Zollicoffer.

Balloons

Aeronautics in the Union and Confederate Armies, with a Survey of Military Aeronautics prior to 1861, by Frederick Stansbury Haydon (Baltimore: Johns Hopkins University Press, 1941).

The Air Arm of the Confederacy, by Joseph Jenkins Cornish III (Richmond: Civil War Centennial Committee, 1963).

The Role of Religion

American Apocalypse: Yankee Protestants and the Civil War, 1860–1869, by James H. Moorhead (New Haven and London: Yale University Press, 1978), delineates how religious beliefs ultimately buoyed Northerners and fired them onward in the war effort and depressed Southerners.

Broken Churches, Broken Nation, by C. C. Goen (Macon: Mercer University Press, 1985), is hard to read, but enlightening and worthwhile.

A Shield and a Hiding Place: The Religious Life of the Civil War Armies, by Gardner H. Shattuck (Macon: Mercer University Press, 1987). The influence of religion is an important and too often neglected topic in military history.

The South and the North in American Religion, by Samuel S. Hill Jr. (Athens: University of Georgia Press, 1980), is a splendid short book of lectures, which suggests that the roots of religious difference, North and South, go far into the past and that by the time of the Civil War the churches were like "third cousins estranged."

Fiction

Confederates, by Thomas Keneally (New York: Harper, 1980), is a wonderful fictional portrait of the poor white soldiers.

The Crisis, by Winston Churchill (New York: Macmillan, 1901), is a classic fictional study about combat motivation.

Johnny Shiloh, by James A. Rhodes and Dean Jauchius (Indianapolis: Bobbs-Merrill, 1959), is a novel based on a true story about the Union's Johnny Clem, the war's youngest soldier.

Miss Ravenel's Conversion from Secession to Loyalty, by John William DeForest (New York: Holt, Rinehart and Winston, 1955), with an introduction by Gordon S. Haight, is a great nineteenth-century novel: DeForest well understood both the Northern and the Southern points of view. Little, if indeed any, other writing surpasses the realism of the war scenes.

Shiloh, by Shelby Foote (New York: Dial Press, 1952), is simply a superb novel about this bloody battle.

A Shipment of Tarts, by Edmund G. Love (New York: Doubleday, 1967), is a delightfully humorous fiction about the Union army's evacuation of some prostitutes from Memphis.

Picture Books

The Image of War: 1861–1865, edited by William C. Davis, 6 vols. (Garden City, N.Y.: Doubleday, 1981–1984), sets a new standard for photographic documentation of the Civil War.

Rebels and Yankees: The Fighting Men of the Civil War, by William C. Davis (New York: Gallery Books, n.d.), offers much good stuff on personal equipage and weaponry and is among the finest of picture books.

Touched by Fire: A Photographic Portrait of the Civil War, edited by William C. Davis, 2 vols. (Boston: Little, Brown, 1985–1986), is a fine supplement to *The Image of War: 1861–1865* above, a potpourri.

PART II

The War in Apparent Stalemate

❧

The rival presidents and their advisers spent the second year of the war trying, with great mental effort and much frustration, to determine the correct strategy and to find the men who could execute it. President Lincoln at this stage of the game was rather too quick to replace a commander who had disappointed him (especially in the politically sensitive eastern theater); conversely, President Davis—particularly in the western theater—too long retained inept commanders whom he regarded as friends.

The Union did, however, surge significantly ahead of the South in the direction of creating an embryonic version of a modern general staff. Abraham Lincoln's energetic secretary of war, Edwin M. Stanton, who assumed the office on January 15, 1862, perceived deficiencies in organization, and so he formed the War Board. It consisted of the heads of the various army bureaus—the adjutant general, the quartermaster general, the chief of ordnance, the chief engineer, and the commissary general—and was chaired by retired Maj. Gen. Ethan Allan Hitchcock. Collectively the War Board became a body of great significance and potency. Coordination between the several bureaus was greatly enhanced, and the War Board provided a source of formal advice on operational questions. But, because Hitchcock failed to become an adequate chief of staff, and because the War Board ceased to formally exist after mid-July 1862, many scholars have not perceived or appreciated its impact. The board spawned a long-lasting effect, through continuing *informal* coordination and cooperation. The War Board, and the residual informal continuation of its work, wrought enormous beneficial impact on the North's war effort. Specific examples of this phenomenon were delineated in the February 1982 article by Herman Hattaway and Archer Jones in the scholarly journal *Military Affairs,* and the essence was incorporated into *How the North Won.*

Another institution, the congressional Joint Committee to Examine the Conduct of the War (hereafter referred to as the Committee on Conduct), had mixed worth. Created in December 1861, it remained active for the rest of the conflict. Dominated by its radical Republican members, the committee tended to promote the fortunes of Republican officers and to bring the dismissal of Democrats—especially those who performed in a faulty or inadequate manner. Generals who appeared to have insufficient antislavery attitudes were doubly likely to feel its sting, and with great celerity.

As the war continued to unfold, it was repeatedly characterized by apparent stalemate, because while armies could, and indeed did, hurt each other mightily in battle, they lacked the combat power to annihilate one another. Commanders slowly (some of them even grudgingly) came to realize and emphasize the importance and inherent value of entrenchments and field fortifications. Even before the use of the spade became commonplace, unentrenched soldiers often spontaneously took advantage of partial cover offered by trees and used bayonets and mess equipment to dig in.

CHAPTER 4

The Peninsula Campaign

Maj. Gen. George B. McClellan succeeded quite well in the task of bringing his forces to combat readiness. His army became a far more formidable one than any ever before mustered by the United States: ninety infantry regiments, twenty artillery batteries with one hundred pieces of field artillery, and nine cavalry regiments—all adding up to approximately one hundred thousand men. Too, by shortly before the end of 1861, the Federals completed construction of a thirty-seven-mile belt of powerful fortifications around Washington (linked together and further strengthened by a brigade of Regular Army cavalry under Brig. Gen. Philip St. George Cooke).

But McClellan resisted forming any organization larger than a division. Not opposed to creating corps, he wanted the army to get some experience in actual campaigning first and for himself to have the opportunity to judge his generals' performances at division level. But political considerations and military judgment commingled in precipitating Lincoln's and Stanton's decision to force McClellan to accept a corps structure.

It began to seem to impatient civilians, however, that McClellan might never be ready for the army to take the field. Earlier, Lincoln had issued a general order that the Army of the Potomac must move forth on or before Washington's Birthday, February 22, 1862. That date came and went, and nothing happened. As the weeks and months slipped by and spring arrived, the victorious Confederate army under Gen. Joseph E. Johnston, headquartered at Manassas (only thirty miles from the Federal capital), was not only an embarrassment to the United States but it was increasing in readiness as well.

Urged by Stanton and by the Committee on Conduct, Lincoln issued a second general order on March 7, 1862. McClellan's army was restructured into four corps, and Lincoln promoted a coterie of good Republicans to take their command: Maj. Gens. Irvin McDowell, Edwin V. Sumner, Samuel P.

Heintzelman, and Erasmus D. Keyes. A fifth corps—not under McClellan's immediate operational control but rather under Maj. Gen. Nathaniel P. Banks (a token Democrat elevated to high command)—was organized from the forces in the Shenandoah valley.

The Siege of Yorktown

McClellan evolved an audacious plan reminiscent of Winfield Scott's brilliant captures of Vera Cruz and Mexico City. The Union navy was to provide the vital lines of communications and to transport the invasion force to some appropriate point on the coast. McClellan's first intention was to land near Urbana, Virginia (hence its initial name, the Urbana Plan), so that he could exploit use of railroad trackage between Richmond and West Point, Virginia. The Confederates, however, abandoned their advanced positions near Washington, thus inducing McClellan to land instead near the tip of land between the York and James Rivers, an area called "the Peninsula."

On March 17, 1862, McClellan's huge force began moving onto the Peninsula. At Yorktown, the Rebel Maj. Gen. John B. Magruder, who had only 12,000 men, magnificently played the role of delayer. Magruder deceived McClellan into thinking Magruder was stronger than he was, by "strengthening" his defenses with fake cannon (tree trunks painted black, so-called Quaker guns) and by parading his men into and out of sight to suggest that there were more than there really were. So McClellan concluded that to take Yorktown positively would necessitate a methodical siege. All the while, Magruder's strength gradually increased, and by April 11, his number of troops had more than doubled to 31,500.

To aid in their unorthodox defense, the Confederates used land mines at Yorktown. These were a modified form of booby trap that one of the Confederate division commanders, Brig. Gen. Gabriel J. Rains, had first implemented twenty-two years earlier in the Second Seminole War. At Yorktown, a hapless Federal rider and his horse were thrown some distance by the initial explosion, but the larger effect was psychological: thereafter soldiers occasionally thought they saw torpedoes everywhere.

McClellan was outraged at what he believed to be an uncivilized act of barbarism, and even the Confederate high command gave sober thought to that possibility. After pondering the issue, the Confederate secretary of war made a ruling that it all depended on how the torpedoes were used: to kill pickets with them *would* be gratuitous murder, but it would be acceptable to use them to kill generals if that could be accomplished. A strange set of unofficial "rules" eventually evolved. Mines should not be used to kill merely for the sake of killing. They would, however, be used to delay pursuits, repel attacks, and protect rivers and harbors.

Torpedoes of various types were rapidly deployed in virtually all of the South's inland and coastal waterways. The Federals, in turn, were induced to devise defensive mechanisms, the world's first "mine sweepers." The initial use of such a device occurred on April 30, 1862. Essentially a huge rake, it was sixty-five feet long and affixed to it were large numbers of grappling hooks, pushed ahead of a lead vessel.

Otherwise, the Federal campaign made very slow progress; and McClellan failed to appreciate the political situation. He arrogantly blamed meddling politicians in Washington, even the president, for spoiling his chances. Just as McClellan had departed Washington, Lincoln had insisted that one corps be detached from McClellan's invasion force and retained to protect the capital.

Johnston elected to evacuate Yorktown on May 3, 1862, and, though he fought a delaying action at Williamsburg on May 5, he continued to withdraw toward Richmond. At this point, however, McClellan's thinking began to blur. His intelligence-gathering section was a poorly functioning assemblage headed by the civilian detective Allan Pinkerton. Not totally inept as sleuths, Pinkerton and his men were simply inadequate as army spies. They relied much too implicitly on information reported to them by frantic civilians and escaped slaves.

Stonewall Jackson in the Shenandoah Valley

Meanwhile, the Confederates had been doing something constructive about their situation. Stonewall Jackson conducted his important Valley campaign: at its conclusion, in two weeks his men had marched 170 miles, routed a total of 12,500 Federals, and occupied the attention of some 60,000 other troops. Although the Confederates eventually increased his strength to 16,000 men, Jackson was always outnumbered at least seven to three. Nevertheless, every time he engaged he was able to hit fractions of his enemy with the bulk of his own command. Out of six engagements, Jackson won all but the first.

It was this campaign that made Jackson a revered Southern folk hero. Called "Old Jack" by his troops (never "Stonewall"), now thirty-eight years old, Jackson had been in the West Point class that graduated in 1846, the same one as McClellan, and the two knew each other well. Unlike McClellan, however, Jackson had never manifested brilliance; he always had to work hard to survive, but that is exactly what he did. And he tended to extract a similar intensity of effort from his men, for, unlike McClellan who possessed a cool analytical intellect, Jackson had an "inner fire" of inspiration.

In its totality, the Valley campaign covered a period of three months, from mid-March to mid-June 1862. The combatants marched up and down the valley five times, or two and one-half round-trips. At the outset, Jackson possessed but forty-two hundred men, located in Winchester. In opposition stood slightly more than twenty thousand Union troops under Major General Banks, a former speaker of the House of Representatives who had been appointed to his rank primarily for political reasons, and another fifteen thousand men—farther to the west—under Maj. Gen. John C. Fremont. Although a professional, Fremont was a topographical engineer and had scant combat or command experience, save for an undistinguished performance earlier in Missouri.

McClellan's intent had been for Banks to push Jackson's men quickly out of the valley and for Fremont to hold that area secure while Banks then moved east to Manassas to protect Washington during the thrust up the Peninsula. When Banks crossed the Potomac in early March, Jackson evacuated Winchester, and Banks proceeded to occupy it. Then, leaving a garrison behind, Banks pursued the southwardly moving Jackson with eighteen thousand men. The somewhat complicated ensuing campaign can best be understood as four separate and distinct episodes.

The first one was the March 23, 1862, First Battle of Kernstown. Banks followed Jackson southward until he became convinced that the Rebels were evacuating the valley, and so Banks turned toward Washington. But Jackson's aim was to minimize aid being directed in favor of McClellan's campaign. Jackson turned and moved rapidly to attack Yankee troops at Kernstown. In the prolonged struggle the Confederates were defeated and driven from the field. But their tactical loss was turned into a strategic gain, when President Lincoln reacted by ordering the corps of forty thousand men under Major General McDowell to interpose between Jackson and Washington, instead of joining McClellan as had been planned.

More than a month later came the second episode, the May 8, 1862, Battle of McDowell. Under orders to force Jackson from the valley, Banks began to thrust southward. But the Union movement was slow and took a full month just to reach Harrisonburg. In cooperation, Fremont moved some of his troops toward Staunton. Jackson left a small covering force to watch Banks and proceeded with the bulk of his force, now some ten thousand men, deceptively appearing to be withdrawing to Richmond. Near Charlottesville the Confederates loaded on trains, and to the surprise of many, the trains headed west, not east. The troops unloaded amid a cheering citizenry at Staunton and marched rapidly toward the town of McDowell. Just short of their goal, some six thousand of Fremont's men attacked them. In severe fighting, the Union forces were compelled to retreat, and the Confederates pursued. The Federals set the woods afire, thus enabling them to get back to safety in the vicinity of Franklin. Jackson then returned to the Shenandoah valley and proceeded north.

The third episode constituted two battles, Front Royal and Winchester, on May 23 and 25, 1862, respectively. Instead of continuing northward along the Valley Turnpike, as it seemed logical he would do, at New Market on May 20 Jackson suddenly veered to the right, across Massanutten Mountain to Luray. There he was joined by troops under Maj. Gen. Richard S. Ewell, bringing Jackson's force to a total of sixteen thousand men. On May 23 Jackson entered Front Royal and easily defeated a small garrison, some eight hundred men, capturing many of them. Jackson's rapidity and victory at Front Royal attracted attention in Washington and inspired a plan to try to entrap and possibly destroy him, using McDowell's corps from the east and Fremont's force from the west. Meanwhile Banks, incredulous that Jackson's men could march so fast, fled to Winchester, where on May 25 he tried to make a stand but was badly defeated. Here much ammunition, other supplies, and numerous wagons fell into Jackson's hands.

Finally came the conclusion at Cross Keys on June 8 and at Port Republic on June 9. Unable to catch Jackson until they reached the ground of his choosing, part of Fremont's force was vanquished from the west and part of McDowell's from the east, a frustrating dual defeat in detail. Both Federal columns then retreated northward. McDowell's orders to proceed toward Richmond were canceled again. But the Valley campaign now ended. Several days later Jackson's men slipped away to join the main Confederate army near Richmond.

The Confederates, now with the knowledge of the great extent that Lincoln would go in ensuring the safety of Washington, would take advantage of that knowledge again in the future. Jackson had demonstrated himself to be a master of strategy and deployment—and his Valley campaign would eventually be much studied by military men around the world. It stands as a quintessential example of successful application of Jominian principle, especially the one that prescribes maneuvering "to engage fractions of the hostile army with the bulk of one's forces."

Fair Oaks (Seven Pines)

By May 9 McClellan had made such headway up the Peninsula that the Confederates felt compelled to evacuate Norfolk. This important depot and port was a severe loss, and, worse, it left the CSS *Virginia* without a home base. The Confederates soon decided to destroy the vessel.

On May 31, with McClellan's advanced elements only five miles away from Richmond (Union troops could actually see the church spires inside the city), General Johnston concluded that the time had come when he must try *something.* McClellan provided the inviting opportunity by dividing his army, placing two corps south of the Chickahominy River and three to the north. Normally the river was not difficult to cross, but heavy rains during the preceding month had swollen it, and on May 30 a terrific storm turned the river into a raging torrent, washing over the bridges.

On May 31, in a battle that saw one of the war's several instances of women exhorting the troops and trying to influence the outcome, the Confederates attacked the two southernmost Federal corps, near a plantation called Seven Pines. In conception, the attack plan was a good one, but instead of providing his subordinates with detailed written instructions, Johnston issued verbal orders that proved to be overly intricate, and the commanders mismanaged their execution. Thus, this is a classic example of Johnston having violated what would later be known as one of the fundamental principles of war: simplicity.

Leaving the road, Confederate Maj. Gen. D. H. Hill's division sloshed through swampy and wooded terrain. The division's four brigades slammed piecemeal, instead of in the intended three-pronged assault, into Major General Keyes's position. The fighting was ferocious and the casualties costly. Keyes's line eroded, and only a spirited bayonet charge by one Federal brigade saved the Union artillery. Methodically, Keyes managed to establish a new line and then was joined by reinforcements. When Confederate attacks crushed the Federal right, some of the Union troops fled to Fair Oaks, a railroad station about a mile north of Seven Pines. Late in the day, the Southerners again assaulted at Seven Pines. The Federals withdrew to a third line, and by 6:00 P.M. the action subsided.

The woman who became involved in the melee was a nurse called Bridget Divers (her real name was Deavers), who had attached herself to the First Michigan Cavalry when her husband had enlisted early in the war. Nicknamed "Michigan Bridget," she earned much fame, then and later, for her bravery under fire in removing wounded men from the battlefield. At one moment she picked up a fallen soldier's gun and fought for a time alongside the men.

The largest battle yet in the eastern theater now ended in stalemate. The assaulting Southerners had lost six thousand men, while the Unionists had sustained about five thousand casualties. Both retained their original positions. The really big loss for the Confederates was General Johnston: In the twilight he had ridden along the lines to make a visual estimate of the situation and sustained several wounds that disabled him for nearly six months. A musket shot pierced his right shoulder, and a few moments later a shell fragment struck him in the chest, knocking him off his horse.

Gen. Robert E. Lee now left his post as chief of staff and took the field at the head of the army. Dispatching himself (and indeed the staff he had assembled as well) outside of Richmond was intended to be only temporary. But Johnston did not recover as promptly as had been expected. Lee would prove to be an energetic and able campaigner; he never returned to his full-time staff duties in Richmond. Not replacing Lee and his staff at Richmond was a grave Confederate mistake. Davis failed to perceive what he had momentarily accomplished in moving toward modernity in military management. And because the staff officers themselves departed from the War Department, the Confederacy would *not* benefit from ongoing informal organization as was the case residually in the North following the formal dissolution of the War Board. On the other hand, Lee and his staff from the first brought a new and higher level of managerial capability to the field army.

The Seven Days Campaign and Malvern Hill

The Seven Days campaign, an interrelated series of engagements fought between June 25 and July 1, 1862, was a fluid and ongoing battle (somewhat like a World War II style of operations). On June 1, 1862, Lee possessed in his command about seventy-two thousand men. The Union army lay in an awkward, potentially vulnerable position. McClellan had some seventy thousand troops situated south of the Chickahominy River, while another thirty thousand men (Maj. Gen. Fitz John Porter's reinforced V Corps) stood north of the river.

On June 12 Lee dispatched his brilliant and flamboyant cavalry chieftain, Brig. Gen. James E. B. Stuart, to reconnoiter. In a bold three-day ride, led by an able scout (the later famous Lt. John Singleton Mosby), Stuart's cavalry rode completely around McClellan's army. The horsemen learned that the Federal army's right flank (northern side) lay unanchored—that is, unprotected—because it was not shielded by any natural feature.

Lee acted daringly: leaving only twenty-five thousand men south of the Chickahominy, Lee deployed his other forty-seven thousand men against Porter's corps, simultaneously recalling Maj. Gen. Thomas J. Jackson's eighteen thousand men from the valley. Meanwhile, having become wrongly convinced that the Confederates outnumbered him two-to-one, McClellan remained excessively cautious. The ensuing campaign turned into a series of frontal assaults fomented by the Confederates. McClellan rather ill-managed his responses to Lee's attacks, but—though forced to move rearward some twenty miles—the Union force inflicted significantly more casualties than it sustained. McClellan ordered that his base be changed from the York River southward to the James River. While he called this retrograde a strategic withdrawal, McClellan's critics suggested that it was a "great skedaddle." (Later it looked even worse when it became known that some of McClellan's subordinate generals had perceived how weak the Confederate defense before Richmond actually was. McClellan had rejected their counsel to press on more vigorously when the army had been so near the city.)

For the next three days, June 28–30, Lee vainly tried to destroy portions of McClellan's force, especially its huge wagon train, and to ensnare its cattle herd. But Lee's plans proved too complicated, his staff bungled in its vital workings, and as a result the Confederate movements were ill-coordinated. Poor and inadequate maps plagued both sides. Several Southern divisions attacked in piecemeal fashion, on June 29 at Allen's Farm, at Savage Station on the Richmond and York River Railroad, and on June 30 in a thoroughly disjointed and diffused battle, variously named White Oak Swamp (an area described by one observer as a "nightmarish morass"), Frayser's Farm, or Glendale. Indeed, fierce fighting occurred, but still the Union retrograde continued.

Commencing at 9:00 A.M. on June 30, Porter's V Corps began organizing a strong natural position on Malvern Hill for defense. Throughout June 30 and into July 1, more and more of McClellan's army filtered into Porter's position. Malvern Hill is a stark elevation (some 150 feet above the surrounding terrain), and ravines deeply cut the slopes to each flank of the Union emplacement while elsewhere swamps offered further protection from attack on either side. Toward the northern front stretched an open plateau.

This time the artillery would come into effective play, for Col. Henry J. Hunt, commanding the Union artillery reserve, had time to post some 250 guns: 100 in front and the rest in reserve and on the flanks. Some of these latter pieces were guns with extremely long range and of huge caliber—such as twenty-pounder Parrotts. Gun crews with mule teams had labored through the night to haul them up from boats on the James River.

Despite having been warned by a member of Maj. Gen. D. H. Hill's staff who was familiar with the region that Malvern Hill was a place that McClellan could render virtually invulnerable, on July 1 (having overestimated the damage the Army of the Potomac had suffered) Lee chose to attack. Jackson's three divisions were to proceed in column down the Willis Church Road toward the point where it turned obliquely to climb the rise of Malvern Hill. Magruder's three divisions, trailing Jackson's command, were to supplement the assault by forming on Jackson's right. Then, still further to the Confederate right, Maj. Gen. Benjamin Huger's command was to hit the Union left center. Maj. Gens. James Longstreet's and A. P. Hill's troops constituted the reserve.

The Confederates moved disjointedly, and things went amiss from the first. Jackson, harassed by Union artillery, suspended movement while he attempted to reconnoiter. Magruder was delayed by taking a wrong route. Lee hastily changed Huger's assignment, now giving him Magruder's sector. Confederate artillery massed behind Huger and one of Jackson's divisions and commenced a bombardment. One of Huger's brigade commanders was supposed to give a signal for the subsequent general-infantry advance. But the Union artillery responded, and for more than two hours the Confederate batteries were subjected to an effective and damaging long-range pounding.

Then, about 3:30 P.M., the lead brigade started forward, though without the expected artillery support because many of the forward Confederate batteries were now inoperative. There was reserve artillery, more than eighty guns, but apparently no one thought to order them up, nor did their commander take any initiative. The Union batteries concentrated on the lead attack brigade, halted and pinned it down, and there it had to remain until dark.

Magruder finally arrived, and Lee ordered him into the fight. But Magruder haphazardly managed to deploy only about one-third of his fifteen thousand troops, and they suffered severely from canister and shells that raked their lines. On the left D. H. Hill belatedly pushed his men forward, and huge numbers of them were mowed down. Most of the attackers never got much beyond the foot of the slopes, halfway to the Union guns. A scant few went farther: one small group got close enough to a Union battery that one of the officers fired at them with his revolver. All of the charges were easily repulsed. Eight additional Southern brigades entered the fighting; all were chewed to pieces. Darkness finally brought an end to it.

This bloody Southern defeat—5,355 Confederate and 3,214 Union dead—concluded the campaign. For the week, Lee had sustained a staggering casualty total of 20,141; the more numerous Federals had lost 15,849. Combined with the related Battle of Seven Pines, the Confederates had lost nearly 30 percent of their available force, whereas, fighting on the defensive, the Federals had lost only about 20 percent of the men they had engaged. But the threat to the Confederate capital had been diminished, and the war's future course in Virginia was altered fundamentally.

McClellan withdrew from Malvern Hill to his new base at Harrison's Landing and there entrenched. McClellan in truth had lost rather little, but he suffered loss of status, and there was little doubt in the minds of much of the Northern populace who had won. The Confederates captured more than forty pieces of artillery during the Seven Days campaign, but, perhaps reflecting even more unfavorably on McClellan's management, one-fifth of the Federal command was now ill, and scurvy was breaking out.

President Lincoln was displeased, even appalled, with matters in the East. He soon decided to place his hopes on a different principal commander, a successful campaigner recently brought from the western theater, Maj. Gen. John Pope. As it would turn out, Pope was the wrong man for what Lincoln had in mind, for he would prove inadequate in army command. But Pope's harsh attitude toward Rebels harmonized with the mind-set that the president had come to espouse in the spring of 1862. Whereas Lincoln had at first gingerly toyed with appeasement, his attitude had changed, and he had come to feel that the war must be escalated so that civilian morale might be crushed. He was now ready for the war to become "hard."

Some of the Union troops, even with the tacit approvals of their commanders, had already taken overt actions that reflected abandonment of conciliation. Athens, Alabama, was sacked wantonly on May 2, 1862; and there had previously been some mayhem in Huntsville. The unit historian of the Ninth Ohio, a regiment already known for its dealing roughly with civilians, wrote that "Fires sometimes broke out in local Rebels' houses. Of course we, in our innocence, never know how they started. In our honest way we helped with rescue and salvage; and the 35th Ohio was our staunch ally in this work of mercy. We carried beds out-of-doors, for example, and threw glasses and porcelain out of windows."

CHAPTER 5

A Rival Displaces McClellan;
and a Second Chance

A graduate of West Point, class of 1842, who had served in the Mexican War, Pope appeared competent. The truth, though not so immediately evident, was this: Pope was a genuinely good general officer but out of his element in army command.

A new (and destined to be short-lived) Army of Virginia was formed for him on June 26, 1862, the same day that Robert E. Lee had initiated the Seven Days campaign. Numbering initially about forty-seven thousand men, the new army had three corps.

"I have come to you from the West," Pope grandiloquently proclaimed, "where we have always seen the backs of our enemies." Pope's phraseology did not go over well, and it earned him much enmity, especially among the numerous McClellan partisans, one of whom remarked that Pope "has now written himself down [as] what the military world has long known, an ass." Samuel Sturgis, another McClellan partisan, not long after this himself delivered what would become the most famous of all utterances about Pope: "I don't care for John Pope a pinch of owl dung." Another critic opined that "If John Pope possessed a coat of arms, it would have been bombast rampant upon an expansive field of incompetence." Nevertheless, what Pope had said was true; he was facing problems of demoralization, and he was genuinely trying to boost morale.

Between July 18 and 25, 1862, Pope issued four general orders that spelled out the government's new harder approach to warfare. His army would "subsist upon the country," and Rebels would feel the pinch of deprivation. Further, Rebel civilians would be "held responsible" if Union supply or communication lines were hampered or if unconventional attacks were made upon army personnel. Southern civilians within areas under Union control would be compelled to swear an oath of allegiance to the United States or else they would be forced to evacuate their homes and sent within Rebel lines. Lincoln's own directives harmonized with those of Pope.

The president ordered the preparation of an executive order authorizing field commanders "to seize and use any property, real or personal," that might serve the enemy war effort; and although he discouraged wanton or malicious destruction, he announced that he would permit the destruction of any civilian property "for proper military objects."

Second Bull Run

On July 14 Pope started toward Gordonsville, Virginia; Lee had to act. Lee possessed but eighty thousand men standing against McClellan's force (which still numbered nearly 90,000) to his front, and Pope's forty-seven thousand men were converging from the north. With McClellan apparently inert, Lee dispatched Jackson with twelve thousand troops toward Gordonsville. On Jackson's heels followed A. P. Hill with an additional twelve thousand. As Pope's Federals proceeded slowly to Culpeper, Jackson saw an opportunity to strike the advanced enemy corps (under the command of Banks, whom the Confederates held in low regard—because they had already captured so many stores from his units, they called him "Mr. Commissary").

But Jackson's men moved slowly, largely because he failed to keep his division commanders informed of his changing plans and subsequent modifications. So, instead of Jackson's intended assault, *his* two forward divisions were hit by the lead Federal corps at Cedar Mountain on August 9. Although suffering mightily themselves the Unionists inflicted grave casualties, until A. P. Hill's reinforcements counterattacked. It was an ill-fought and mismanaged battle for both sides, costing 2,353 Federal casualties and 1,338 Confederates. Ironically, it caused the Confederates to deduce that Pope was launching a major southward offensive when actually Pope had orders to hold steady until the bulk of the Army of the Potomac and other reinforcements could unite with him. Maj. Gen. Ambrose E. Burnside's corps from the Carolina coast had already reinforced Pope.

The Army of Northern Virginia was now restructured into two wings, a larger one of four (later increased to five) divisions under Longstreet, and a smaller one of three divisions under Jackson. It would take a number of weeks for additional tinkering, made more difficult by the ongoing campaigning, but

Lee ultimately achieved a new standard of excellence in his organization by restructuring the arrays of artillery and cavalry. (They continued to enjoy and to benefit from this superiority until midwar, when the Union army at last also achieved good restructure.) Confederate artillery was now to be doled out much less than before to brigades or even to smaller-size units. Instead, it was to be concentrated in battalion-size artillery units attached at least as high as division level and kept well toward the front, with the exception of an army reserve. The army artillery reserve was a reinforced battalion of eighteen guns commanded by Col. Stephen D. Lee.

When R. E. Lee learned that McClellan's army was being depleted and the troops being sent to Pope, he decided to exploit his interior lines and launch another offensive. Concentrating most of the Confederate army on the Rappahannock River, Lee sought to turn Pope's right. Daringly, Longstreet's corps deployed to distract Pope, while the other corps under Jackson successfully passed to the west, reaching the Federals' base at Manassas Junction. Jackson's men gleefully proceeded to consume much, and destroy more, of Pope's provisions, which included such delicacies as boned turkey, canned beef, lobster salad, oysters, and even Rhine wine and whiskey.

Pope was now compelled to make a difficult choice: either retreat to Washington or attack Jackson to recover the supply line. Longstreet's corps was following Jackson's route, but lagged two days' march behind. Pope could exploit his position, use his interior lines, and hit Jackson, and if they moved quickly enough, the Federals could attack with a two-to-one advantage.

The maneuvers that led to the battle proper opened on August 26, 1862. The perspicacious modern historian of Second Bull Run, John Hennessy, has recently shed new light on our understanding of the subtleties of the campaign's unfolding. Confederate cavalry under Maj. Gen. Fitzhugh Lee entered Manassas Junction as Jackson's troops began leaving their position below the Rappahannock. The next day Pope sent troops toward Manassas and several other points. On the following day, Jackson concentrated just above Groveton, north of the Warrenton Turnpike. When Pope's troops approached along that road, Jackson's men assaulted. A vicious stand-up fight ensued, and both sides lost heavily. Pope mistakenly concluded that he had caught Jackson in the process of retreating and ordered concentration for an all-out assault. Jackson, though, was not in retreat: he was instead taking an admirable defensive position behind an unfinished railroad bed.

The Yankees failed to act in concert. Indeed, on August 29 a portion of Pope's command attacked Jackson's Confederates near Groveton, but Federal

Maj. Gen. Fitz John Porter failed to support the assault as he had been ordered. (Later Porter became a scapegoat for Pope's ultimate failure.) During that night, Longstreet's corps began to arrive, stretching out in lines at an angle next to Jackson's force. The Confederate army now occupied a four-mile-long line shaped like an open V, facing the enemy to the east.

Most significant, just before dawn on August 30, Col. S. D. Lee's reserve artillery battalion, with the last of Longstreet's forces, reached the center of the Confederate line. The artillery position could have hardly been better: the battalion could fire completely across Jackson's front. The guns nestled along a commanding ridge about one-quarter of a mile long. The field of fire embraced some two thousand yards—more than one mile. Immediately opposite Jackson's lines stretched an open field, any part of which Lee's fire could sweep.

During the morning and first half of the afternoon of August 30 the two sides exchanged long-range fire. At 3:00 P.M. a huge concentration of Federals advanced in heavy force against Jackson's left. When the Yankees moved directly toward Jackson's line, Lee's fire hit them in perfect enfilade. A few of the attacking troops did manage to get quite close to Jackson's line—so close, in fact, that some of Jackson's men hurled rocks at their foes. Despite two attempts to rally it, the main assault force was thrown back.

Thousands of reserve troops who stood ready to exploit any success, intimidated by S. D. Lee's effective enfilade artillery fire, never moved up. Two Federal regiments haplessly tried to charge the guns, and some of the attackers got dangerously near, but they were stymied by canister. The Northerners should have made a more determined effort to overrun S. D. Lee's position, but even if they had, the Rebel guns still would have been relatively safe, because by happy accident the gunners enjoyed cover and concealment from a stone wall just to their front. (The presence of that stone wall has been little noted, but its remnants are present to this day.)

The Union charge turned into a retreat. R. E. Lee had not issued any advance order for a counterattack, but, anticipating such an order, Longstreet promptly launched one. (After the war Longstreet became the victim of a character assassination, so many accounts of the battle were later distorted, asserting untruthfully that he culpably delayed for an unjustified period of time.) Hitting hard and inflicting severe punishment, the Confederates thrust forward for more than a mile and a half. One Federal regiment, Duryee's Fifth New York Zouaves, suffered the heaviest losses of killed and wounded of any Civil War regiment on any day in the entire war. One Texan remembered that, from a distance, the dead Zouaves, with their colorful uniforms, lay so thickly that it reminded him of a field full of posies. The total Confederate casualties amounted to 9,187, while Pope lost 16,054.

The last fighting of the campaign occurred on September 1 at Chantilly, or Ox Hill, Virginia (where two of the Union army's more promising general officers, Philip Kearny and Isaac I. Stevens, were killed). Lee edged his army toward Leesburg, where they would cross the Potomac River.

Lincoln was again ready for a change in eastern army command, but fortuitously for Pope there was a new assignment for him in Minnesota (a challenge he would prove equal to meeting). Not long after the U.S. army had withdrawn from its posts in Minnesota, the Santee Sioux decided it was an opportune time to attack the whites whom they resented for having encroached on Sioux lands. Led by their chief, Little Crow, they spent much of the summer of 1862 raiding up and down the Minnesota River valley and killed more than 800 whites. Militia first clashed with the Sioux, and, on September 23, 1,400 of the volunteers under Col. Henry Hastings Sibley (not to be confused with Henry *Hopkins* Sibley) won a victory in the Battle of Wood Lake.

Little Crow managed to flee with many of his followers to Dakota Territory, but about 1,500 of the Sioux were captured. Eight days before the battle, Pope had arrived to assume command of the Department of the Northwest. A military court sentenced 307 of the captives to die for having committed atrocities, but Lincoln pardoned all but 38. These last were publicly hanged in December. Pope then had the duty of setting up Federal garrisons to guard outlying settlements and to post border detachments to keep the remaining Sioux bottled up in Dakota Territory, safely away from the growing white settlement in Minnesota. Sporadically, renewed Sioux attacks again erupted during the spring of 1863, but they were minor, and Pope's remaining tenure passed in relative tranquility.

Antietam

The Federals meanwhile strove to achieve unity of command, having named —earlier in the summer—Maj. Gen. Henry W. Halleck to be general in chief. Halleck, who reached Washington during what he regarded as a "time of great peril," had ordered an immediate increase of the concentration around Washington. Troops were to come by rail from western Virginia, Burnside's corps to return from North Carolina, and what then remained of McClellan's army should come by boat. After Pope's defeat, Halleck and Lincoln elected once again to rely on McClellan to cope with Lee in the field.

The Confederate incursion into Maryland was intended to be a raid, not an invasion, for Lee expected to have to return to Virginia at least by the winter. There were hopes that many Marylanders might rally to the Confederate cause and join the Southern army as it moved through the state, but these hopes proved to be in vain. Either the Marylanders were not sufficiently pro-Confederate or they were appalled by the tattered and bedraggled condition of the Rebel troops. Perhaps it was partly because, as some claimed, one could *smell* the army coming before it could be seen. "They were," reported one witness, "the dirtiest men I ever saw, a most ragged, lean, and hungry set of wolves. . . . Yet there was a dash about them that northern men lacked."

Lee mainly wished to feed on the enemy's country, while also protecting the harvest in Virginia. He needed at least a rudimentary line of communications to bring him ammunition and other basic supplies, and for this he intended to use a wagon route from Winchester, Virginia, through Harpers Ferry into Maryland: but a large Federal garrison held Harpers Ferry. Jackson's corps was diverted to take that place, and it proved quite a prize: the Confederates seized seventy-three pieces of artillery, thirteen thousand small arms, two hundred wagons, and 12,500 prisoners. This was the largest single surrender of U.S. troops during the war (indeed, the largest *ever* until the fall of Corregidor in 1942).

But this promising beginning went sour, when on September 13, a copy of Lee's plans, carelessly lost by an officer who had used it to wrap three cigars, fell into McClellan's hands. Lee initially elected to withdraw south of the Potomac— if that was possible—to avoid battle for which he felt unprepared, but news reached him that Harpers Ferry had fallen on September 15. The Confederates managed a last-minute concentration, near Sharpsburg, Maryland, and there awaited McClellan's onslaught.

"Now I know what to do!" McClellan had gleefully chortled upon his first quick reading of the famous Lost Order, which revealed to him that Lee's army was beyond South Mountain divided into four widely separated parts. "Here is a paper," McClellan said to one of his generals that evening, "with which if I cannot whip Bobbie Lee, I will be willing to go home." Although on September 14 there was very heaving fighting at three gaps in South Mountain, McClellan, as was typical, did rather little to hasten things. He allowed two and one-half days to be consumed in moving his army to its assembly area for what became the Battle of Antietam. Even then, on September 16 when he could have attacked, he chose to delay further. How ironic, for not until midday on September 16 did Stonewall Jackson's troops begin arriving at Sharpsburg from Harpers Ferry. More arrived all during the day and evening, and two more divisions came up at dawn on September 17. Three and one-half days had passed since finding the Lost Order.

Making ready to attack, the Union troops formed just to the east of Antietam Creek. That stream flows southward into the Potomac a few miles below Sharpsburg. Three bridges spanned the creek: the Rohrbach Bridge (to become known as the "Burnside Bridge") to the south, just below Sharpsburg; the Middle Bridge; and the Upper Bridge. There were also several places where the water could be forded. McClellan's plans were vague and his instructions unclear. Worse, he made some last-minute command changes that blurred the unity of command in Burnside's corps—a violation of another fundamental principle of war.

What McClellan wanted were major thrusts, both from above and from below the enemy position, with supporting attacks creating diversion along the entire center. Actually, considering the terrain and the Yankees' two-to-one numerical advantage (although "the Young Napoleon" believed it was the other way around), the planned double envelopment was a wise choice; but Major General Burnside, the wing commander to the south, misunderstood. Burnside thought that his offensive was merely a secondary attack.

As the daylong fight ensued, the Federals launched five successive but poorly coordinated assaults, unfolding serially from north to south. And then stalemate ended the struggle. The defending Confederates were able to prevent a debacle. But because they were unentrenched, as well as seriously outnumbered, they suffered heavily.

The opening assault, in "Miller's corn field," commenced at 6:00 A.M. The defenders were driven very slowly but steadily rearward. But Major General Sumner's corps was held back until 7:20, and in the meantime, Rebel infantry, supported by forward batteries, stormed out of the West Woods in powerful counterattack.

McClellan had wigwag flag communications with his two corps attacking from the north, but Burnside, obscured from direct view, could exchange communications with headquarters only by courier—a much slower process. Burnside became stalled east of the Rohrbach Bridge and in repeated attempts, failed to take the bridge until much later; at 1:00 P.M. he finally succeeded in doing so.

In the meantime, the advantage of possessing interior lines allowed the Confederates to diminish the forces facing Burnside and redeploy them at more seriously threatened points. By midmorning the focus had shifted to the Rebel center. There, a farm lane, worn down below the adjacent surface by weather and long use, formed a natural trench that the Confederates had bolstered with a breastwork of fence rails. Later called Sunken Road, and by others Bloody Lane, this sector became the scene of the most awful slaughter: one Federal division lost 40 percent of its men, another 30 percent. A Confederate officer wrote that his unit's first volley "brought down the enemy as grain falls before a reaper." Suddenly, however, a mishap in Confederate command caused a gap to be opened in the defensive line, the Rebels' sole serious tactical error of the day. McClellan could have exploited his good fortune, because the position was clearly visible from his headquarters, but he did nothing, choosing to rely on Burnside's anticipated success.

Burnside's men were badly battered in taking the bridgehead, and then they required more time to reorganize and replenish their ammunition. At last, around 3:00 P.M., Burnside's troops thrust strongly toward Sharpsburg, closing with the weary and demoralized defenders. Then, suddenly, another dramatic turn of events occurred. The last Confederate division arrived from Harpers Ferry, that of Maj. Gen. A. P. Hill. It surged into the hard-pressed lines making a slashing attack on Burnside's unguarded left flank.

Scurrying back toward the bridge, Burnside's corps managed to retain its possession and assume a more secure defensive stance. The Confederates were too spent to drive Burnside any farther, and nightfall at last brought the end to this the single bloodiest day of the Civil War, and indeed in all of the American military experience. The South lost 13,724 to McClellan's 12,469 casualties, but also another 12,500 Federals had been taken at Harpers Ferry. Photographers reached the Antietam battlefield before the dead were buried—a seminal event in American history—and the horrifying pictures, widely distributed, shocked as well as entranced a jolted Northern public.

Both armies had hurt each other tremendously, but neither had gained any advantage, and no further engagement seemed promising. The battle dictated that the campaign now end. Lee's army could neither be supplied nor forage, so the Confederates disengaged and withdrew back into Virginia, considerably earlier than Lee had hoped.

The aftermath brought the end to McClellan's military career. Abraham Lincoln could not understand or tolerate that no effective pursuit or further destruction of Lee's forces followed. "He is an admirable engineer," the president said of Little Mac (a nickname that had come to be frequently used), "but he seems to have a special talent for a stationary engine." On November 7, seven weeks after Antietam, McClellan was relieved. But it was the lack of follow-up—not the battle—that Lincoln could not tolerate. Although extremely disappointed, the president regarded the battle itself as a sufficient victory to justify—without seeming to reflect any tinge of desperation—his issuance of a preliminary proclamation of emancipation.

McClellan never internalized the reality of Antietam, and just as Andrew Jackson had ceremoniously relit a candle from his headquarters tent on the anniversary of the Battle of New Orleans, each year McClellan celebrated the anniversary of Antietam. "Those on whose judgment I rely," he had exulted, "tell me that I fought the battle splendidly and that it was a masterpiece of art." His family shared the attitude; his daughter, who later married a European and lived in France, named her home the "Villa Antietam." But McClellan received no more command assignments. When R. E. Lee was informed of McClellan's removal, he remarked to Longstreet, "I fear they may continue to make these changes 'till they find someone whom I don't understand."

After the Battle of Antietam and the Army of Northern Virginia's retreat from Maryland, R. E. Lee most wanted a quiescent situation for the remainder of the fall and winter. Save for a major battle in mid-December at Fredericksburg, he was successful in fulfilling his hope to rest and refit his army.

Aside from this, until well into 1863, about the only thing of significance in the East—and this was even before McClellan was relieved—was a second ride around the Union army by J. E. B. Stuart's Confederate cavalry. On October 9, 1862, Stuart's men, some eighteen hundred strong, began their venture and on the next day crossed the Potomac. They went rapidly into Pennsylvania, appearing suddenly at Chambersburg. There they proceeded to seize horses and destroy public stores. They cut telegraph lines and snatched all the military equipment they could carry away, demolishing the rest. They wrecked railroad machine shops, depots, and several trains. Then, in the afternoon of October 11, they moved eastward to Cashtown, Pennsylvania, and subsequently south through Emmitsburg, Maryland. On October 12, after brief skirmishing near the mouth of the Monocacy River, they forced their way and recrossed the Potomac near Poolesville, Maryland. Spectacular only on the surface, the four-day venture was relatively insignificant, but it lifted Southern spirits and was a further embarrassment to McClellan. Now, however, much attention shifted from affairs in the East to events in the western theater.

CHAPTER 6

The Abortive 1862 Confederate Invasion

Kentucky and Middle Tennessee

After the siege of Corinth, General Beauregard's health—which had been poor for months—continued to plague him, and he departed from the army on sick leave. Confederate officials had come increasingly to regard him as unfit for major field command; therefore, on June 17, 1862, Gen. Braxton Bragg was named commander of the Confederacy's Western Department, and head of the principal force therein, soon renamed the Army of Tennessee.

Bragg was vexed with grave problems: many men had deserted, subsistence was scant, transportation inadequate, and the telegraphic link to Richmond was often disrupted. Bragg had to rely on the regular mail in order to communicate with President Davis. But Bragg possessed keen organizational skills, and the army began to revive: health and general spirits picked up, an improved water supply and good weather produced good effects; the troops secured new clothes, rested, and became ready once again for an aggressive campaign.

Sadly, however, while Bragg was able to cause improvements in the health of his army, his own health—physical and mental—was often iffy. Bragg sent thirty-five thousand men to Mobile, Alabama, while the garrison at Mobile was dispatched by train to field duty in east Tennessee. Employing six different railroads, Bragg used track as if it were a pipeline, redeploying troops over a 776-mile distance in record time.

The Invasion of Kentucky and the Battle of Perryville

Late in July 1862 Bragg reoccupied Chattanooga and late in August proceeded to march through middle Tennessee, proclaiming on September 5 the state as thus restored to the Confederacy. Bragg then commenced his invasion of Kentucky. He had not initially intended to invade the Bluegrass State, thinking that merely redeeming middle Tennessee would force Federal General Buell to retreat in order to regain his lines of communication.

Unfortunately for the Confederates, however, the fundamental principle of war—unity of command—had not been achieved in the West. Bragg counted on cooperation with an army of ten thousand men under Maj. Gen. Edmund Kirby Smith, but both Bragg and Smith were independently inclined individuals and failed to work well together. The plan had been for Smith to thrust from Knoxville early in August against Federal forces at Cumberland Gap. Bragg intended to join him there, and united they would invade middle Tennessee. But General Smith delayed, ineptly conducting his turning movement, and entered Kentucky even while the Yankees still held Cumberland Gap (though they subsequently abandoned it).

With Lee's Maryland raid underway by this time (and in simultaneous coordination with it), Bragg moved into Kentucky, successfully bypassing Buell's Federal Army of the Ohio at Nashville. From September 15 through 17, 1862, Bragg's army besieged Munfordville, Kentucky. The Federal garrison, numbering slightly more than four thousand men, surrendered the town on the same day as the Battle of Antietam.

Bragg next went north toward Louisville, then veered east, occupying Bardstown on September 21. Bragg then traveled to Frankfort to oversee the installation of a Confederate state government, while the two wings of his army led by his subordinates, Leonidas Polk and William J. Hardee, screened the area southeast of Louisville. Through September, Buell's army operating out of Nashville had responded, although timidly, to the movements of Bragg's army and had then fallen back to cover Louisville and Cincinnati, reaching Louisville on September 25. Bragg meanwhile raided into the bluegrass.

In the field both armies suffered from unusually high temperatures and the worst drought in years. On October 1 Buell's nearly fifty thousand men left Louisville in four columns: one directly east to make a feint at Frankfort, the other three to converge first upon Bardstown; subsequently (it was intended), all four were to reunite at Harrodsburg. Poor intelligence induced Bragg to expect a major attack upon either Frankfort or Versailles, some fifteen miles south.

As the head of the Federal column neared Frankfort, Bragg mistakenly believed it was the vanguard of Buell's main force and concentrated General Smith's army there to block it, while General Polk's wing maneuvered to attack the south flank of that column. Thus, the target was much smaller than the Confederates had suspected, which was all the more reason therefore that the Confederates could have demolished this one-quarter of the Federal army had Polk followed his orders and moved rapidly. But, on October 3, choosing to interpret for himself reports from the cavalry, Polk decided to retreat to Danville. Hardee, meanwhile, concentrated his wing near Perryville, both for protection and to get badly needed water from Doctor's Creek, a tributary of Chaplin's Fork of the Salt River. Toward that same water source, and desperate for some of it, on October 7, approached the three main Union columns.

The Battle of Perryville on October 8, 1862, was Kentucky's major engagement of the war. It developed quite disjointedly, for neither commander realized what he faced. Bragg persisted in believing that only a small enemy fragment was at Perryville, and he expected to dispatch it easily and quickly. Buell meanwhile erroneously estimated that the whole enemy force was nearby, which induced him not to launch a uniform attack. In fact, a queer atmospheric phenomenon prevented battle noises from being heard behind the lines, and Buell did not realize the engagement's extent until late in the day. About 1:00 P.M. the Confederate force thrust forward. In some of the war's most reckless and vicious hand-to-hand fighting, the Federals ebbed back under the steady pressure. A reinforcing brigade was too late to bolster the faltering Federals, and the Confederates drove the brigade back, capturing its commander.

The uncoordinated battle ended at dark. The Federals had employed but nine of their brigades while another fifteen remained unoccupied, although they were within supporting distance. The Federals lost 846 killed, 2,851 wounded, 515 captured or missing; and 510 Confederates were killed, 2,635 wounded, 251 missing, nearly one-quarter of the possibly 16,000 Rebel effectives who fought. Both sides had won a partial victory. Many Confederate soldiers expected to fight again the next day, but Bragg ordered that they retire to Harrodsburg before morning. Minor skirmishing on the roads constituted a mere anticlimax to the now terminated campaign.

Bragg's withdrawal into east Tennessee, combined with R. E. Lee's recent return to Virginia from Maryland, concluded a major phase of the Confederacy's ill-fated grand strategy. Grady McWhiney, in his fine partial biography of Bragg, offers much insightful analysis concerning Bragg's election to abandon Confederates in Kentucky—which in retrospect was one of the most controversial decisions of the war. Leading to his conclusion that Bragg was quite unfit for army command, McWhiney observes that Bragg had placed an undue hope in Kentuckians to keep him informed of the enemy's movements: when they did not, Bragg was befuddled. There were other factors involved too: Bragg got a report that forces under Earl Van Dorn and Sterling Price, which he had expected would be advancing into Tennessee, had been defeated in a battle at Corinth, Mississippi, on October 4; Confederate quartermasters had failed to send up sufficient food for Bragg's army in Kentucky; and, last, Bragg was much discouraged by the scanty numbers of recruits he had been able to glean in Kentucky. One Confederate captain, E. John Ellis, observed: "We found indeed 32 men who were willing to be Colonels, 32 willing to serve as Lieut Cols and Majors, any quantity ready to tack on their collars the bars of a Captain or Lieut, but few, very few willing to serve in the ranks. *Kentucky is subjugated.*" This, of course, was true, but it was largely due to Bragg's utter failure.

The Battle of Stones River

On October 27, 1862, Federal Maj. Gen. William S. Rosecrans replaced Buell as commander of the principal Union force in Kentucky and renamed it the Army of the Cumberland. Rosecrans advanced that force to Nashville. Convivial and likable, Rosecrans merited the enthusiasm of his admirers, who called him "Old Rosy": handsome, red faced, excitable, known to be aggressive and brave, like McClellan he was loved by his soldiers. The troops particularly liked the way he inspected regiments: whenever he spotted soldiers with worn clothing or equipment, he would urge them to demand what they needed from their superiors. He explained that strong demands for relief would flow upward through regiment, brigade, division, and corps until they reached army headquarters, and, he exclaimed, "I'll see then if you don't get what you want!" The men knew that Rosecrans worked long and hard. Stories circulated—and they were true—that he often labored far into the night, always until two (and usually until four) o'clock, and occasionally he did not sleep at all.

Rosecrans spent nearly two months preparing an offensive, and on December 26, 1862, he marched his forty-seven thousand men southeastward toward Murfreesboro, where Bragg's force had been encamped for weeks. Bragg, who had taken much censure for his indecisive Kentucky campaign, now stood strongly with thirty-eight thousand men on the defensive astride Stones River. That narrow stream loops off northward to join the Cumberland River. To the east of Stones River, on low hills that dominated the terrain, Bragg had posted a detached division of Maj. Gen. John C. Breckinridge. West of the river, where a heavy growth of scrub cedar obscured vision, Bragg deployed his main force along a four-mile front. The usually rather shallow river was well above its normal level, having been swollen by recent heavy rains.

On the evening of December 29, Rosecrans's army began arriving in the vicinity of Murfreesboro. By nightfall two-thirds of the force was in position just seven hundred yards in front of the Confederate army, assembled along the Nashville Turnpike. In bizarre coincidence the opposing commanders plotted mirror-image battle plans: each decided to hold with his right and attack with his left. Obviously, whoever moved first would have the advantage. But neither showed much celerity, and another day passed. Then, the Confederates made the initial thrust: at dawn on December 31 Lieutenant General Hardee's corps circled around the Union right flank with clocklike precision, and his men surprised the Federal soldiers (some of whom were cooking breakfast).

The Union right was squashed. Brigade after brigade was forced rearward, one of them suffering five hundred casualties in the initial minutes, until an entire corps had fallen back three miles before rallying on the Nashville Turnpike. By 10:00 A.M. the Union line had been turned almost ninety degrees. Although the Union troops fought valiantly, they soon began to run out of ammunition because Confederate cavalry raiders had intercepted the Federal ammunition train coming from the northwest on the Nashville and Chattanooga Railroad. Nevertheless, the day was not totally lost for the men in blue: a division under Brig. Gen. Philip H. Sheridan fought stubbornly and long held its ground before making an orderly retreat. Maj. Gen. George H. Thomas directed his corps in a rally that by 4:00 P.M. had reformed and stabilized a new Union line. Further Confederate charges were repulsed, and the day ended with the Federals compactly ensconced in a salient around Rosecrans's headquarters.

Bragg believed he had scored a major triumph and that Rosecrans would surely pull back the battered Federal army to Nashville on the next day: "God has granted us a Happy New Year," Bragg exultantly telegraphed Richmond. But in truth the battle was not yet over. It was to continue, though not on the next day during which both forces stood steady in their positions. Both commanders seemed to expect the other to make the first move, and neither did. The cold and fair day passed tensely but with only minor skirmishing. Rosecrans then made several rearrangements: he pushed one division across Stones River, strengthened the forward line along the west bank, and sent more protection to the supply trains. Bragg misinterpreted all this to be in preparation for the Union retreat he expected. Thus, he was appalled on January 2, 1863, to discover the entire enemy army still confronting his force.

The morning and most of the afternoon passed. Then at 4:00 P.M., almost precipitously, Bragg ordered Major General Breckinridge's division to dislodge the enemy division east of Stones River. The forty-five hundred men in the initial assault drove their enemy off a ridge they occupied and across the river. Pursuing to the banks the attackers soon discovered—to their enormous surprise, and at the cost of eighteen hundred casualties—that the Federals were well prepared to resist, aided by the concentrated fire of fifty-seven cannon. That night Bragg learned that reinforcements were being sent to Rosecrans. Thus, the Confederate general would have to eat his words about having proclaimed victory after the first day. It would not be his enemy but he himself who would have to extricate troops from the field.

Because he had retained possession of the battleground, Rosecrans declared Stones River a Union victory. In truth, it was a stalemate; the fight had cost 1,730 Union dead, 7,802 wounded, and 3,717 missing; Bragg had fared only a little better, sustaining a loss of 1,294 dead, 7,945 wounded, and 1,027 missing. The Army of Tennessee withdrew toward Shelbyville. Rosecrans chose not to pursue, electing instead to occupy Murfreesboro. Thus, the Confederacy was not only eliminated from enjoying any presence in Kentucky but forced out of much of Tennessee as well. Meanwhile, however, a spectacular debacle had befallen Union forces in the East.

CHAPTER 7

The Fredericksburg Campaign

A Study in Generalship

R. E. Lee heads almost any list of the Confederacy's greatest generals, and surely he *was* remarkable, in many ways a great combat commander. But Lee is not without his critics. The historians Thomas Lawrence Connelly Jr. and Allan Nolan have recently opined that Lee was too provincial, concerned almost exclusively with the war in Virginia; and worse, he was too aggressive, far too reckless, and willing to spend much of the South's undeniably limited resources and numbers for inadequate return. Occasionally Lee enjoyed good luck, and certainly any general's performance improves when fortune favors his endeavors. At Antietam, for example, he was simply lucky that McClellan did not annihilate his army. Within the nine months following, President Abraham Lincoln would employ a series of three new eastern army commanders. Against Ambrose E. Burnside, at Fredericksburg, Lee enjoyed the great luck of having his opponent hurl a fatal assault frontally into well-emplaced defenders.

Maj. Gen. Ambrose E. Burnside in Army Command

"Burnside is a brick!" or so did many persons proudly proclaim as they repeated the most often spoken assessment of the new Army of the Potomac commander. Elevated to his position on November 9, 1862, Burnside was considered well qualified for army command, but in truth his selection was hard to justify. Following his 1847 graduation from the Academy, he had seen only garrison duty before resigning his commission in 1853 to enter business.

Manufacturing a type of breech-loading carbine he had invented, Burnside had hoped to achieve financial independence. The carbine was a reliable and very accurate single-shot weapon that used a special brass cartridge. During a test in 1859, one of them was fired five hundred times, without cleaning and without misfire, only a few of the shots failing to hit a target five hundred yards away. The army purchased 55,567 Burnside carbines and 21,819,200 of its special cartridges.

At the onset of the Civil War, Burnside organized a Rhode Island infantry regiment, one of the first during the early crisis to reach Washington, and this earned him promotion to a brigade command. At its head he performed well at First Bull Run. He also became something of a favorite of President Lincoln, and that helped ensure Burnside's appointment to command the early 1862 expedition against the coast of North Carolina. Success in this brought him promotion to major general. Furthermore, he was a close chum and protégé of McClellan's—until the Maryland campaign during which their relationship soured and McClellan placed much blame on Burnside for the failure.

Now thirty-eight years of age, Burnside impressed people with his flashing eyes and otherwise quite imposing appearance and with his soft-spoken good nature. Most notable was his beard, trimmed to the "Burnside cut" with a lush mustache running across his upper cheeks into long and fluffy side whiskers (which was the origin of the term *sideburns* in popular American language). But Burnside simply did not measure up to his new assignment; and, deep down, he tended to realize, possibly even to magnify, his inadequacies. He drove hard, overworked himself, slept very little, and became physically ill. He proved the weakest of all the Federal opponents that Robert E. Lee faced.

The Battle of Fredericksburg

From mid-October 1862 into November, Union troops gradually shifted southeastward. Slowly, Burnside assembled a sufficiently large number of troops so located that Lee felt forced to respond. First Longstreet's corps was ordered to move to Culpeper and thence to Fredericksburg; Jackson's men would subsequently follow. Burnside's choice in the matter was diminished by the Union high command's impatient desire for action, especially for an eastern advance that would be in concert with activities then occurring in the western theater. Thus, the two armies came into concentration, the one north of the Rappahannock just above Fredericksburg, the other in and around the city and to the south and southwest.

Burnside, with his army of some 120,000 arrayed into three grand divisions under Maj. Gens. William B. Franklin, Joseph Hooker, and Edwin V. Sumner, intended to penetrate the enemy lines and thrust due south to Richmond. Sumner's Right Grand Division would cross the river on three pontoon bridges immediately opposite the city; Franklin's Left Grand Division would cross on three other bridges farther downstream; and Hooker would support their attacks and constitute the general reserve. The menace of Burnside's advance had impelled the Confederates to shift troops from western Virginia and to seek still other reinforcements from elsewhere, so that the Southern army had come to number about 74,000.

Burnside's pontoon bridges were delayed in arriving, and by the time he was ready to cross the river, Lee's army was stretched out in defensive array some six miles along the heights overlooking Fredericksburg. On the foggy morning of December 11, the Federal engineers began laying the pontoon bridges. On the Union left, there was no opposition, and three bridges were laid easily, despite the work being hampered by ice forming on the water. But it was a different matter with the bridges just opposite the city. Numerous times, Confederate sharpshooters drove the bridge builders away. Finally, in boats, a four-regiment Union task force crossed the river and drove away the harassing enemy. The bridge building at last was completed.

By nightfall one of Sumner's divisions occupied Fredericksburg and sacked the town (certainly a vivid illustration of how the nature of the war was changing!). During the next day, December 12, all the remaining Union forces (save for that part of Hooker's grand division in general reserve) crossed the river. The Confederates, however, were ready.

The Southern army occupied strong positions along the irregular edge of the plateau parallel to the river. The left, held by Longstreet's corps, was the stronger part: Longstreet's was the larger of the two Confederate corps, the terrain was more favorable for defense, and some of Jackson's men would not arrive until just before the battle.

The dominating terrain feature in Longstreet's sector was an elongated steep elevation known as "Marye's Heights." To the front was a wide canal and a drainage ditch, either or both of which Union troops assaulting in this sector would have to cross. Then, near the base of the hill, ran an old sunken road, and in front of that stretched an old stone wall, behind which the most advanced of the defenders would enjoy formidable cover. Union soldiers thought that the wall was much lower than it turned out to be; when the depth of the sunken road was figured in, the wall was some four feet higher on the Confederate side than on the other. Furthermore, Longstreet's artillery was carefully and well emplaced. The artillerist E. Porter Alexander boastfully proclaimed, "We cover that ground now so well that we will comb it as with a fine-tooth comb. A chicken could not live on the field when we open on it!"

During the night a Union council of war reached the wise decision to direct the main attack against Jackson's corps, deployed on the Confederate right along a long, low, but heavily wooded, ridge. But just before the battle Burnside made some hasty and thoroughly unwise modifications; worse, perhaps, his new orders were somewhat vague. Instead of the whole of the Left Grand Division thrusting forward in full force, the bulk was to be retained in line along the Old Richmond Stage Road. A force consisting of one lead division, under Maj. Gen. George G. Meade, supported on the right and left by two others, would attempt first to "carry" the high ground on the Confederate right flank, thought vulnerable, at Hamilton's Crossing, and then try to make a penetration in the woods.

Even this diminished thrust, however, made good headway for a time. The morning was very foggy, and, until the fog lifted, the Confederates could not see the approach. Then, twenty-three-year-old Confederate Maj. John Pelham detected the enemy advance. Pelham, who had enrolled in West Point in 1856 and had been a cadet for nearly five years under the experimental extended curriculum, had excelled in artillery studies. At the Academy and subsequently in the more than sixty Civil War battles and skirmishes in which he would take part (before he sustained a mortal wound in March 1863), Pelham did much to refine the concept of a "flying battery," that is, extremely mobile field artillery. He was a favorite of General Lee, who had nicknamed him "the Gallant." Now, galloping past Hamilton's Crossing with two artillery pieces, Pelham held the Union thrust in check for a critical thirty minutes. Pelham stood firm until, with one of his guns disabled and nearly out of ammunition, he had to withdraw at last.

Jackson, meanwhile, managed to redeploy his artillery and became ready to oppose any renewed Union advance. Union guns on Stafford Heights opened fire, and for one and one-half hours a long-range artillery duel ensued, eventually silencing Jackson's artillery. Meade's forward elements, shielded by woods, made enemy contact and found a weak spot. Inadequately supported, however, they could not hold the ground they took, which was regained by a Confederate counterattack under the leadership of Brig. Gen. Jubal Early and A. P. Hill. Then, however, the Southerners too were halted.

At the opposite end of the battle line, events unfolded considerably the worse for Burnside. Sumner's men, and then Hooker's reserves, with incredible bravery, haplessly assaulted Marye's Heights not once, but fourteen times. Some got within twenty-five yards of the stone wall, but could go no farther. Soldiers fought until late in the afternoon under murderous fire, gaining little more than feet or yards. One reporter later summed up the battle by opining, "It can hardly be in human nature for men to show more valor, or generals to manifest less judgment." It was a futile, wild, fantastic, direct slam against a well-entrenched enemy, and it failed miserably. One Union officer later recalled that

> The whole plain was covered with men, prostrate and dropping. . . . I had never before seen fighting like that—nothing approaching it in terrible uproar and destruction. . . . As they charged, the artillery fire would break their formation and they would get mixed. Then they would close up, go forward, receive the withering infantry fire, . . . the next brigade coming up in succession, . . . and melt like snow coming down on warm ground.

General Longstreet remarked that "The Federals had fallen like the steady dripping of rain from the eaves of a house." A Federal general said, "It was a great slaughter pen . . . they might as well have tried to take Hell." (During the few lulls that occurred in the firing, heaven—not hell—had *its* representative on the field in the person of Sgt. Richard Kirkland of the Second South Carolina Volunteers. Laden with several canteens of water, he bravely made his way to numerous wounded Federal soldiers and gave them aid. Later, quite the talk of both armies, he became known as "the Angel of Marye's Heights.")

And so the battle ended. The cost in killed, wounded, and missing was heavy: 12,653 Federals to 5,309 Confederates. "God! It is horrible—horrible!" the newspaperman Horace Greeley moaned, "130,000 magnificent soldiers so cut to pieces by less than 60,000 half-starved ragamuffins!" "What luck some people have," Confederate Gen. Joe Johnston, then in the western theater, remarked when he learned about what had happened at Fredericksburg. "Nobody will come to attack me in such a place." And the battle occasioned Lee's now classic remark to Longstreet: "It is well that war is so terrible—we should grow too fond of it."

Burnside stupidly considered renewing the assaults the next day. He even issued orders to that effect—and planned on (suicidally perhaps?) leading them in person—but his more prudent subordinates persuaded him to refrain. Two days later, on December 15, the humiliated Federal army withdrew unmolested to the north bank of the Rappahannock.

Of his impatient critics who asserted that Lee should have counterattacked, that he missed a golden opportunity, Lee remarked privately to J. E. B. Stuart: "No one knows how *brittle* an army is." Lee might well have added that no one adequately apprehended the strength of the defense and that once Burnside had retreated it was Lee who stood ready to repulse any rash frontal onslaught that might be launched.

Aftermath: The "Mud March"

While the Union army completed its northward crossing of the Rappahannock, its officers bickered, grumbled, and second-guessed Burnside's decisions. As the troops settled into positions along Stafford Heights, Burnside traveled to Washington, where on December 21 he had a conference with Lincoln. The president called the defeat an "accident," clearly intending to retain Burnside in command. Halleck, the general in chief, reminded Burnside in writing, and Lincoln endorsed the letter, that "our first object was, not Richmond, but the defeat or scattering of Lee's army." The main problems now, however, were the weather and, specifically, the poor condition of the roads.

At least Burnside had learned something from the disaster at Fredericksburg, and so he hatched a new plan. Now he would try to march swiftly upriver and cross with the pontoons at United States Ford: Lee would thus be outflanked, forced either to abandon his position or, under adverse conditions, to attack Burnside's army. But Lee was even more keenly aware than Burnside that United States Ford offered a dangerous passage to his rear and was timely in ordering a Confederate force to dig in there.

On January 20 Burnside selected Banks Ford, near Falmouth, and ordered that the bridges, other necessary equipment, and supporting artillery be brought there by dawn the next day. That evening it started to rain: a slow drizzle fell at first, and then commenced a steady downpour, accompanied by a howling wind. What had passed for roads began to totally disappear, even while the pontoons and guns were being dragged through the mud. Burnside later admitted, "From that moment we felt that the winter campaign had ended." The men pitched their tents in the icy rain and with great difficulty built smoky fires. All the wagon trains were far to the rear, so the only food that the men had to eat was the morsels in their haversacks.

When morning came the rains grew worse. When the troops resumed their dreary slog through the mud, big globs stuck to each boot with every step, and still more went wrong. Two corps met at a muddy crossroad: faulty orders called for them to pass the same spot heading in different directions. The pontoon trains became intermixed with the artillery and caissons on the same pathways, inducing them to attempt even poorer parallel paths and plantation lanes.

Axles mired, and wagon beds sank flat to the level of the mud. So too did the quartermaster wagons, ambulances, battery wagons, and all of the army's wheeled vehicles. By ten in the morning on January 21, every vehicle was stuck, and even the draft animals were belly-deep. Men oozed down knee-deep at every step, until at last they had managed to cover a few miles. Details formed to try to move the mired equipment, but even sixteen horses and all the men who could get hands on to help could not move a single pontoon. Long ropes were employed, with 150 men pulling on a piece, laboriously achieving a few feet. All day it went like this, and the rain that continued seemed to the men to be ever harder and colder.

Many of the soldiers eventually responded with humorous resignation to their pitiful situation. They laughed hysterically; and the Rebels across the river, many of whom could see what was going on, laughed too, teasing and shouting jeers. One officer put in a requisition for "50 men, 23 feet high, to work in mud 18 feet deep." By the time night came even the food left in haversacks was soaked and ruined. Cold salt pork was all anyone had to eat. But Burnside refused to cancel his plan, and he still intended to somehow cross the river the next day and fight the Rebels.

In the morning a few supply wagons did get forward, and some units were issued a whiskey ration. To one brigade the amounts dipped out were too generous and, on empty stomachs, this resulted in an entire brigade becoming inebriated. A fight broke out, and soon a general melee erupted. By noon even Burnside saw the hopelessness of it all, for as one private later wrote, "It was no longer a question of how to go forward, but how to get back." And back they trudged, reaching their camps at Fredericksburg on January 23, the "mud march" a miserable failure. Two days later, Major General Hooker replaced Burnside in command of the army.

CHAPTER 8

The Chancellorsville Campaign

"Fighting Joe" in Army Command

Quick acting (sometimes too quick and therefore rash), frank, outspoken, and quite nervous, Joseph Hooker nevertheless normally exhibited courtesy, polish, grace, dignity, and generosity. He knew that his first task was to reorganize the army and to revive its fighting quality. This he accomplished well. Abandoning the grand-division concept, he skillfully restructured the Army of the Potomac into seven infantry and one cavalry corps, a total force that by the spring numbered about 135,000 well-prepared men.

Now fifty-three years of age, Hooker had been twenty-ninth in the 1837 class of fifty U.S. Military Academy graduates. He had experienced combat in the Second Seminole and Mexican Wars, and served as adjutant at West Point. Still only a captain after sixteen years of service, however, he resigned his commission in 1852, farmed for five years, and in the late 1850s became superintendent of military roads in Oregon. Early in the Civil War he rather brashly talked his way into a brigade command, and by good performance rose to the head first of a division and then of a grand division just before Fredericksburg. His haste in sending a one-word dispatch, "Fighting" (which he signed "Joe Hooker"), at Williamsburg on May 5, 1862, where he displayed great bravery, suggested the nickname "Fighting Joe," which newspaper reporters then pinned on him. He was clean shaven and red faced, with white hair and blue eyes. Some people were reminded of the American flag when they saw him, but he recently had made public statements that threw his patriotism into question: he had suggested that the president and his administration were imbeciles and that the Union needed a military dictator.

Knowing Hooker well, Lincoln sent him a meticulous letter containing these remarkable statements:

> There are some things in regard to which, I am not quite satisfied with you. I
> believe you to be a brave and skillful soldier, which, of course, I like. I also believe
> you do not mix politics with your profession, in which you are right. You have
> confidence in yourself, which is a valuable, if not an indispensable quality. You are
> ambitious, which, within reasonable bounds, does good rather than harm. But I
> think that during Gen. Burnside's command of the Army, you have taken counsel
> of your ambition, and thwarted him as much as you could, in which you did a
> great wrong to the country, and to a most meritorious and honorable brother
> officer. I have heard, in such way as to believe it, of your recently saying that both
> the Army and the Government needed a Dictator. Of course it was not *for* this,
> but in spite of it, that I have given you the command. Only those generals who
> gain successes, can set up dictators. What I now ask of you is military success, and
> I will risk the dictatorship.

Hooker also received from the president a general charge to seek "military success" but "beware of rashness." In addition to Lincoln's forbearing trust, however, two big reasons Hooker got the command was that he was a darling of the radical Republicans and the Committee on Conduct rated him highly.

Quite popular with the men in the ranks, Hooker genuinely deserved their adulation. He ordered the issue of tasty rations to include fresh vegetables and soft bread instead of only hardtack, supervised a thorough cleanup of unsanitary camps, instituted liberal furlough policies, and induced paymasters to come up with the soldiers' six months of back pay. To levels not seen since the days of McClellan, before long flagging, morale began to soar. Health conditions improved, causing long sick lists to shrink.

Hooker also further developed the use of divisional patches, which had first been devised in 1862 by the late Maj. Gen. Philip Kearny. He assigned to each corps its own distinctive identification symbol, such as a star, a Greek cross, or a crescent, and within each corps the badge of the first division was colored in red, the second in white, and the third in blue. Other Federal armies soon heard about this system and adopted it.

Still, Hooker had his critics, and some of what they said was true. The most legitimate mark against Hooker was that he had been insubordinate and quite disloyal to poor Burnside. Always known for his hard drinking, Hooker was termed by one critic "a noisy, low-toned intriguer," under whose influence the army headquarters became "a place to which no self-respecting man liked to go, and no decent woman would go. It was a combination of barroom and brothel."

Many persons later believed he prodigiously patronized whorehouses, although in truth this distorted allegation grew out of his efforts to combat widespread venereal disease within the ranks. Men were constantly cycling in and out of the capital, but a grave problem existed: Washington, D.C., like all of the larger cities, North and South, was rife with prostitutes. Hooker attempted to corral them into one area and to police them better. The red-light district in Washington, bordered by Pennsylvania and Constitution Avenues and Twelfth and Fifteenth Streets, came to be called "Hooker's Division."

Hooker's Plan and Lee's Response

During the late winter and early spring of 1863, Lee was genuinely mystified as to Hooker's intentions. On one thing, though, Lee correctly banked: Northern public opinion and political realities would induce the eastern army to take the offensive again. Hooker mapped out a plan to meet the demand. The main maneuver element in Hooker's plan would consist of three corps, swinging northwest of Fredericksburg, along the Rappahannock, and then crossing that river and subsequently the Rapidan. Two corps would stay in front of Fredericksburg, holding the Confederates in their defensive positions. The remaining two corps would be held in reserve, ready to exploit any advance. Each man would carry sixty rounds of ammunition and eight days' rations, consisting of twenty-four pounds of food apiece. To facilitate more speedy movement, for the first time in the eastern theater, most of the usual supply wagons would be replaced by a train of two thousand pack mules.

To enhance his chances of success Hooker sought to divert Lee's attention by sending the Federal cavalry on a raid to try to disrupt Lee's communications. The infantry got underway on April 27. This was a propitious time because Longstreet was far away with much of his corps on a foraging expedition around Suffolk; Lee stood in position with only sixty thousand men.

On April 28 and 29 the three attack corps, forty-two thousand strong, under Maj. Gens. George G. Meade, Oliver O. Howard, and Henry W. Slocum, forded the Rappahannock and Rapidan Rivers. By April 30, having used the better part of four days to complete a flanking march of some forty miles, the lead elements reached Chancellorsville, a strategic crossroads situated on the northeastern edge of the area called "the Wilderness." Thus, indeed, Lee had been turned. On April 30—using words that would come back to haunt him—a confident Hooker told his men: "The operations of the last three days have determined that our enemy must ingloriously fly, or come out from behind their defenses and give us battle on our ground, where certain destruction awaits them."

By April 29 J. E. B. Stuart's Confederate cavalry had captured enough Federal stragglers for Lee to conclude that although Hooker had split his army, either of the parts might be as large as the whole of Lee's sixty thousand men then present. The logical Southern response seemed to be to retreat to the North Anna, the next river line southward, and try there to reunite with Longstreet's large foraging party. But Lee guessed that this was exactly what Hooker expected, so Lee boldly elected to attack one of the three separated bodies of Federal troops.

The units opposite Fredericksburg offered the less promising of the two targets; so Maj. Gen. Richard H. Anderson's division and part of Maj. Gen. Lafayette McLaws's division, the principal portion of Longstreet's corps still with Lee, would march westward during the remaining hours of April 29 and on April 30. They were to reach a point just southeast of Chancellorsville, eventually to form a battle line below Matt's Run. There they would be joined by most of Jackson's corps, moving rapidly in hoped-for deception, leaving only Jubal A. Early's thinly spread division to hold the heights at Fredericksburg.

The Battle of Chancellorsville

The three slowly progressing Federal corps soon found themselves within that dense forest of second-growth pine and scrub oak known as the Wilderness, an extremely thick and overgrown area choked with small maple, ash, cedar, and fir trees, heavily interlaced with vines and brambles. Only here and there was there a small open space or a patch cleared by some farmer. Otherwise the dense vegetation was heavily punctuated by numerous creeks, gullies, and swamps. It was an extremely difficult zone for any maneuver.

The Federal corps commanders expected, and impatiently awaited, orders to advance. Finally, late in the morning, Hooker sent Meade's and Slocum's corps forward. Contact was made about three miles southeast of Chancellorsville. But suddenly Hooker ordered a disengagement and a fallback. Both corps commanders objected strenuously, for their men then held the higher ground. "If he can't hold the top of the hill," Meade grumbled, "how does he expect to hold the bottom of it?" Despite Hooker's earlier and possibly justified boast that "My plans are perfect, and when I start to carry them out, may God have mercy on Bobby Lee; for I shall have none," the commanding general had lost his nerve. "I just lost confidence in Joe Hooker," he later admitted.

Stuart now brought Lee a report that the Federal right flank extended westward from the Wilderness Church along the turnpike, and, while refused slightly, it was not resting on any natural obstacle—the units there seemed unprepared to offer any significant resistance. In a flash Lee realized that he had been presented with a precious opportunity. He determined to make that the main point of an attack by twenty-six thousand men of Jackson's corps (Early's division would still remain in place before Fredericksburg). It was risky, because it meant further dividing his already outnumbered army and that Jackson's force would have to make a flanking march of some twelve miles across the Union army's front. But, that night, in council of war, Lee and Jackson reached a final decision. (This meeting, which turned out to be the last that these two men would have with each other, for Jackson was to receive a mortal wound the next evening, became the subject of the most famous—and most beloved, in the South—of the postwar paintings depicting episodes of the conflict: *The Last Meeting* by E. B. D. Fabrina Julio.)

A local guide knew a seldom used trail that would keep Jackson's men out of sight of the Federals most of the way. For diversion Lee directed the seventeen thousand men that remained southeast of Chancellorsville to exert as much pressure as they could. Stuart's cavalry would screen the movement. In the clear and hot morning of May 2, 1863, Jackson's column, stretching out six miles, began stepping its way across the Union front.

Federal observers, perched near the tops of tall trees, spotted and reported heavy enemy movement on the III Corps commander's—Maj. Gen. Daniel E. Sickles's—front. Sickles requested permission to attack, but Hooker hesitated; finally, at noon, Hooker instructed Sickles to "move out cautiously and harass the movement." Sickles sent two divisions forward, and at about 2:30 P.M. this force encountered the Confederate rear guard, near Catherine Furnace. The Federals killed or captured nearly the whole of one regiment, but by then Jackson's lead regiment was already forming up for their assault.

More and still more Confederate regiments arrived. Though partially concealed in wooded areas, enough of the Southern forces could be seen by various Union pickets to indicate clearly that something big was about to happen. Junior officers tried frantically to alert higher headquarters, but Major General Howard shared Hooker's assumption that Lee was retreating and believed that the thick woods would preclude any major assault against his flank. At 5:00 P.M. Jackson was ready to unleash onslaught. Many of the Union soldiers had stacked arms and were preparing supper, some were playing cards, and others were dozing.

Suddenly, much startled wildlife scurried out of the woods, just ahead of Jackson's men who stormed forward, shrieking the shrill Rebel Yell. In a milewide assault wave, they slammed into the Federal flank and began rolling it up. Howard's XI Corps quickly shattered; frightened and disorganized, these Union soldiers streamed in panic toward Chancellorsville. One combatant later remembered, "Along the road it was pandemonium; on the side of the road it was chaos." Hooker's extreme right, where Howard's men had been, virtually evaporated. Fresh Union troops and artillery stabilized the situation somewhat, but it was only disorganization within the Southern units and approaching dusk that finally stopped the Rebel juggernaut. Hoping that he might continue the assault, possibly even in the darkness and certainly by the next light, Jackson rode forward on the turnpike to study the exact Federal positions. As his party returned, at about 9:00 P.M., a North Carolina regiment fired at what it thought to be Yankee cavalry. The famed hero fell from his saddle, hit three times. (This particular regiment later had a famous motto: "First at Bethel, farthest to the front at Gettysburg, last at Appomattox." Sarcastic historians have suggested that they also should have added "and the only one to kill Stonewall Jackson.")

The wounding of Jackson ended all hope that the Confederates could press any more until the next morning. Jackson was taken on a bumpy ride five miles in an ambulance wagon to a field hospital; by the time the wagon arrived Jackson had gone into shock. Every hope still existed for his eventual recovery, although at 3:00 A.M. a surgeon amputated his left arm. Stuart temporarily assumed command of Jackson's corps.

Meanwhile, during the night Howard's corps had reorganized, and strung out in new battle array along a road above Chancellorsville. Maj. Gen. John F. Reynolds's I Corps came over from its positions near Fredericksburg and established a new and much more secure right flank, the northern extremity reaching to the Rapidan River. Indeed, the Confederate army now stood in grave danger of being destroyed in detail. All of Sickles's and most of Slocum's corps stood squarely between one force comprised of Anderson's and McLaws's division to the southeast of Chancellorsville and Stuart's command to the west. Further, near Fredericksburg, Maj. Gen. John Sedgwick possessed in his VI Corps some twenty-eight thousand men who were in place opposite positions held by Early's scant ten thousand. The Army of the Potomac had not been *disabled*, indeed not even seriously hurt. True, Howard's corps had been routed, but it lost a total of 2,412 total casualties for the whole campaign— a not out-of-line number. Hooker still possessed a huge manpower margin over Lee.

By the morning of May 3, the Federal army was quite ready to fight and could have mounted an offensive. Hooker's nearly ninety thousand men stood concentrated, facing Lee's divided force of forty-eight thousand. But Hooker long since had surrendered his offensive will. When the Confederates renewed their assault early in the morning, the two divided bodies of men fought desperately trying to reunite, and Hooker suddenly made it easier for them to do so. First he ordered Sickles's and Slocum's corps rearward, seeking to simplify and shorten his defensive lines. This allowed Lee's divided forces to rejoin at the flanks and also to seize high ground at Hazel Grove, just south of Chancellorsville. There the Confederates emplaced artillery, and harassing cannon fire forced the Federals to pull Sickles's III, Slocum's XII, and Maj. Gen. Darius N. Couch's II Corps entirely from the vicinity of Chancellorsville northward behind a new main battle line, manned by the corps of Reynolds, Meade, and Howard.

Shortly after 9:00 A.M. a minor disaster befell Hooker: he was leaning against a column of the Chancellor House, his headquarters, which was suddenly struck by a Confederate shell; splinters of all sizes flew wildly, and Hooker was stunned senseless; and the reinforcements and supply trains were scattered. Rumors flew through the ranks that Hooker had been killed, and indeed for a few moments his aides did think he might be dying, but his medical director managed to revive him. Hooker struggled to mount his horse and ride toward the rear, but he was not again fit to exercise command during the remainder of the campaign: he suffered intense pains, was occasionally faint, and his right side was partially paralyzed—and he was livid for weeks afterward.

Meanwhile, Sedgwick tried to push Early from the heights below Fredericksburg, hoping to seize and secure them and then march to the aid of Hooker. Sedgwick's men made quick work of the weak Confederate holding force, scattering Early's men with a dramatic bayonet charge. Then Sedgwick began moving westward, along the Plank Road. But when Lee learned that Early had lost the heights, and that Sedgwick's corps was on its way, he dispatched McLaws's division to block the road. The advance units of both forces came into contact near Salem Church, and during the later part of the afternoon numbers of Sedgwick's troops gradually came up and engaged the Confederates in close combat.

Anderson's division was dispatched to go to McLaws's aid while Early, bolstered by one of McLaws's brigades, began reorganizing a few miles southeast of the church. So, on May 4, Lee had a detached force of twenty-one thousand men ready to attack the bulk of Sedgwick's corps. As conflict commenced and the Confederates managed to make progress, Sedgwick's flanks began to bend backward, and thus the Union corps came to be pressed from three directions. Sedgwick wisely abandoned any hope of joining Hooker, fought hard for the remainder of the day, and during the night crossed Scott's Ford and withdrew to safety north of the Rappahannock.

Lee promptly resecured the heights to the south and west of Fredericksburg, leaving token forces to hold them; the rest of the weary men rapidly marched back toward Chancellorsville. On May 6, Hooker disengaged, crossed United States Ford, and retreated. The Chancellorsville campaign was over. Helping to shield Hooker's army as it retired, Maj. Gen. Winfield Scott Hancock added significantly to his already stellar reputation. He deployed parts of three regiments in a skirmish line, a man posted every three yards, which successfully resisted a series of Confederate rearguard attacks. This kind of formation came to be regarded as the standard defensive protection for a disengaging main force.

The Union loss stood at 17,287; the Confederate casualty list numbered 12,821. The most immediate and obviously crushing Rebel loss was General Jackson. Taken from the field hospital by wagon to a farm twenty-five miles away, he was expected to recuperate. "Give [Jackson] my affectionate regards," Lee told one of Jackson's chaplains who visited his headquarters on May 7, "and tell him to make haste and get well, and come back to me as soon as he can. He has lost his left arm, but I have lost my right." On that very day, however, Jackson's physician diagnosed that pneumonia had set in. Nothing could be done. Jackson died at 3:20 P.M. on May 10, 1863. His last words, which became a Southern euphemism for death, were "Let us cross over the river and rest under the shade of the trees."

Conclusion

The second year of the war ended with the Union seemingly little closer to subduing the South than it had been at the outset. Despite obvious successes, essential stalemate *still* prevailed in the West; and, in the East, Lee's Army of Northern Virginia seemed unbeatable. To have accepted the engagement at Antietam was nearly the worst of all Lee's decisions; and to stand fast a second day was sheer folly. But he did both, and thanks to the tactical mastery with which he and his subordinates managed that unwanted battle, and McClellan's ineptitude, Lee had avoided tragedy. The twin debacles of Fredericksburg and the Mud March, and the subsequent spectacular victory at Chancellorsville, gave Southerners much reason for buoyant morale—and Northerners much cause to hope for better things from other commanders. One scholar, Michael C. C. Adams, has suggested that, in the East, the Southerners enjoyed a psychological dominance over their foe. On the other hand, it seems plausible to suspect that by this moment in time the Confederates might have been suffering from overconfidence.

Too, the Chancellorsville campaign had taken a more costly toll on Lee's army than it had appeared at first. General Jackson's loss was bad enough, but even more serious was the loss of numerous other important or promising officers; Southern command resources were beginning to diminish. Indeed, Lee previously had concluded that an infantry corps with thirty thousand men or more was too large for a commander to handle, especially in wooded situations. He had, however, refrained from restructuring so long as he had the two extraordinarily capable men, Longstreet and Jackson. Now he felt forced to divide the army into three infantry corps with three divisions each. Richard S. Ewell was promoted to the rank of lieutenant general and replaced Jackson; and Ambrose P. Hill, also raised to lieutenant general, was made commander of the new Third Corps.

It is amazing, given the several occurrences of happenstance that produced entrenchments or fortifications, that the Civil War's second year still did not see the universal adoption of them. The Hornet's Nest at Shiloh, the unfinished railroad cut and the stone wall in front of S. D. Lee's artillery position at Second Bull Run, the sunken road at Antietam, and the stone wall at Fredericksburg should have been more than enough to show even the most unprescient that trenches or field fortifications should always be constructed (on the occasions when good fortune did not render them as a given). And, because the muzzle-loading rifles required that the soldier stand, or be behind an embankment or wall that provided at least a forty-five-degree upright position, when they could be so constructed, trenches had to be deep. When rifle-armed troops were well emplaced defensively, there seemed to be no way to dislodge them by frontal attack. More and more, wise commanders would attempt flank attacks or turning movements. One of them, U. S. Grant, would choose to lay siege when his assaults failed.

SUGGESTED READINGS

Special Studies of Note

"Abraham Lincoln, John Pope, and the Origins of Total War," by Daniel E. Sutherland (*The Journal of Military History* 56 [October 1992]: 567–86), is an insightful and important piece.

Confederate Strategy from Shiloh to Vicksburg, by Archer Jones (Baton Rouge: Louisiana State University Press, 1961, 1991). Although Jones asserts that he no longer believes the correctness of much herein, he is nevertheless the master student of Civil War strategy—and always stimulating.

Davis and Lee at War, by Steven E. Woodworth (Lawrence: University Press of Kansas, 1995), should have been volume 2 and matched with *Jefferson Davis and His Generals* below. It thoroughly cements the case, if the first one had not been sufficient, that Woodworth has a place among the small group of the greatest younger Civil War historians.

Jefferson Davis and His Generals, by Steven E. Woodworth (Lawrence: University Press of Kansas, 1990), is totally slanted to the western theater but is very important and provocative. Woodworth has recently completed the necessary companion volume, and that together with this one well complements T. Harry Williams's *Lincoln and His Generals* below.

Lee's Tigers: The Louisiana Infantry in the Army of Northern Virginia, by Terry L. Jones (Baton Rouge: Louisiana State University Press, 1987), is a great unit-level history.

Lincoln and His Generals, by T. Harry Williams (New York: Knopf, 1952), is my mentor's most popular book.

Our Masters the Rebels: A Speculation on Union Military Failure in the East, 1861–1865, by Michael C. C. Adams (Cambridge: Harvard University Press, 1978). As the title implies, Adams imputes a psychological dimension to the poor performances of the Union's earlier eastern generals.

The Story the Soldiers Wouldn't Tell: Sex in the Civil War, by Thomas P. Lowry, M.D. (Mechanicsburg, Pa.: Stackpole Books, 1994), affirms what the soldiers denied and offers the statistics on incidence of venereal diseases. Lowry tells about such things as the small pornographic books that soldiers could purchase through the mail, the bawdy songs they sang, and the sexually oriented smutty poems and jokes they told. However, this book is about not only the seamy side of love but also true romance.

Battle and Campaign Studies

Antietam: Essays on the 1862 Maryland Campaign, by Gary W. Gallagher (Kent: Kent State University Press, 1989).

The Campaign of Chancellorsville, by John Bigelow (New Haven: Yale University Press, 1910), is a masterful study.

Fredericksburg, a Study in War, by George William Redway (New York: Macmillan, 1906), is a classic campaign study.

Landscape Turned Red: The Battle of Antietam, by Stephen W. Sears (New York: Ticknor and Fields, 1983), is written vividly.

No Better Place to Die: The Battle of Stones River, by Peter Cozzens (Urbana: University of Illinois Press, 1990). Cozzens, an employee of the U.S. State Department, writes intriguing and colorful campaign studies.

Return to Bull Run: The Campaign and Battle of Second Manassas, by John J. Hennessy (New York: Simon and Schuster, 1993), is now *the* standard work on the subject, and its style is so graceful that one adulator has been induced to exaggerate that Hennessy is this generation's Douglas Southall Freeman.

The U.S. Army War College Guide to the Battle of Antietam: The Maryland Campaign of 1862, by Jay Luvaas and Harold W. Nelson (Carlisle, Pa.: South Mountain Press, 1987), is the finest of several extant battlefield guidebooks and is quite helpful.

Memoir

Fighting for the Confederacy, by Edward Porter Alexander, edited by Gary W. Gallagher (Chapel Hill: University of North Carolina Press, 1989). Gallagher has found previously lost material and thus makes an important fresh contribution.

George B. McClellan

The Civil War Papers of George B. McClellan: Selected Correspondence, 1860–1865, by Stephen W. Sears (New York: Ticknor and Fields, 1989), is a stacked deck and *probably* unfairly anti-McClellan but is nonetheless most interesting.

George B. McClellan: The Young Napoleon, by Stephen W. Sears (New York: Ticknor and Fields, 1988), is the best anti-McClellan study.

McClellan's Own Story, by George B. McClellan (New York: C. L. Webster, 1887), shows his pomposity.

Other Biographies

Bold Dragoon: The Life of J. E. B. Stuart, by Emory M. Thomas (New York: Harper and Row, 1986), is good and sound scholarship.

Braxton Bragg and Confederate Defeat, vol. 1, *Field Command,* by Grady McWhiney (New York: Columbia University Press, 1969). McWhiney is a most worthy student of the great David Donald. This is the start of a brilliant biography, but Bragg proved too sour and unpleasant a topic, so McWhiney left completion to one of his friends, Judith Hallock.

Breckinridge: Statesman, Soldier, Symbol, by William C. Davis (Baton Rouge: Louisiana State University Press, 1974), is the prize-winning biography of the Kentucky-born vice president who became both a general and a secretary of war in the Confederacy. Davis is the undisputed dean of the nonacademics who write Civil War history. He has been most prolific—and all of his works have been noteworthy and worthwhile.

Commanders of the Army of the Potomac, by Warren Hassler (Baton Rouge: Louisiana State University Press, 1962). Hassler, now retired, was a military historian with a gifted touch.

John Pope, a Biography, by Trenerry Walter and Wallace Schultz (Urbana: University of Illinois Press, 1990), offers, at last, something more than the "owl dung" story on Pope.

Lee, by Douglas Southall Freeman (New York: Scribners, 1961), is a one-volume abridg-
ment of the prize-winning and much heralded four-volume biography edited by
Richard Harwell. While Freeman's work may not be without considerable flaw, all
students of the Civil War owe it to themselves to read *something* by him.

Lee the Soldier, edited by Gary W. Gallagher (Lincoln: University of Nebraska Press,
1996), is a good sampling of "just about everything one could possibly want to look
at" that has been written about Robert E. Lee.

The Life of the Gallant Pelham, by Philip Mercer (Macon: J. W. Burke, 1929). It is said
that when Pelham died, numerous girls—each thinking herself to have been his
fiancée—put on mourning costumes.

Mighty Stonewall, by Frank E. Vandiver (New York: McGraw Hill, 1957), is said by some
to be the best writing ever about Jackson. But some expect James I. Robertson Jr.'s
new biography of Jackson to surpass this one.

Robert E. Lee: A Biography, by Emory M. Thomas (New York: Norton, 1995), is the
most modern and most highly revered one-volume biography of the "great man."
Thomas claims to be a "post-revisionist." That means that he falls somewhere
between Douglas Freeman (who loved Lee to the point of blindness in judgment)
and modern critics such as Thomas L. Connelly and Allan Nolan (who were both
harsh and sometimes obtuse in their attempts to grasp the realities of Lee's possible
"feet of clay").

Stephen Dodson Ramseur: Lee's Gallant General, by Gary W. Gallagher (Chapel Hill:
University of North Carolina Press, 1985).

Stonewall in the Valley, by Robert G. Tanner (Garden City, N.Y.: Doubleday, 1976), is
essential popular history.

Fiction

The Red Badge of Courage, by Stephen Crane (New York: Appleton, 1896). The battle in
this great classic of war literature, a timeless work of fiction, is Chancellorsville. The
reader is especially urged to seek out a scholarly edition with commentary, such as
the one edited by Sculley Bradley, Richmond Croom Beatty, E. Hudson Long, and
Donald Pizer, 2d ed. (New York: Norton, 1976.)

The River and the Wilderness, by Don Robertson (New York: Doubleday, 1962), is a vivid
novel about General Burnside at Fredericksburg and in the Wilderness campaign.
It contains several lurid love stories that some might call vulgar.

Picture Book

Antietam: The Photographic Legacy of America's Bloodiest Day, by William A. Frassanito
(New York: Scribner's, 1978). All of Frassanito's works reflect blending of the author's
expertise as both a historian and a photo analyst.

PART III

The Great Turning Points

❧

The Vicksburg and Gettysburg campaigns are perhaps the two most captivating and striking extended episodes of the war. More than 1.5 million people visit the Gettysburg National Military Park each year, and there the term *turning point* is so common that it is even the name of a nearby motel. Vicksburg, while not quite as popular, is also a much visited national park. The conclusion of these two campaigns at the same time, early in July 1863, seems to many students to "mark the beginning of the inevitable end." Such a concept is too simplistic. While they are campaigns of enormous significance, it is crucial to remember that the war then entered into the period that might best be described as the "long pull," and there would still be much evidence of continuing Confederate viability—punctuated most notably by a stunning Rebel triumph in September: the Battle of Chickamauga.

But how well would the people of one side or the other bear up under a "long pull"? The Southerners needed to follow up on and capitalize gains from their victories, and ultimately they did not do this. Too, as Mark Grimsley has pointed out, "the year 1863 marked a significant watershed, because during that year one can see the emergence of large-scale destruction carried out, in fairly routine fashion, by large bodies of troops." That did much to depress popular morale.

CHAPTER 9

The Confederate "Jewels" on the Mississippi
Vicksburg and Port Hudson

Control of the entire Mississippi River had been a principal Union war aim from the outset. By early 1862 the North had seized all but a 110-mile stretch. At the endpoints of that river segment lay Port Hudson, Louisiana, 25 miles north of Baton Rouge, and Vicksburg, Mississippi, a commercial city near the mouth of the Yazoo River at the terminus of an important rail line. The Confederates had managed to tenaciously hold these two points. They were strong as well as valuable places. Port Hudson sat on an almost precipitous bluff where the river made a sharp turn (which enhanced defense of the place). Vicksburg was called the Gibraltar of the West and seemed impregnable because of its location on high bluffs and the rough, and in places swampy, surrounding terrain.

In late 1862 the Federals commenced an onslaught at both ends of the segment, commencing on November 16 when a Federal fleet steamed upriver toward Port Hudson and briefly bombarded the batteries. The boats withdrew and left things quiet in that sector for nearly a month, but on December 13 they returned and resumed pressure. U. S. Grant, too, before the year's end, launched the first of his efforts against Vicksburg, this one culminating in the Battle of Chickasaw Bayou.

The Chickasaw Bayou Campaign

The Chickasaw Bayou campaign (December 1862–January 1863) was one that lent some credence to the later myth—popular in some quarters—that Southern generals in the main were superior to Northern generals. Many years after the war's end, die-hard Rebels still remembered and spoke of campaigns such as this one where the recently promoted Brig. Gen. Stephen D. Lee, as they put it, "gave old Sherman a good drubbing." Indeed, one Southern newspaper even proclaimed that the Chickasaw Bayou battles "deserve as historic a place in history as that of Thermopylae."

Vicksburg is situated at the end of a long series of hills running inland from the water almost at a right angle. The Yazoo River touched the foot of these hills at Haynes' Bluff where it then swung away and emptied into the Mississippi about six miles north of the city. Most of the ground in the triangle delineated by the bluffs and the two rivers was low, marshy, cut by lakes and bayous, and heavily wooded with dense undergrowth, except where there were clearings for a few small plantations. Beginning at the foot of the bluffs farthest from the city, and running for a distance of nearly fourteen miles, there was first a good road, then swamp, then a series of connected lakes that had once been a bed of the Yazoo. This stretch of water was too deep to be forded except at three or four places. A specially constructed floating obstruction blocked the Yazoo and proved to be sufficient to stop all Federal attempts to get up the river.

Grant planned a three-pronged attack. He suggested that Maj. Gen. Nathaniel P. Banks (in charge of Northern forces in Louisiana, but not subject to Grant's command) should lead a force up the Mississippi River. Meanwhile, Major General Sherman would move down the river from Memphis, and Grant himself would bring troops southward through central Mississippi toward Grenada, then turn west in a coordinated attack upon Vicksburg. Banks, however, refused to cooperate, and Confederate troops under Major Generals Van Dorn and Forrest thwarted Grant with brilliant cavalry raids on his line of communications. Indeed, at Holly Springs, Van Dorn's men destroyed supplies worth $1.5 million and took fifteen hundred prisoners, though they were at once paroled. Julia Dent Grant, the general's wife, was present, but neither she nor any of the civilians were taken captive. Her carriage was burned and the Confederates made off with her team of horses, but the Confederates did not stay long in Holly Springs, and Mrs. Grant soon rejoined her husband. Grant terminated this phase of the campaign, but Sherman's force was left to continue alone toward Vicksburg.

Sherman was by no means being sent to certain defeat, for he had thirty-three thousand men aboard sixty transports accompanied by seven gunboats. To oppose this Stephen D. Lee (recently transferred from the eastern theater) had a "reorganized brigade" of twenty-seven hundred men, and there were twenty-four hundred other Confederate soldiers stationed in and around Vicksburg. On Christmas Eve 1862, Sherman's flotilla neared, but Southerners had telegraph outposts along the river and so were warned. Early on December 26, Sherman's forces debarked twelve miles up the Yazoo. General firing commenced and continued throughout the day with little effect save to slow the gingerly advancing Federal troops. Confederate counterassaults regained all lost ground. The same sequence recurred several times the next day. This time the Confederates gradually fell back under the weight of far superior numbers, until well-emplaced and well-directed Confederate artillery stopped the Union advance. General skirmishing resumed throughout December 28. That night Sherman made a reconnaissance and determined upon a grand assault, snorting that it would probably cost the Union five thousand men before they got Vicksburg and they might as well lose them here as anywhere else.

Stephen Lee correctly guessed the main assault would be at Chickasaw Bayou, so he bolstered his line there and set a trap: he decided to allow an initial progress in order to draw as many Federals as possible into a killing zone. Following a tremendous barrage, three brigades of the Union division commanded by Brig. Gen. George W. Morgan advanced the three-quarters of a mile over fallen timber before reaching the wood's edge. As Lee had intended, the terrain provided a "funnel effect," as a morass of mud and water necessitated that many men had to cross a log bridge. The attackers managed to advance to within 150 yards of Lee's rifle pits before a withering "storm of shells, grape and canister, as well as minie-balls which swept the front like a hurricane of fire" shattered their ranks and forced the survivors to retreat. It was "a repetition of Balaklava, although mine was infantry and Earl Cardigan's force was cavalry," lamented Brig. Gen. John Milton Thayer, one of Morgan's brigade commanders. The Federals had not lost 5,000 men, as Sherman had predicted, but had not taken Vicksburg either. Their casualties numbered 1,776 (1,439 of them from Morgan's division). The Confederates lost a total of 207. Sherman floundered but did little beyond have his men entrench. On December 31 a truce was arranged for the burial of Union dead, and then Sherman reloaded onto the transports and steamed back to Memphis.

The Final Struggle for Control of the Mississippi River

January 1863 passed in relative quiet, but on February 2—demonstrating that it *could* be done—the Union ram *Queen of the West* ran past the Vicksburg batteries. The vessel was struck twelve times but was not seriously damaged. Until she was lost a dozen days later, this warship wreaked havoc upon both the Mississippi River and the Red River. The Union enjoyed a tremendous

Stephen D. Lee. Starting only as a captain he made lieutenant general at the age of thirty—the war's youngest to attain that rank on either side. He was above all else conscientious and competent, and his importance, as well as his multifaceted involvement in the war, has too often been unnoticed. (courtesy Leib Image Archives, York, Penn.)

advantage in the struggle for the river because the Confederacy never managed to develop sufficient naval strength. The Federal navy now possessed a fleet of new boats specifically designed for river warfare. This naval power proved to be one of the keys to Grant's campaign.

Grant immediately set into motion a series of schemes to get at Vicksburg. An unsuccessful attempt was made to deflect the waters of the Mississippi by hand-digging an alternate channel; Union gunboats tried haplessly to get into the Red River from above Vicksburg; an expedition was sent toward Yazoo Pass via a bayou, but was blocked at Fort Pemberton; a number of complex and fruitless campaigns were conducted north of Vicksburg in expeditions on Deer Creek, Steele's Bayou, and Rolling Fork. Grant later asserted that he had only scant hopes that any of these schemes might work. He was saving his major effort for the spring and summer: to have *empty* vessels, shielded by cotton bales, run southward past the Vicksburg batteries while Grant marched overland with the troops.

The struggle meanwhile continued unabated, though also stalemated, at Port Hudson. That place actually would continue to hold out until after Grant finally reduced Vicksburg, which rendered its further defense pointless. While it had been successfully passed on March 14, 1863, by a few warships commanded by Rear Adm. David G. Farragut, the episode proved only the strength of the place and that reduction of its batteries could be accomplished only by land action. Banks's Army of the Gulf made two attempts to storm the place: on May 27 and on June 14. In the first, Federal losses amounted to 1,995, contrasted with 235 Confederate casualties; in the second, the Unionists suffered 1,792 casualties to the Confederates' 47. The struggle continued as a siege.

In mid-April, Grant managed to force things to a head. Several diversionary thrusts were made: (1) Maj. Gen. Frederick Steele's division moved by water from Young's Point to Greenville, Mississippi, and then inland to maraud; (2) Col. Benjamin H. Grierson led one thousand cavalrymen on a raid from Grand Junction, Tennessee, through east Mississippi to Baton Rouge; and (3) Sherman's corps made an elaborate feint from the north. On April 16, in the middle of the night, Rear Adm. David D. Porter's fleet ran past the city. Even though often hit by enemy fire, all but one of the boats passed safely. They met Grant at Hard Times, Louisiana, to which the troops had marched overland.

Confederate defenders stymied the initial crossing attempt, but Grant moved rapidly to a position opposite Bruinsburg. There, outnumbering the Rebels by more than two-to-one, Grant was able to cross, force Grand Gulf's evacuation, and quickly take Port Gibson. Here Grant's men stymied a plucky resistance that was aided by difficult terrain (steep, sharp ridges and gullies covered with thick vines and dense undergrowth). Grant had hoped to live off the country but could not move rapidly enough to avoid depleting resources in the army's immediate vicinity, so he reopened supply lines, the navy running four hundred thousand rations past the river batteries.

By now the numbers of Confederate troops in Mississippi had increased considerably beyond the puny levels that had been committed the previous December: Lt. Gen. John Clifford Pemberton now commanded an army of some thirty-two thousand men, while Gen. Joseph E. Johnston had another force of some six thousand with more reinforcements arriving. Grant campaigned against these enemy armies with his own field force of forty-one thousand men. For a successful conclusion of Grant's venture, it was crucial that Maj. Gen. William S. Rosecrans remain sufficiently strong and adequately active in Tennessee to prevent Gen. Braxton Bragg from sending significant reinforcements to Pemberton. Rosecrans accomplished this well in his unheralded, underrated, and relatively bloodless Tullahoma campaign.

∾

Herman Hattaway and Archer Jones saw so much of an interrelation between the Vicksburg, Gettysburg, and Tullahoma campaigns that in *How the North Won* they discussed all three of them together in a single long chapter. The Tullahoma campaign stretched from June 23 to July 3, 1863. At the outset, Rosecrans's Army of the Cumberland was at Murfreesboro, Tennessee, where it had been gradually strengthened during the six months that followed the Battle of Stones River. Bragg's Army of Tennessee was screening the Federal force by maintaining a fortified line from Shelbyville to Wartrace, Tennessee.

Fearing that Bragg would dispatch troops to aid Pemberton at Vicksburg, Lincoln and Halleck pressed Rosecrans to take the offensive. This he did, first feinting toward Shelbyville but moving in main force toward Bragg's right. There the Federals achieved a penetration, inducing Bragg to give ground. Rain slowed the Yankee advance, but by June 26 they had occupied Manchester, Tennessee, and there they were a threat to Bragg's Shelbyville-Wartrace line so he pulled back to Tullahoma.

On June 28 Rosecrans sent a rapidly moving column to strike the railroad in Bragg's rear. While it arrived too late to destroy the bridge across the Elk River before the Rebels posted strong defenders there, the column did tear up hundreds of yards of track near Decherd. This induced Bragg to decide that his situation in middle Tennessee was untenable, and so he withdrew across the Cumberland Plateau into a new position behind the Tennessee River. Rosecrans having lost only 560 men had finessed Bragg into withdrawing eighty-five miles, and, furthermore, the Yankees had seized 1,634 Rebels who had fallen prisoner and snatched eleven cannon and large quantities of supplies.

By the middle of the second week of May, as Grant's resupplied army began its advance, the Confederates stood divided. On May 12 an engagement erupted at Raymond, fifteen miles from the Mississippi capital. In several hours of fighting, both sides sustained about five hundred casualties, but the outnumbered Rebels were gradually forced toward Jackson. At the same time Sherman's men were clashing with enemy skirmishers along Fourteen-Mile Creek. Grant used one corps as a covering force to hold Pemberton at bay while the other two Federal corps concentrated against Johnston. On May 14, outnumbered almost five-to-one, Johnston withdrew northward. In brief fighting that afternoon Grant seized the state capital. Leaving a minimal guard under Sherman to protect against any sudden return by Johnston's men, Grant turned his main force toward Vicksburg.

On May 16 Pemberton attempted to hold Grant east of the Big Black River by accepting what proved to be a major battle. This, the Battle of Champion's Hill, was the bloodiest of the series of conflicts preliminary to Grant's beginning of a siege at Vicksburg. The hill is a crescent-shaped ridge, about seventy-five feet in elevation. The Confederate line stretched out about three miles. During the preliminary fighting the northern portion was gradually forced to bend back so that eventually the Rebel position somewhat resembled the number 7. Pemberton expected a main attack along the verticle, but it actually came from the horizontal above. It was a bloody battle, described by one Union brigade commander as among "the most obstinate and murderous conflicts of the war." In the contest Federal effectives numbered about 29,000 and they sustained a total of 2,441 casualties. The Confederate effectives, probably numbering under 20,000, suffered 3,851 casualties. The Confederates were outgeneraled, outmaneuvered, and finally finessed. Fearing disaster, Pemberton elected to withdraw into the Vicksburg defenses, fighting delaying actions along the way.

On May 18 the siege of Vicksburg began. Johnston subsequently received additional troops from Tennessee and South Carolina, but the Union high command reinforced Grant much more heavily. Grant tried two major assaults, the first on May 19 and the second three days later. In the first, Grant harbored hope that the Confederates might be caught not fully ready and that a sudden rush against the entire defensive perimeter would succeed. But the fortifications were already well prepared, and the onslaught failed. The Federals suffered some one thousand casualties. In the second assault, responding to the faulty advice of the militarily inept political major general John A. McClernand, Grant focused on a selected three-mile section of the defenses, trying to penetrate it by concentrating for a maximal hammer-blow against six selected strong points. Gunboats and siege mortars brought up the Yazoo supplemented the firepower. But there occurred only one successful though brief breakthrough, near a railroad redoubt, and that breach was quickly reclosed by counterattacks. Otherwise the assaults were suicidal and losses were heavy.

It was obvious that a conventional siege was necessary. Grant made no further attempt to take the city by assault, but as the siege progressed several attempts were made to demolish the defenses by mining under them and blowing them up. On June 25 twenty-two hundred pounds of powder were detonated in a tunnel that had been run under the Third Louisiana Redan. Two regiments stormed into the gap thus created, but a second defensive line had already been prepared slightly to the rear as insurance against what had happened, and troops therein prevented any further Union advance. On July 1 another mine was exploded but the breach was not as large as they had hoped, so the Federals elected not to try storming through. A third mine was set to explode on July 6 in conjunction with an attack that Grant planned for that day, but that attack proved unnecessary (because by then the Confederates had capitulated).

Union communications along the Mississippi, protected by gunboats, remained secure, and Grant had only to apply the rules of military science and wait (while enjoying tactical security) until Pemberton—trapped against the river—was forced to surrender because of depleted supplies. From boats on the river and from troops in the encircling lines, the Vicksburg populace and defenders suffered onslaughts against their nerve and will. Union gunboats lobbed into the city huge mortar shells that made craters as deep as seventeen feet. On the field, the situation was described by Confederate Cpl. Ephraim Anderson:

> The enemy continued to prosecute the siege vigorously. From night to night and from day to day a series of works was presented. Secure and strong lines of fortifications appeared. Redoubts, manned by well-practiced sharpshooters, . . . parapets blazing with artillery crowned every knoll and practicable elevation, . . . and oblique lines of entrenchments, finally running into parallels, enabled the untiring foe to work his way slowly but steadily forward.

Large numbers of wounded men, some eight hundred or more in early June, suffered mightily in the Vicksburg hospitals—many of which were located in residences converted for the purpose. Some twenty or more men died each day. Chaplain William Lovelace Foster of the Thirty-fifth Mississippi Infantry described the horrors in a moving letter to his wife:

> On passing through the hospital what a heart-rending spectacle greets the eyes! Here we see the horrors of dreadful war! . . . The weather is excessively hot and the flies swarm around the wounded—more numerous where the wound is severest. In a few days the wounds begin to be offensive and horrid. . . . Nor can this be avoided unless a nurse were detailed for every man—but there is only one allowed for every eight men. . . . Never before did I have such an idea of the cruelty and the barbarism of war.

As the city trembled from the bombardments, the people therein gradually reduced their daily meals to one-half and then to one-quarter rations. Soldiers were obliged to eat mule meat, rats, and young shoots of cane. One of the entrapped civilians later recalled that her servant found rats dressed and for sale in the market. A Confederate enlisted man wrote that rats, when fried, had a flavor "fully equal to that of squirrels." One Missouri soldier stoutly held that "If you did not know it, you could hardly tell the difference, when cooked," between mule meat and beef.

Not only food, but even adequate drinking water, for some, became scarce. Here, we see an example of some less-than-noble quality, a disinclination to share one's resources, in a certain quarter of the civilian populace: Dore Miller, wife of a Vicksburg lawyer, who had a private supply of fresh water, even while many other persons suffered from thirst. She wrote, "We hear of others dipping up the water from ditches and mud-holes. This place [her "bomb proof"] has two large underground cisterns of good cool water, and every night in my subterranean dressing room a tub of cold water is the nerve-calmer that sends me to sleep."

At last, after forty-seven days of siege, Pemberton and all but two of his officers agreed that they should surrender on July 4, 1863. The Federal losses amounted to 4,910 during the siege, while the Confederates had suffered casualties amounting to 1,872 before they capitulated. The captives numbered 2,166 officers, 27,230 enlisted men, and 115 civilian employees; all were paroled save for 1 officer and 708 men who preferred to go north as prisoners. The Rebel army also yielded its entire equipage: 172 cannon, large amounts of every ammunition type, and some sixty thousand shoulder weapons.

There served in the Union ranks during the Vicksburg siege a woman—Albert D. J. Cashier (whose real name was Jennie Hodgers). There are a number of mentions in both Northern and Southern records of women who dressed as men and joined the fighting. Mary Livermore—a prominent activist with the U.S. Sanitary Commission—noted in her diary that the total number of women among the Civil War soldiers was probably about 400, and many writers have since accepted and repeated her unsoundly underpinned estimate. Lauren Cook Burgess is now thoroughly researching the topic and thus far has documented some 150 women combatants. Best of all, she has found that some of them got promoted (never being found out)—several became sergeants, a few became lieutenants, and at least one rose to captain! All women whose sex was discovered were immediately discharged and sent home. A few of them perhaps were insane (as usually it was assumed whenever any of them was found out), others no doubt desired to be near a husband or lover who also was a soldier, and some simply were gutsy and patriotic and wanted to serve.

Cashier was a true and permanent transvestite. Enlisting in Company G, Ninety-fifth Illinois Infantry on August 6, 1862, she served honorably not only

Pvt. Lyons Wakeman (actually Sarah Rosetta Wakeman), a female
soldier about whom we know a great deal—thanks to the trove of
letters saved by her family and provided to Lauren Cook Burgess,
who edited and published them. (courtesy of Lauren Cook Burgess)

throughout the Vicksburg campaign (where her name was later inscribed along
with all the others from Illinois on that state's monument in the Vicksburg
National Military Park) but also in the 1864 Red River campaign, in operations
against Nathan B. Forrest's cavalry in north Mississippi, in the Battle of Brice's
Crossroads (June 10, 1864), in the pursuit of Maj. Gen. Sterling Price who raided
into Missouri in the fall of 1864, in the Franklin and Nashville campaigns, and
in the early 1865 seizures of forts near Mobile, Alabama.

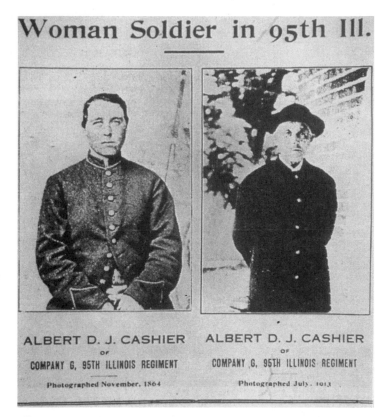

Albert D. J. Cashier (actually Jennie Hodgers) was one of at least 150 women who served quite well in combat—disguised as men. (courtesy of the Illinois State Historical Library)

After the war she worked as a farmhand and handyman. She kept her sex a secret until 1911, when it was discovered by a physician attending to a broken leg she had suffered in an automobile accident. In old age she collected an invalid soldier's pension and was very active in the Union veteran's society, the Grand Army of the Republic. She died in 1915 and was buried in uniform with full military honors.

The embittered people of Vicksburg did not again celebrate the 4th of July until patriotic fervor and love for the United States was rekindled during World War II. But the capitulation in July 1863 was hailed all over the North with exuberance and exultation, especially when, just a few days later, Port Hudson also surrendered. Taking that place had cost nearly ten thousand Union men—

dead, wounded, or physically impaired from disease or exposure—compared with the Southern losses of only 871. Now, however, "The Father of Waters," as President Lincoln gratefully proclaimed, again flowed "unvexed to the sea," and the Confederacy was split in two.

CHAPTER 10

The Gettysburg Campaign

A period of preparation in the middle of May 1863 marked the beginning of the Gettysburg campaign. Owing to a singular claim made by Confederate Postmaster General John H. Reagan in his 1905 memoirs, many students have been drawn to conclude falsely that strategically the Confederate high command conceived the campaign as being a distracting counteroffensive, alleviating their dismal situation in the West. Even before the Chancellorsville campaign, Lee had contemplated a thrust into Pennsylvania and in February 1863 had directed the engineer officer Jedediah Hotchkiss to prepare a map of the Shenandoah valley extended to Harrisburg and even to Philadelphia.

Now, having scored two major victories within the past five months, morale and optimism were high, and Lee felt ready. Lee's real motives for the Gettysburg campaign were these: he wanted to stymie any Federal plan for a summer campaign in Virginia; he hoped to crush the Federal troops then occupying the lower (northern) end of the Shenandoah valley; much as had been the case in September 1862, he wanted to give the people of Virginia a respite from the nearness of war and a chance to produce a good crop; above all he wanted to spend the summer maneuvering and absorbing supplies in south-central Pennsylvania; for, last, he also much hoped to increase the level of Northern war weariness.

Lee's Initial Movements and Hooker's Response

The end of May 1863 saw the two armies gazing at each other across the Rappahannock River. Always wary about the numerous fords, the two forces kept particularly close watch on them. Lee's army, reinforced to a strength of about seventy-five thousand, detached its first elements on June 3, 1863. Hooker countered by shifting troops toward the upper fords; but he ignored reports

Arlington House. Mrs. R. E. Lee's inherited ancestral home, shown here with Federal soldiers lolling. She never resigned herself to losing it, and when a friend asked her what she would do with the Federal graves if she did succeed in getting it back, she replied, "My dear, I would smooth them off and plant my flowers." (courtesy Leib Image Archives, York, Penn.)

that suggested Lee was swinging in a much wider arc and kept the bulk of the Federal army concentrated near Falmouth. Hooker guessed that Lee was trying to repeat the Second Bull Run campaign. So on June 6 Hooker ordered Major General Sedgwick's VI Corps to make a reconnaissance in force in front of some pontoon bridges just south of Fredericksburg. Sedgwick's troops skirmished with A. P. Hill's men for several days.

Hooker's cavalry, meanwhile, gleaned information that an enemy force of six brigades was located at Culpeper Court House. On the afternoon of June 7, Hooker decided to hit that force. He dispatched his cavalry, with three thousand specially selected infantrymen, under Brig. Gen. Alfred Pleasonton. The Rebel force numbered about ten thousand men, under the command of Maj. Gen. J. E. B. Stuart. Hooker had sent a like number, enough men to make a good showing but not enough to destroy them. What ensued on June 9, 1863, proved to be the greatest cavalry battle ever fought on American soil: the nearly twelve-hour-long Battle of Brandy Station.

On the night of June 8, Pleasonton had pulled his men up to the east bank of the Rappahannock. His divided force was to unite at Brandy Station, four miles southwest of Beverly Ford, and from there push toward Culpeper, six more miles to the west. Stuart meanwhile was engaged in presiding over a resplendent review of five brigades on parade, a proud display for R. E. Lee prior to commencing the upcoming campaign. After the parade, the units encamped, with orders for an early start the next day, June 9. Just before dawn a Confederate picket at Beverly Ford was startled by the crack of a Sharps carbine, followed by the splash of oncoming Federal cavalry crossing the river.

Though surprised, the Confederates responded well and slowed the enemy. By 10:00 A.M. the Southerners mounted a counterattack. Both sides fought with great determination and skill. It was a cavalry fight of the most classic kind: bugles sounding, sabers flashing, revolvers blazing, dust and smoke and confusion everywhere, and the outcome long in doubt. But there was no outcome, really. By late afternoon both sides had had enough, and the Federals withdrew, unmolested, back across the river. The casualties included 81 Federals killed, 403 wounded, 382 missing; total Confederate losses were estimated at 523. An unusually large number of the wounds sustained were caused by sabers, more than in any other Civil War battle. The episode was somewhat symbolic: no longer was the Federal cavalry regarded as notoriously inferior to the Confederate horse soldiers. Otherwise, there was not much military significance to the Battle of Brandy Station.

The next day Hooker pieced together the bits of information that he had obtained, trying to decide what to do next, and concluded that it was a propitious moment to attack Richmond. President Lincoln, however, responded immediately and emphatically in the negative. "I think *Lee's* Army, and not *Richmond,* is your true objective point. . . . Fight him when opportunity offers. If he stays where he is, fret him and fret him."

Incoming reports finally convinced Hooker that he should transfer his headquarters to Dumfries; but he seemed incapable of suggesting to the Union high command any plausible countermeasures to Lee's maneuvering. Late in the afternoon on June 14, Lincoln wired Hooker, "If the head of Lee's army is at Martinsburg and the tail of it on the Plank road between Fredericksburg and Chancellorsville, the animal must be very slim somewhere. Could you not break him?" On the next day, June 15, 1863, Lee's advanced units began forcing their way across the Potomac River.

Long marches each day in high heat took a toll, but on June 18 a weather front brought heavy rains, cooler temperatures, and even some small-sized hail that resembled sleet. Some Confederate elements encountered resistance, and a few clashes occurred, but Lee got his army easily into Pennsylvania. His men then commenced a lavish ingathering of all manner of goods. They also seized numerous blacks who supposedly were escaped slaves and sent them southward. The northeastern public panicked at Lee's advance, and Lincoln called out one hundred thousand militia.

Nevertheless, the president remained calm, reasoning correctly that Lee was making not an invasion but a raid and would be vulnerable so far from his base. This presented the Union forces with "the best opportunity," the president proclaimed, "we have had since the war began." Some twenty-five thousand reserve troops were sent to Hooker.

As the days of June trickled away, however, Hooker used the last chits of confidence that Lincoln and Halleck might have had in him. On June 24 Hooker asked for orders, since, he said, except in relation to his own army, "I don't know whether I am standing on my head or feet." On June 27 Hooker was relieved, and one of his corps commanders, Maj. Gen. George G. Meade, was given command of the Army of the Potomac; for, among other reasons, Lincoln believed that this Pennsylvanian "will fight well on his own dunghill."

George G. Meade and the Battle of Gettysburg

Now forty-eight years of age, Meade was tall and spare but stooped, though graceful and soldierly. His slightly curling dark-brown hair was streaked heavily with gray, and he was balding. Sometimes prone to self-pity and self-depreciation, he was quite touchy and concerned with "getting his just rewards," and this propelled him occasionally into awkward situations. He had a hair-trigger temper and a penchant to speak in the heat of the moment in a quite offensive and abrasive manner, and that, in addition to the dark circles under his eyes, brought him his revealing nickname: "a damned old goggle-eyed snapping turtle." But he was a solid, honest, and somewhat gifted, though not brilliant, officer. Nineteenth in the 1835 West Point class of fifty-six graduates, and commissioned in the Topographical Engineers, he had experienced combat during the Second Seminole and Mexican Wars. He nurtured his keen ambition for promotion, and from the outset of the Civil War he had served competently as a brigade, division, and then corps commander. He was a master of logistics and had an extraordinary eye for topography. Altogether he made a dull, but very steady, army commander.

Lee rated Meade as more able than Hooker but assessed that the change of command, coming at a critical moment, would cause difficulty in transition. Thus, Lee's blinding exhilaration continued and doubtless affected his poor performance during the ensuing battle into which he blundered. Too, Lee would be ill-served by Richard S. Ewell, underscoring how much Stonewall Jackson was missed; the latter probably would have expanded appropriately upon unspecific orders, while the former showed inadequate initiative and excessive prudence. Ewell may even have had severe mental problems. His appearance suggested to some observers that he looked birdlike; legends persist that he sometimes hallucinated that he *was* a bird: for hours at a time he would sit in his tent softly chirping and at mealtimes would eat only sunflower seeds or grains of wheat.

The battle occurred, almost by accident, at the insignificant little town of Gettysburg. Most unfortunately for the Confederates, Stuart with the bulk of the gray army's cavalry was absent on a detached raid, and this prevented Lee from learning of the Federal army's nearby presence until June 28. Early that day, Lee, still ignorant of the enemy situation, ordered Ewell to cross the Susquehanna and seize Harrisburg. The other two Confederate corps were to move forward from the vicinity of Chambersburg and Greenwood, Pennsylvania, ultimately to join Ewell. That night a spy in Longstreet's employ came in with a rather accurate, and surprising, report of the enemy troop locations. Lee was forced to recall his advance units from Carlisle and York and begin an immediate concentration around Cashtown and Gettysburg.

Meade planned to maneuver through Frederick toward Harrisburg and thus menace Lee's line of communications while keeping between the Confederates and Washington. A chance engagement commenced a couple of miles west of Gettysburg, shortly before dawn on July 1, 1863. Brig. Gen. John Buford's two cavalry brigades, scouting ahead of the main Union forces, clashed with James J. Pettigrew's Confederate brigade (Henry Heth's division of A. P. Hill's corps), which was moving toward the town hoping to capture a supply of shoes incorrectly believed still to have been there. (Jubal Early had passed through the town several days before, taking everything that was of any use.) Buford recognized the potential strategic importance of the numerous roadways that crossed at Gettysburg and also noted the imposing high ground to the south. Thus, he organized his badly outnumbered cavalrymen and offered a stout defense. His dismounted troopers were able to hold off increasingly strong infantry assaults until Federal infantry reinforcements could join them, the first ones starting to arrive at about 10:30. Although Federal resistance stiffened, the Confederates built up superior strength, captured McPherson Ridge, and pushed toward Seminary Ridge. Around noon the fighting died down.

Just after one o'clock, Ewell's corps began arriving from the north and by coincidence commenced threatening the exposed Federal north flank. Union reinforcements maneuvered to counter this danger. Ewell's men continued driving and pushed the Federals back with heavy losses. Union forces were driven to Cemetery Hill, where they rallied. By midafternoon Ewell's corps had swept through and captured the town, but they failed to push on to secure the heights below the town, as Lee had indicated he wished done "if practicable." By evening the Federals had extended their position to Culp's Hill.

Meade persevered in his decision to concentrate near Gettysburg, even though his engineers had already laid out a defensive line some distance to the southeast. Lee, however, was able to concentrate quicker than Meade, and during the night of July 1 and—except for Pickett's division and Stuart's cavalry—his whole army assembled, strung out in a line along Seminary Ridge. Meade's men proceeded to occupy most of what became known as the "inverted fishhook" formed by Culp's Hill, Cemetery Hill, Cemetery Ridge, and the two formidable hills called the Round Tops. Ironically, a sign was posted on the arched gateway to the cemetery that warned, "All persons found using firearms in these grounds will be prosecuted with the utmost rigor of the law."

While it took considerable time for them all to arrive, Meade's fifty-one brigades of infantry and seven of cavalry eventually stretched along a formidable three-mile line. Lee's thirty-four brigades of infantry and one of cavalry occupied a five-mile semicircle. In artillery, Meade's 354 guns outnumbered Lee's 272, but Lee had the advantage of being able to concentrate his artillery anywhere he might choose, and his position allowed more mobility for the guns.

For the second day of the battle, July 2, 1863, Ewell and his principal subordinate division commander, Early, talked Lee out of his first-choice option, an assault upon Culp's Hill and subsequently Cemetery Hill. Without Stuart's cavalry, Lee lacked adequate information about both terrain and enemy dispositions, which led him to the erroneous suspicion that the main Federal defensive line was along the Emmitsburg road, with its flank near the Wheat Field. Lee therefore decided to try turning the Union position, with Longstreet's corps slamming into the Federal left, which was then rolling northward along Cemetery Ridge. To prevent Meade from shifting troops in response, Ewell was ordered to make a diversionary attack at Culp's Hill.

Longstreet got his men up to the battle area in the quickest time he could, but circumstances forced him to delay the actual assault. When the head of his column finally approached the assembly area he noticed that his movements could be observed by a Union signal station on one of the Round Tops, so he countermarched and approached by a different route, resulting in another delay of three and one-half hours. Unenthusiastic about the attack, Longstreet also consumed much time in aligning his corps. At the outset of Longstreet's attack there were few Unionists situated on Little Round Top, because on moving to his assigned sector, Gen. Dan Sickles had gone somewhat forward, without explicit permission. This resulted in the formation of "Sickles's salient," which included these soon famous spots: the Peach Orchard, the Wheat Field, and "the Devil's Den."

After many delays, the assault at last commenced at 4:00 P.M. Meade, meanwhile, continued to bring up more troops. Although there were some tense moments on Little Round Top and Cemetery Ridge, by 6:00 P.M. the Federals were quite secure, had numerical superiority, and the left flank was well covered. And, luckily for Meade, Federal Brig. Gen. Gouverneur K. Warren, the army's chief engineer, had seized the initiative at Little Round Top and forced the defensive deployment of Col. Strong Vincent's brigade in the nick of time. Attacked, Vincent's front began to crumble, but it was quickly reinforced and stabilized by Stephen H. Weed's brigade. Weed (who on June 6 had been jumped in rank from captain to brigadier general) urged his men to superhuman effort, and by sheer will and strength they managed to get a battery of six three-inch rifles up the rugged slope.

The story of the exploits of Vincent's lead regiment (Col. Joshua Chamberlain's Twentieth Maine) became legendary. Rushed into position on the southern side of Little Round Top, Chamberlain's hastily redeployed men fought precariously, holding the extreme left of the Union line. They fended off repeated Confederate attacks. By late in the afternoon most of Chamberlain's men had exhausted their ammunition. Onward came the Confederates in still another charge. Chamberlain ordered his gutsy men to fix their bayonets and boldly led them in a furious charge. Hand-to-hand combat turned back the onslaught. (Chamberlain, probably the North's most popularly renowned nonprofessional high-ranking officer was a college professor and later became president of Bowdoin College and the governor of Maine. Thirty years after the war he received the Medal of Honor for his brave actions at Little Round Top.)

One of Longstreet's divisions, under John B. Hood, fought most furiously, and some of the men did push to quite near the summit. Leading, in the thick of the fray, Hood himself was badly wounded, permanently losing the use of his left arm. There were several more hours of desperate and vicious fighting,

Joshua Lawrence Chamberlain. An amateur warrior, famous for his regiment's bold performance at Gettysburg, he would be given the honor of presiding over the surrender parade at Appomattox. (courtesy Leib Image Archives, York, Penn.)

especially in the Devil's Den, and even more so in the Wheat Field, where six charges and countercharges swirled, but the attack fizzled with the nightfall.

During the night, despite Longstreet's vehement objections, Lee decided to assail on the next day the Federal center with fifty regiments (eleven brigades drawn from four divisions). Lee and Longstreet both had to be aware of how unlikely it was that any group of soldiers could cross the slightly more than one mile of artillery-swept ground, slightly uphill—an eighteen- to twenty-minute rapid walk directly into the face of enemy fire—and arrive with enough cohesion and vigor to break a line of determined defenders. But it was only four years since Napoleon III at Solferino had smashed the Austrian center, exploiting a heavy bombardment followed by a frontal assault. Lee wrongly believed that the Yankees were now demoralized and that having tried attacking both ends the enemy must be weakest in his center. In his worst moment of anachronistic thinking, Lee convinced himself that the Napoleonic model deserved a try.

The charge was co-led by one of Longstreet's division commanders, Maj. Gen. George E. Pickett, his own division comprising about one-third of the assault force, and James J. Pettigrew of Hill's corps, who would command the wounded Heth's division, which would be the main assault force on the Confederate left. Far from being unplanned, as the charge often is depicted as having been, it was worked out in detail—even the careful selection of which tunes the regimental bands would play. The name "Pickett's Charge," first given by the Richmond press, is a misnomer, just as it is an untruth that those men who made the charge were almost all Virginians. Pettigrew commanded at most only a few hundred less than one-half of the troops and ultimately got all the way to the stone wall himself, while Pickett stopped at a house at least six hundred yards from it.

Pickett, one of the most unfortunate characters in American military history, had graduated last in the West Point class of 1846—in the same class with McClellan and Stonewall Jackson. Pickett had enjoyed one exquisite taste of glory. During the Mexican War he had been the first American to scale the ramparts at Chapultepec. Thus far, however, his performance in the Civil War had been quite unspectacular, but now at last came a leading role, and he grasped it eagerly. In the aftermath, he too came to wish that the attack *had* been named "Longstreet's assault."

A terrific artillery bombardment preceded the "charge," during which the Federal infantrymen simply lay secure under cover. Capt. Charles Phillips of Battery E, Massachusetts Artillery, recalled that "the enemy opened a heavy fire from a long line of batteries, which was kept up for an hour, but beyond the noise which was made no great harm was done." Blue-clad gunners responded to the fire, and for a time there was a terrific artillery exchange, so loud it reportedly could be heard 150 miles away. When the Federal artillery chief, Brig. Gen. Henry J. Hunt, pulled his gunners back to safety, the Confederates wrongly concluded that they had disabled the Union army's guns. Brigadier General Hunt always claimed that had his superiors allowed him, he could have stopped Pickett's Charge with artillery alone.

One of the seminary professors recorded the temperature at 3:00: eighty-seven degrees. "General, shall I advance?" Pickett inquired of Longstreet. So overcome by his feelings that he could not speak, Longstreet bowed his head. The lines were dressed, flags unfurled. At 3:10, 10,500 men moved forward, in

George H. Pickett. Perhaps the war's most unfortunate officer—he was a coleader of the unsuccessful charge at Gettysburg that bears his name. (courtesy Leib Image Archives, York, Penn.)

two main ranks followed by a thinner third line of file closers. The men moved deliberately, at route step—110 a minute. In perfect order and at steady advance, with every passing minute they covered just less than a hundred yards.

In the first part of the charge, the Confederates were hit by long-range artillery, then by rifle fire that continued in salvos, and by Napoleons that were firing canister. Pettigrew rode on horseback, close behind his line. His horse was hit. Dismounting, he sent it back with a wounded man and stayed with his line. Grapeshot smashed the fingers of his right hand. On and on he and his men pressed. He could see clearly the stone wall on Cemetery

Ridge. Having covered nearly half the distance in about eight minutes, the Confederates reached a swale, which sheltered them from most of the incoming fire. They halted and redressed the lines. Up to this point, while their losses were far from insignificant, they had by no means been crippled or demoralized. Onward they continued.

At one-quarter of a mile from the enemy (less for Pickett's men) the Confederates halted and delivered a volley. Then they went on. But only about five thousand of the assaulters managed even to get to Cemetery Ridge; the most valiant of them—only a handful—poured over the stone wall at about 3:30. Some men in a few Federal regiments did break and flee, but the attackers were easily handled as heavy reinforcements of Yankees rushed up. The hand-to-hand fighting lasted somewhat less than two minutes—in later recountings of the battle, declared to have been the most dramatic "hundred seconds of the Confederacy." One Confederate brigadier general, Lewis A. Armistead, and 150 of his men momentarily drove some Yankee cannoneers from their pieces. Putting his hand on one of the cannon barrels, Armistead shouted, "Give them the cold steel!" But a moment later he was shot and mortally wounded. He and five other Confederate generals died as a result of wounds sustained at Gettysburg.

And then the pitifully crushed and vanquished remnants began making their way back—while numbers of the victorious Yankees shouted, "Fredericksburg! Fredericksburg!" Relatively little musketry fire hampered the retreaters, however, because many Federals stopped shooting, partly out of chivalry, partly from feeling that there had been enough killing, and largely because many Federals were occupied in rounding up prisoners.

Pickett had lost all 3 of his subordinate brigadier generals, and of his 13 colonels, 8 were killed and the other 5 were wounded. Of his 35 officers above company-grade rank, only 1 came back unhurt. Of the 10,500 men who made the advance, 5,675 were killed or wounded—54 percent. The Federals captured thirty of the thirty-eight regimental flags that were carried up near the stone wall on Cemetery Ridge.

The cost was bitter, even staggering; the Federals had lost 212 killed and wounded out of each 1,000 engaged; the Confederates lost 301 per 1,000. Over the three days of battle, the Federals sustained a total of 23,049 casualties; the Confederates' losses amounted to 28,063. The Gettysburg battle represents the worst aspect of the Confederacy's offensive-defensive strategy. It would have been advantageous to seize the *strategic* offensive, but to seize also the *tactical* offensive against a superior foe resulted in the South's squandering lives—and the North was more able to sustain losses than was the Confederacy. Lee was ill-influenced by Napoleonic warfare, but perhaps too (for him as well as for numerous other Civil War generals) the Mexican War also provided an unwise motivation. In that conflict, fought mostly with premodern weaponry, assault tactics had been successful. But *why* had they been successful? The Civil War generals seem not to have understood.

As an interesting aside, both sides also sustained the loss of a woman as a result of the combat. A twenty-year-old Gettysburg resident, Jennie Wade, while baking bread in the home of her sister, was struck fatally by a stray bullet. At least one of the Confederate combatants was female, dressed in uniform. It is believed that she was the wife of a Confederate soldier who had chosen to accompany him into war. Both were killed in Pickett's Charge and were buried by a detail of the victorious Yankees on the hillside that became known as "the high water mark of the Confederacy."

"Too bad! Too Bad! Oh, too Bad!" Lee cried out in anguish the night following Pickett's Charge. "The task was too great," Lee told the survivors of the assault and admitted that it was all his fault. Indeed, it *was* Lee's fault: he had fought his worst battle and had lost miserably. But, and again to Lincoln's great disappointment, no mop-up pursuit followed the great battle at Gettysburg. Brig. Gen. John D. Imboden's cavalry covered the Army of Northern Virginia as it disengaged and limped southward, crossing the Potomac back into Virginia on July 14. Ironically, in a meaningless rearguard action, at Falling Waters (near Martinsburg), West Virginia, the gallant General Pettigrew—who had gone relatively unscathed all the way forward and back in Pickett's Charge—was mortally wounded.

After the war Longstreet would become the victim of an organized character assignation, led by a rabidly pro-Lee group of Virginians. Much myth grew— and some of it even still persists in some circles—that Longstreet, not Lee, was responsible for the Confederate failure at Gettysburg. This phenomenon was playfully condemned by the historian Gaines M. Foster, who, in his book *Ghosts of the Confederacy,* suggested that "Longstreet blew it at Gettysburg," which was one-half of a chant that went with a Rebel "Ghost Dance"—the other half being "overwhelming numbers and resources."

CHAPTER 11

The "Long Pull" of the War

It is too easy, and misleading, to think of the Civil War's outcome as already decided by early July 1863. As to its total duration, the conflict was then but only a little past the halfway point. Williamson Murray in his article "What Took the North So Long," published in the 1989 volume of *MHQ: The Quarterly Journal of Military History,* observed that the length of the Civil War had much to do with the immensity of the geographic area of the Confederacy as well as with the complexities of modern war.

The Confederacy was larger than any European nation except Russia and Turkey. "Taken together, Mississippi and Alabama are slightly larger than present-day West Germany," Murray pointed out, and "The distance from central Georgia to northern Virginia is approximately the distance from East Prussia to Moscow." Furthermore, "The distance from Baton Rouge to Richmond exceeds the distance from the Franco-German border to the current Soviet-Polish frontier." While the eastern theater was relatively close to the centers of Northern industrial power, the vast western regions were sparsely populated, rough, and substantially primeval wilderness. Murray's insightful conclusion is, "Without railroads and steamships, the North would not have been able to bring its power to bear and probably would have lost the war."

True, after Gettysburg R. E. Lee's eastern army was weakened significantly, and in the West the Confederacy had been split geographically, but the Confederacy still retained a remarkable degree of viable potency. It proved able to redeploy internally and score a morale-boosting victory by the early fall of 1863. And in addition to triumph in battle, determination and popular will, effective propaganda, political manipulation, guerilla activity, raids, and technical achievement all *can* contribute to the final results in warfare. To be sure, however, the Confederacy would ultimately come up short.

Davis and Lincoln as War Leaders

Historians laud Lincoln for his achievement in presiding over the Union's ultimate victory, while Davis's performance has elicited much controversial commentary—often in a quite negative vein. As one might expect, it is a strong temptation to make Davis look bad when he is depicted as a foil for Lincoln. This phenomenon was described and ridiculed by Ludwell Johnson in a compellingly interesting and aptly titled 1981 essay, "Jefferson Davis and Abraham Lincoln as War Presidents: Nothing Succeeds like Success," which was published in the scholarly journal *Civil War History*. Of *course* Confederate strategy was *not* foredoomed inevitably to fail. What then of Davis as opposed to Lincoln as war leader?

Archer Jones and Thomas Lawrence Connelly Jr. amply showed in *The Politics of Command* that Jefferson Davis started with much superior military knowledge and experience and gradually improved as generalissimo, but he peaked late in 1863, and thereafter his competence deteriorated. The lost key to Confederate victory lay in a national application of ideas best understood among the Southern generals by Beauregard, who *could* have been the architect of success had not unfortuitous circumstances (and the personal enmity that festered between him and Davis) destroyed his opportunity.

Davis needed better input than he got, such as that which would have been provided by a staff with a capable chief. Davis never escaped tension and discord, standing squarely in the middle between his powerful and trusted adviser on the one hand, Robert E. Lee, and what Connelly and Jones call "western concentration bloc" on the other. Lee made valuable but too provincial and too costly contributions. He was a reflection of Frederick the Great, the great Prussian general; but, as Connelly and Jones aptly opined, "unfortunately for the Confederacy, he was only a Virginia Frederick." The western concentration bloc desired to take advantage of dispersal in the western theater and to launch a series of concentrations exploiting interior lines, allowing effective operations against the most vulnerable and inviting Union armies. These ideas (Connelly and Jones concluded) were too belatedly adopted, were ill-executed, and never unreservedly pursued. (But Richard McMurry, in *Two Great Rebel Armies*, offers many reasons that the South's western army was inferior and therefore a western concentration probably could not have worked anyway.)

Last, Davis made a chronically unsatisfactory use of the Confederate military department system. This territorial system in some respects was well suited to the Confederacy's inherent parochialism and state-rights philosophy, but it

Jefferson Davis. The Confederate president—was he, as Clement Eaton suggested, "the sphinx of the Confederacy"? or will we someday have a *truly* satisfying biography of him? Did he "believe in the Confederacy with his head but not his heart"? or is there some other explanation for his failure to induce very many others to believe in "the Cause" as passionately as he did? (courtesy Leib Image Archives, York, Penn.)

became too much of an intertwined part of Davis's strategy. Davis placed great (though—to be fair—by no means unbending) emphasis on the need to protect *all* territory. The real flaw was that few of the officers who served in department command were fit for their jobs (mainly because there was no universal and clear job description for their position)—and, worse, there was no official to oversee and to ensure that coordination and interdepartmental cooperation were achieved. Too often either men or resources or both were ineffectively allocated. (This would be illustrated in sharp relief at the end of the war when fewer than one-third of the Rebels still under arms were arrayed in contention against either of the two main Yankee armies.)

But perhaps Davis's ultimate failure as a war leader was in not being able to keep the Southern people as dedicated to the continuation of the military

struggle as he. By early in 1865 Davis had become willing to accept the oblitera-
tion of slavery, if only that might bring Confederate independence. There had
long been much grumbling about "a rich man's war and a poor man's fight," but
to give up the true reason for waging it in the first place indeed was too much
for a very great many of the Southern people to bear. And (in stark contrast
to Lincoln's keen ability) Davis seemed unable to bestir the Southern people
with his words. This is a bit baffling, because Davis was regarded by many
persons—especially before and long after the Civil War—to be a captivating
public speaker. Even if it is not true—as has been said—that "he believed in
the Confederacy with his head but not with his heart," Davis could not convey
an adequate element of civil religion. He converted to Episcopalianism, prayed
much, and proclaimed several national fast days of supplication: all to no avail.

Abraham Lincoln possessed virtually no military knowledge at the war's
outset, but he was a quick learner. As Herman Hattaway and Archer Jones
delineated at length in their December 1980 article in the scholarly journal
Civil War History, Lincoln became a conventional mid–nineteenth century
military strategist who fully shared the ideas of his West Point–trained generals.
Both he and they analyzed operations in terms of lines of operations, rightly
believed in the superiority of the defensive over the offensive, and saw in turning
movements the best way to overcome the power of the rifle-strengthened
defense. Lincoln derived these ideas primarily from his generals but also from
the military realities as he perceived them in the course of the war.

Lincoln grasped by early 1862 (about the same time that he also began to
regard a "hard war" policy as acceptable and appropriate) that battles were
unlikely to be decisive and that the means of victory lay in occupying the
enemy's territory and breaking his lines of communications. To do this it was
necessary to overcome the enemy's advantage of enjoying interior lines. Quite
early Lincoln explained that his "general idea of the war," was that

> we have the greater numbers, and the enemy has the greater facility of concentrat-
> ing forces upon the points of collision; that we must fail unless we can find some
> way of making our advantage an overmatch for his; and that this can be done by
> menacing him with superior forces at different points, at the same time; so that
> we can safely attack one, or both, if he makes no choice, and if he weakens one to
> strengthen the other, forbear to attack the strengthened one, but seize, and hold
> the weakened one, gaining so much.

But Lincoln also pushed generals to fight battles—and to win victories.

Abraham Lincoln. Shown here beardless, and hence shortly *before* he became president. He was a *great* war leader and deservedly became one of the most beloved American presidents because of his keen intellect, his wonderful way with words, his mastery in interpersonal relationships, and his (perhaps cosmic) ability to practice, and therein to inspire others with, a potent civil religion. (courtesy the Civil War Library and Museum MOLLUS, Philadelphia, Penn.)

The idea of simultaneous advance continued to be refined in Lincoln's mind, and it became a controlling idea of his and the overall official Union strategy. This was the concept upon which Lincoln had based the abortive order he issued in 1862 for all Federal armies to begin an advance on Washington's Birthday. There followed three simultaneous Union advances producing mixed results:

Halleck and McClellan in the spring of 1862; Grant, Rosecrans, and Burnside in the fall of 1862; and Grant and Hooker in the spring of 1863. It was not that the strategy could not work, or that Lincoln became apprehensive of it; the difficulty was, until Lincoln at last found (and adequately appreciated) Grant he did not have anyone who could implement it adequately on a grand scale.

The fundamental problem was that Lee's army was too strong and taking Richmond too difficult. So Lincoln and his de facto chief of staff Halleck came to accept stalemate in Virginia, stressing the western theater instead. Yet, the strategy for the West differed from that in the East: it aimed at territorial and logistical objectives, because the goal was not necessarily total military victory but a breaking of the Southerners' will to continue the contest.

In the meantime, until that could be achieved, Lincoln somehow had to keep Northern will sufficiently buoyant and cohesive. There would be a close call, for soul-searing battle deaths and an apparent impossibility of achieving victory *soon enough* nearly eroded Northern morale—especially when the 1864 Federal elections loomed and Lincoln (with good cause) feared he might not be reelected. But things did work out in Lincoln's and the North's favor, owing more than a little to Lincoln's masterful practice and conveyance of civil religion. He did not belong to any church, though fervently (even if not in formal fact) he *was* a Christian (as will be demonstrated in a forthcoming book by the minister and popular writer Peter Marshall Jr.). Conveying at least to a sufficiently large segment of the Northern populace a degree of his own feeling that the Union was an object of transcendent worth, Lincoln held it up to the American people as being "the last best hope of mankind on the earth."

Last, Lincoln's *most* masterly handling of the military problem was in achieving not only emancipation but also the integration of black troops into the Union army—for they not only much helped the Northern cause, but the defection of tens of thousands of slaves into Yankee uniforms doubly hurt the South.

Psychological Implications of Radical Change: Troubled Minds and Mixed Attitudes and the Implementation of Military Conscription

When on January 1, 1863, as earlier he had promised he would, Lincoln issued the Emancipation Proclamation, the war took on a new character. The conflict previously had by no means been one that had as its primary aim the eventual elimination of slavery in the United States. Beyond emancipation, it seemed only a short logical step to the North's employment of black troops (which would be the first time that the nation had done so since the War of 1812). Prejudice against blacks, and the belief that they were incompetent and incapable of being good soldiers, was quite potent above as well as below the Mason-Dixon line; hence, many Northern whites resisted taking such a step. Southern whites, meanwhile, were indignant at the North's presumption of declaring blacks to be emancipated, and beyond that they were thoroughly horrified and repulsed at any prospect of blacks being used as soldiers fighting against the Confederacy. The North's choice to commit blacks to combat spurred Southerners to a more intense psychological commitment, making the ultimate breakdown of Southern will all the more problematic.

The Lincoln administration had grave problems in maintaining national cohesion, cooperation, and commitment—and it quickly found how serious those problems might be when it finally felt compelled to resort to national conscription. The draft was enormously unpopular in the North, much more bitterly and intensely so than in the South, where to be sure it was not altogether welcome. Four different enrollments occurred as a result of the North's Conscription Act: June–August 1863; and March, July, and December 1864.

The first enrollment dragged on so long because it was bitterly and violently resisted in a number of locations, but especially in New York City. There, on July 13, 1863, began five days of vicious and bloody antidraft and antiblack rioting. In the end the riot was quelled by five regiments dispatched from Gettysburg. It so happened that R. E. Lee retreated his army south of the Potomac on the same day that the riot had commenced, making this redeployment practicable. Unhappily, this riot was not the only instance of nasty behavior and demonstration against blacks, the draft, or both. Nonetheless Lincoln's political management of the draft issue was masterly as also was the subsequent ongoing maintenance of peace in New York City, overseen by Brig. Gen. Edward R. S. Canby. With subtle concessions, civil order was restored, reasonably well maintained, and conscription continued. This abatement of an otherwise near disastrous outcome was crucial to the continuation of the war's momentum.

Altogether the enrollments called nearly one-quarter of a million men into service. About one-third of that number, however, paid the allowed commutation fee of three hundred dollars and thus were excused from service. Only 46,347 men responded to the draft by actually serving; another 116,188 furnished substitutes. Others enlisted before they were actually called, in order to avoid the stigma of conscription.

Employment of Black Military Laborers and Black Troops

From an early date both sides exploited black labor. Southerners used slaves in all sorts of projects, but many escaped, made their way into Union lines, and were put to work for the North. They performed all manner of tasks ranging from trench and grave digging to cooking, cleaning, and maintenance. More came than the army could accommodate, and eventually the government employed masses of liberated slaves to cultivate abandoned plantations. These, however, became favorite victims of Confederate raiders and guerrillas, so protecting them required much diversion of Union manpower.

Ever since the fall of Fort Sumter, many Northern blacks had been requesting to serve in the Union army. Lincoln long resisted this and even overturned Maj. Gen. David Hunter's March 1862 order to free all the slaves in Georgia, South Carolina, and Florida; Lincoln overturned a similar proclamation that John C. Fremont had issued in Missouri. At first the Union's policy actually was to cooperate in the return of escaped slaves to their owners. The first black units came into being extralegally. In the late summer of 1862, Brig. Gen. Jim Lane commenced forming a black regiment, the "First Kansas Colored." Also in the late part of 1862, the famous Fifty-fourth Massachusetts was formed by state authority and mustered officially into national service early in 1863. The first official black unit organized by the Federal government was the First South Carolina Volunteers (later renamed the Thirty-third U.S. Colored Infantry), comprised of liberated slaves and commanded by the longtime abolitionist Col. Thomas Wentworth Higginson. The Union promised automatic and permanent freedom from slavery to all blacks who enlisted and to their families as well.

Because so many Northern whites needed persuasion if they were to tolerate black troops, and so many persons had doubts about their abilities, several discriminatory measures were implemented: blacks served in segregated units, almost all of the officers were white, and blacks received less pay. This last provision induced an ironic result: to the enormous disgust of whites, on July 20, 1863, the provost marshal general ruled that, although blacks were subject to the draft, a black was not an acceptable substitute for a white draftee. The pay scale was revised and made equal for both races in mid-1864; and retroactive remedy of inequity was approved by Congress early in March 1865.

While some whites of inferior ability obtained commissions to lead black units, the quality of these officers was generally high. Indeed, because white units often had the prerogative of choosing their officers by popular election, the ironic truth may be that black units almost universally had better officers than did white units. Nearly 80 percent of them had previous combat experience, and the selection process was keen: only about one in every four applicants managed to qualify. While a few blacks were able to secure commissions as regimental chaplains or surgeons, combat leaders—no matter how superior their performance—found it nearly impossible until late in the war to be appointed or promoted beyond noncommissioned levels. In 1862 Brigadier General Lane appointed a black captain, and Maj. Gen. Benjamin Butler appointed some seventy-five free black militiamen to company-grade positions, but those positions subsequently were systematically eliminated. Only after January 1865 were restrictions on promoting black officers lifted. Records reveal the names of 109 black officers, only 2 as high as major.

A series of significant engagements in mid-1863 brought black combatants considerable public notice and much recognition for their toughness and dedication: an assault on May 27 against Port Hudson, Louisiana; a battle at Milliken's Bend, Louisiana, on June 7, which proved to be one of the most vicious engagements of the entire war, resulting in 30 percent of the blacks being killed or wounded; and on July 18 a grand assault on Battery Wagner, located on Morris Island at the entrance to Charleston Harbor. This last engagement became one of the war's most famous episodes, a dramatic and costly bayonet charge. No black regiment had attracted as much public interest as the one engaged here. It was Col. Robert Gould Shaw's Fifty-fourth Massachusetts (Colored) Infantry, with the ranks comprised only of volunteers—free blacks and runaway slaves—including two sons of the most prominent black American of the era, Frederick Douglass.

In their desperate and unsuccessful attempt to capture the battery, which was never *taken* (the Confederates elected to abandon it on September 6, 1863), the Fifty-fourth Massachusetts paid a fearful price. The task of taking Battery Wagner was nearly an impossible one; the place was a huge and powerful earth fort built across the narrow neck of Morris Island at the harbor's mouth. No flanking approach was possible. Ground troops had no avenue of assault but a frontal one. Unobstructed fields of fire were buttressed by massive emplantations of land mines. The Confederate inventor Gen. Gabriel Rains, had been sent to Battery Wagner to give special attention to the defenses and to the deployment of torpedoes equipped with his new and quite potent Rains fuse. Sand offered perfect camouflage, completely obscuring the shallow emplacement of deadly devices detonated as if by a hair trigger. Though some of the attackers got the regimental colors up to the parapets, they could not penetrate nor could they stay, and the survivors were forced to retreat. The Fifty-fourth Massachusetts lost more than 40 percent of its number, including its prominent young colonel, who was buried in a mass grave with the black soldiers who fell with him.

No longer was there any question: blacks had proved their worth as soldiers, and there was a tremendous increase of their numbers in service. Blacks took part in 449 engagements, 39 of them major. More than one-third of the black troops died in service. An officially recorded number of 178,892 black men served in the Union armies, including some 7,000 noncommissioned officers. Black troops comprised 120 infantry regiments, 12 heavy-artillery regiments, 10 batteries of light artillery, and 7 cavalry regiments, constituting by the end of the war slightly more than 12 percent of the Union's land forces. Quite significantly, the number of black troops in the Union army toward the end equaled approximately the total number of Confederate soldiers still present for duty, a ratio that indeed did have a psychological impact on Southerners. Confederate soldiers found fighting black opponents rather frightening. Southerners made every attempt to harass and abuse the black troops. Sometimes one side or the other, or both, denied quarter in battle, and as the war progressed Confederates tended to become more frustrated, and combat atrocities escalated.

A most notorious episode occurred on April 12, 1864, when 1,500 Confederates under Maj. Gen. Nathan Bedford Forrest stormed into Fort Pillow, Tennessee, on the Mississippi River forty miles north of Memphis, defended by some 585 to 605 Federals, nearly half of whom were black. The Confederates lost 14 killed and 86 wounded while between 277 and 297 Federals, nearly one-half of the garrison, were killed or mortally wounded. Long beclouded by controversy, Southern denials, and claims that the blacks simply refused to surrender, the statistics and other available data do indicate that a massacre of the black defenders occurred. Forrest *did not order* the massacre, but given his totally callous feeling that blacks were nothing more than a commodity to be bought and sold, neither could he have had any grave reservation. In truth, he lost control of the conduct of his men. The crux of this episode is a reflection of the depth of hostile feelings inflamed by racial attitudes.

Military Prisons and Prisoners of War

Quite understandably, men from black units had a morbid fear of falling captive; and, indeed, Southern soldiers especially feared becoming prisoners of

A sharp-looking regiment in the United States Colored Infantry. There were about 180,000 African Americans who became soldiers in the Union army—a bold experiment borne of necessity. They fought splendidly. (courtesy Leib Image Archives, York, Penn.)

blacks. On May 1, 1863, the Confederate Congress passed a resolution declaring that all white officers captured while serving with black troops were summarily to be put to death or otherwise punished at the discretion of a court-martial for inciting insurrection, and the black soldiers themselves were to be returned into slavery. Both sides threatened retaliation in kind against any atrocity inflicted upon a prisoner, and in bitter frustration the South eventually backed down from making good its threats against black prisoners or their officers. An added trump card entered the picture in the person of Confederate Brig. Gen. W. H. Fitzhugh Lee (R. E. Lee's second son), who fell captive while recuperating from a wound he had suffered at Brandy Station and was not exchanged until March 1864.

The issue of blacks totally aside, to be a prisoner of war was, as it always is, a fearsome experience. Even though the people of both sides thought that the other side tortured and otherwise purposefully mistreated prisoners, neither actually had any systematic policy of maltreatment. The problems sprang primarily from exposure, overcrowding, and disease, though sometimes—in that day of primitive medicine—they sprang also from poor medical care and malnutrition. At one time or another the United States captured 462,634 men; the Confederacy 211,411. The Union paroled on the field 247,769, and 25,976 died in its prisons; the Confederacy issued 16,668 field paroles, and 30,218 died in its prisons. The mortality rate was slightly more than 12 percent in Northern prisons and was 15.5 percent in Southern prisons.

Although the South's prisons became the more infamous in history, it was the North at the outset that inclined toward denial of prisoner-of-war rights. Because the Lincoln administration insisted that the Union was inviolable, it therefore refused to agree that captives it might take were anything other than traitors. First Bull Run changed that. There the Confederates captured about fifty officers and approximately one thousand enlisted men. Neither side could afford to callously mistreat prisoners without the other taking reprisal. The main problem, which continued to recur throughout the war, was the unforeseen taking of large numbers for whom there were inadequate prison facilities. The January–February 1862 Burnside expedition against Roanoke Island resulted in the capture of twenty-five hundred prisoners, and when, on February 16, 1862, Grant seized Fort Donelson he took fifteen thousand prisoners. Nothing more than minuscule preparations had been made to receive and properly incarcerate such large numbers.

Things were often pretty rough in the prisons of both regions. The South, much the poorer materially—particularly with the passing of time—in many instances was unable to maintain healthful conditions. The most notorious of the Civil War prisons was Andersonville, Georgia, a huge outdoor stockade occupied between February 27 and September 5, 1864, by an ever increasing number of unfortunate Federal inmates. There are 12,912 known graves there, but some estimates place the total number of deaths at this prison much higher. The North, too, sometimes had heinous problems in prisons, mainly due to overcrowding. Many people believed that Southerners deliberately mistreated the prisoners they held, and this ultimately induced what literally was a war psychosis in the North. Popular clamor demanded tougher treatment of the captive Southerners, and oftentimes officials acquiesced, especially in punitive reduction of food rations.

Informal arrangements were sometimes made between particular generals to exchange or parole prisoners. In July 1862 Confederate Maj. Gen. Daniel H. Hill and Union Maj. Gen. John A. Dix completed negotiations for an exchange cartel. Never completely satisfactory in its operation, since numberless disputes occurred, the cartel nevertheless did result in many thousands of officers and men being paroled and exchanged. On December 17, 1863, owing especially to dissatisfaction with respect to exchanges of black troops and their officers, the North in essence repudiated the Dix-Hill Cartel and appointed Major General Butler as a special agent of exchange to oversee such matters in the future. Special exchanges continued to be carried out, from time to time, until in April 1864 General Grant ordered the cessation of further exchanges, realizing that the North with its much larger manpower resources could stand allowing ever larger numbers of captives to languish in prison much more readily than could the South. It was still another way that the North wore the South down. But it resulted in conditions within the prisons becoming all the more overcrowded and unhealthful for those unfortunates who simply had to wait out the war while languishing in captivity.

CHAPTER 12

Continuing Confederate Viability

Guerrillas and Raiders

The Confederates made significant use of guerrillas and raiders. Ruminating upon the vigorous Confederate guerrilla activity of the 1862–1863 winter, President Lincoln remarked, "In no other way does the enemy give us so much trouble, at so little expense to himself, as by the raids of rapidly moving small bodies of troops (largely, if not wholly, mounted) harassing, and discouraging loyal residents, supplying themselves with provisions, clothing, horses, and the like, surprising and capturing small detachments of our forces, and breaking our communications." The impact of rebel raids and guerrillas caused a tremendous dispersion of Federal forces.

Even when the Union moved on the offensive with its main armies, it stood on the defensive in protecting its communications and its conquered territory. In January 1863, for example, against 13,000 Confederates who menaced north Mississippi and west Tennessee, the Union deployed 51,000 troops in a cordon to cover railroads and the routes of advance of potential raiders. There were 56,000 men guarding Kentucky, West Virginia, and the line of the Baltimore and Ohio Railroad against the potential threat of 15,000 Confederates. Including the garrison of Washington and troops deployed by both sides in Missouri and Arkansas, 190,000 Union soldiers, more than one-third of those in the field, were defending territory and communications against 43,000 Confederates, about one-sixth of all those available. As captured territory increased and communications lengthened, this condition became ever more aggravated. Aware of this, the Confederates dedicated a part of their superior cavalry to fomenting raids that harassed communications and disturbed political conditions.

Three times in 1862 the youthful horsemen under Brig. Gen. John Hunt Morgan (who himself would become known as "the Thunderbolt of the

John Hunt Morgan. The "Thunderbolt of the Confederacy" led some dashing cavalry raids in the western theater. (courtesy Leib Image Archives, York, Penn.)

Confederacy") had swept around the Yankee army and wreaked havoc in Kentucky, destroying bridges, telegraph lines, and supply depots, fighting Unionists who were never quite able to corner them, and scurrying back with horses, prisoners, and material. Morgan's forte was an aggressive independence that led him to employ innovative tactics that confused traditionally inclined opponents. He suffered periodically from chronic mental depression—of which Abraham Lincoln is the war's most outstanding example; yet, for some reason, unduly depressed people often manage to be outstandingly productive and accomplished. Morgan was keenly brash and confident—ultimately overconfident—and this allowed him to take great, daring, and audacious risks. And until his luck played out, he proved a handsomely good practitioner of guerrilla warfare, in part because he much exploited civilian help and because he had little scruple about employing the services of vicious outlaws. (As his able biographer, James A. Ramage, delineates, Morgan became a potent symbol of the Lost Cause Myth after the war.)

Immediately following the debacle at Gettysburg and the fall of Vicksburg, in stark demonstration that the South still had spunk, Morgan conducted one of the war's longest cavalry raids, certainly one of its most spectacular, into Indiana and Ohio. His men were variously armed; everyone had one revolver and some had two, a few preferred shotguns while most carried British Enfield rifle muskets with the barrel sawed off to carbine length. (They disliked captured Yankee carbines because of their smaller caliber.)

Crossing the Ohio River at Brandenburg, Kentucky, they covered seven hundred miles in twenty-five days, almost constantly in combat. The name *Morgan* became something of a household word: *beau sabreur* to Southerners, bandit fiend to Northerners. The raiders captured 6,000 prisoners, diverted 14,000 Regulars from other duty, precipitated the muster of 120,000 militia, destroyed thirty-four bridges, damaged railroads in more than sixty locations, and destroyed hundreds of thousands of dollars' worth of property. Though he was captured, and imprisoned until he succeeded in making a bold escape during the following winter, Morgan managed to give the people of the Old Northwest a brief scare and a taste of what one resident called "the miseries of the South," the sobering spectacle of war on one's own homeland and hearthside.

In the western theater the greatest folk hero of the Confederacy, and deservedly so because of his many exploits that did damage to the Union cause, was Nathan Bedford Forrest. Called "the Wizard of the Saddle" by admirers and "That Devil Forrest" by William T. Sherman, Forrest was something of an untutored military genius. In 1861 he enlisted in the Confederate army as a private, was promoted to brigadier general on July 21, 1862, was elevated to major general on December 4, 1863, and by war's end had become a lieutenant general. He displayed extraordinary capability as a tactician and had a keen insight into strategic possibilities. Allegedly illiterate, though this was not true, his philosophy of war was popularly said to be "Git Thar Fustest with the Mustest." He doubtless never said anything so silly, but he did demonstrate the benefits of getting "there first, with the most men." A modern realist, he admitted that "War means fightin' and fightin' means killin'." General Sherman later suggested that he thought "Forrest was the most remarkable man our Civil War produced on either side."

In addition to two spectacular raids into Tennessee (July 1862 and December 11, 1862–January 3, 1863), several others of Forrest's more noteworthy achievements deserve mention. Shortly before the Battle of Gettysburg, Forrest was guided to a ford (the bridge having been burned) across Black Creek near Gadsden, Alabama, by a local resident, a teenaged girl—Emma Sanson (who

Nathan Bedford Forrest. The war's greatest amateur warrior; William T. Sherman proclaimed Forrest "the most remarkable man our Civil War produced on either side." (courtesy Leib Image Archives, York, Penn.)

after the war was a darling of Confederate veterans and was made a full member of the principal veterans' society). Using this ford enabled Forrest to pursue and capture two thousand Federal raiding troopers under Col. Abel D. Streight. Later, on June 10, 1864, at the Battle of Brice's Crossroads (also called Guntown and Tishomingo Creek), Forrest demonstrated that he was much more than a raider and spoiler: in a head-on engagement, outnumbered three-to-one, against Brig. Gen. Samuel D. Sturgis's combined-arms force of eighty-one hundred infantry and cavalry and twenty-two cannon manned by four hundred artillerists, Forrest and his men inflicted one of the most humiliating defeats in the history of the U.S. Army. (This battle is discussed in detail in Chapter 13, within the thematic context of Forrest's innate mastery of modern warmaking.)

For many partisans, it may always remain one of the Civil War's great "what if's": whether Forrest could have done much more than he did for the Confederacy, whether he would have been equal to the tasks of much enlarged command responsibility. But the truth is, he had risen to his maximal level of competency. He was an unorthodox military man. He positively *had* to be in *personal control* of any situation he managed. He had a volatile, sometimes nasty, personality. He got along with but few of his superiors—only the most forbearing and patient of them. He was a genius, an eccentric one at that, and in no way a military professional. He could *not* have managed a modern army.

On August 20, 1863, some 450 Confederate and Missouri guerrillas under William Clarke Quantrill moved toward the unsuspecting antislavery and pro-Union Kansas town of Lawrence. The next day Quantrill's "bushwackers" sacked the town, burning property worth $1.5 million and killing about 150 men and boys, sparing only women and small children. The hot-blooded Quantrill expected no quarter from his despised enemies and intended to give none. He had issued orders to kill "every man big enough to carry a gun." The guerrilla war in the Far West was typified by this kind of harsh fanaticism.

Other raids continued elsewhere. Beginning on September 22, 1863, Col. Joseph O. Shelby led his band of Confederate light-horse troops on a fast-paced raid through Arkansas and Missouri that lasted until November 3. Despite his having been wounded in July, Shelby and his men slashed their way across fifteen hundred hard miles through enemy-held territory, inflicted more than one thousand casualties, destroyed army and public property worth some $2 million, captured enough goods to completely reequip his command, and returned with several hundred new recruits gleaned from the populace that possessed sorely divided loyalties. From September 30 to October 17, 1863, Maj. Gen. Joseph Wheeler raided communications of the Army of the Cumberland. During most of November 1863 raiders under Maj. John S. Mosby (himself known as "the Gray Ghost") were quite active in northern Virginia. Frequently harassing the rear lines of the Federal army, Mosby estimated that he diverted and kept at least thirty thousand Union soldiers away from the front.

There is considerable reason to believe that had the South emphasized such operations more strongly, it could have dragged the war on longer than it did. But guerrilla raids were contrary to certain social values particularly espoused by upper-class and more refined Southerners. Thus, unlike in the western theater—where generals such as Braxton Bragg, Kirby Smith, and J. E. Johnston appreciated the guerrillas' achievements, and encouraged more such activity—in the East, the Confederate high command tended to discount the value of the guerrillas and raiders and concentrated instead on more conventional operations. It is probably true that, owing to the shorter lines of communications in the East, Mosby did not have the chance to achieve as much as could the westerners. But conventional operations were also still far from over in the West, and what the South achieved, on September 19 and 20,

John Singleton Mosby. The "Gray Ghost" was the most well known of the Confederate guerrillas. (courtesy Leib Image Archives, York, Penn.)

1863, rather starkly demonstrated that the war had not ended with Gettysburg and Vicksburg.

Chickamauga

On August 16, 1863, Union Major General Rosecrans's Army of the Cumberland began to turn the position of the Confederate Army under General Bragg at Chattanooga. Rosecrans had been urged to do this some six weeks earlier, but he had delayed while railroad repairs proceeded, supplies accumulated, and corn ripened. The Federal army would once again sever its own line of communications, depending, as in the Tullahoma advance in June 1863, on what the army could carry with it, on its living off the country, and on what could be brought up by wagon via a circuitous route through rugged country over bad roads. Rosecrans thus faced a far more difficult supply situation than had Grant in his similar move against Vicksburg the preceding May.

Rosecrans managed to distract Bragg, by first moving one corps toward Chattanooga and bombarding the city, while moving the other three Federal corps over the unfordable Tennessee River and around Bragg's west flank. The Confederates then abandoned Chattanooga and fell back to protect the railroad in north Georgia. Rosecrans, overconfident, and lacking information from his inadequate cavalry, erroneously concluded that Bragg was withdrawing to Atlanta. In the ensuing operations Rosecrans even acted as if he had already hit and hurt Bragg and had him on the run. Bragg, however, was strong and would become stronger. Meanwhile, Bragg performed in an uncharacteristically superior manner as he helped to further the notion of a demoralized withdrawal: scores of sham rebel deserters entered the Union lines to spread false stories of depressed Confederate morale because of the Chattanooga loss.

The Confederates were in the process of completing one of the most significant redeployments of the entire war, achieving the most far-flung concentration since Shiloh. Forces came from many directions; most important were two divisions of James Longstreet's corps who traveled by train from Virginia. The Union high command at Washington began to catch glimmers of the danger, and reinforcements were ordered from Grant's and Burnside's commands, but they did not arrive in time; and so Bragg's army outnumbered Rosecrans's seventy thousand to sixty thousand.

Rosecrans believed he would enjoy the advantage of the tactical defensive. Having turned the Confederates and cut their communications, the Southerners would now have to attack or withdraw farther. Suddenly, realizing the danger his dispersed force faced, near the last minute Rosecrans, like Lee before Antietam, succeeded in concentrating. But Bragg had the upper hand, for after five days (September 9–13) of maneuvers and frustrating attempts to precipitate a favorable battle, he learned that Longstreet's corps was rushing to him. On September 16 Bragg began his grand scheme, aiming to sweep through the front of Maj. Gen. Thomas L. Crittenden's corps, pour northward, and interpose the Confederate army between Rosecrans's force and Chattanooga. Then Bragg intended to lunge southward, driving the vanquished Federals into McLemore's Cove, where he planned to destroy them.

During the night preceding the battle, the two armies shifted for position. The area just west of Chickamauga Creek, so named by Indians and meaning "River of Death," was densely wooded; neither side knew exactly where the units of the other stood. On the morning of September 19, Federal Maj. Gen. George H. Thomas ordered a division to reconnoiter toward the creek. They encountered Forrest's dismounted cavalry, drove them back, and the battle began.

The nearest Confederate infantry began to help, and the essentially frontal fighting lasted all day. Neither side gained any decided advantage. Veritable dogfights erupted along the front. Each side fed in divisions, brigades, or regiments as one or the other seemed to be gaining an advantage. On the Confederate left, troops under Maj. Gen. John B. Hood made the most progress. Thrusting their foes back for one mile, they were to be thwarted only when Hood and his staff rode into an unusual battlefield hazard—a nest of yellow jackets. These Confederate leaders were momentarily disabled, and the charge diminished. During the night of September 19, the two forces rearranged their well-concentrated positions. Most important, Longstreet arrived with the rest of his men.

In the fighting on the second day, September 20, Rosecrans's army repeatedly countered Bragg's efforts to overlap its north flank, and ultimately the Confederates felt compelled to resort to frontal assaults. Bragg issued orders for these to unfold successively, north to south. He actually intended the main attack to occur near the northern flank, with a strong secondary attack by Longstreet down near the southern flank. As it turned out Longstreet's men achieved a spectacular breakthrough. Storming rebels swarmed through a gap in the Union line created by a mix-up in Union divisional placement orders. Rosecrans had forgotten the precise alignment, and upon receiving a request that one division close up a gap on the right flank of another, he failed to recall that the Federals had still another division between the two in question. He sent an order to the unit on the extreme right to close on the flank of the specified unit to the left. The division commander so ordered, and Brig. Gen. Thomas J. Wood, who had recently been humiliated for failing to obey orders with sufficient haste, now in a perverse mood, asked for the obviously unwise order to be given him in writing and proceeded to evacuate what turned out to be the very spot that Longstreet's troops slashed into.

Unfortunately for the Confederates, Bragg had failed to provide for any general reserve, and thus they could not fully exploit and follow up Longstreet's sudden success. Even so, the Federals suffered mightily. The jubilant Confederates swept forward, and here occurred a famous and humorous incident. Maj. Gen. Benjamin F. Cheatham cried, "Forward, boys, and give 'em hell!" The excited clergyman, Bishop/Gen. Leonidas Polk, approved of the idea but felt constrained to guard his tongue and so cried out to his men, "Give 'em what General Cheatham says, boys!" The fleeing Federals did not stop until they got to Rossville on the outskirts of Chattanooga, leaving behind eight thousand men who fell captive, fifteen thousand small arms, fifty-one pieces of artillery, and all manner of supplies, animals, and vehicles. Only the magnificent efforts of Major General Thomas saved the blue army from even worse disaster.

"Slow Trot" Thomas, as his contemporaries called him, or "Old Pap" Thomas, as many of his soldiers soon came to know him, would earn a new nickname in this battle. A Virginian by birth, Thomas had married a Northern girl and had renounced loyalty to his native state. A splendid physical figure, he stood six feet tall and weighed two hundred pounds; always neat in dress and appearance, he was also extremely conscious of how his troops looked, often remarking that the fate of a battle might depend upon the condition of a belt buckle. He also carefully looked after his troops' welfare, and they in turn loved him as soldiers loved few other generals of the Civil War.

At Chickamauga he formed a defensive perimeter at a place called "Snodgrass Hill" behind which most of Rosecrans's fleeing army eventually found safety. Rosecrans and his other corps commanders, Crittenden and Maj. Gen. Alexander McCook, fled to Chattanooga, thinking the rebels were destroying their entire army; but Thomas remained on the field. Turning two brigades to block Longstreet, Thomas requested the small reserve corps of Maj. Gen. Gordon Granger to protect the new flank. In splendid battlefield initiative, the reserve commander eventually abandoned his flank-protection duty and moved to join Thomas, whose two brigades by then were quite precariously engaged. As nightfall finally came, they still held their lines.

Bragg correctly assessed that his enemy was still strong and potent, and so he chose not to risk an assault upon Chattanooga. Instead, he proceeded to occupy strong positions on Missionary Ridge and Lookout Mountain and placed the city under siege. Two specific questions pertinent to the evolution of warfare are illustrated by the concluding episode of the Battle of Chickamauga. The first question is why did the Confederates find it impossible to follow up their victory on the battlefield and effectively pursue the fleeing Union army into, and even through and beyond, Chattanooga? The answer is that under Civil War–era conditions, even a vanquished defense could always muster sufficient firepower to fend off total destruction.

The second question is what made it possible for Thomas to form the army-saving defensive perimeter? One would be much tempted to credit it all to technology: several of Thomas's units possessed breech-loading weapons. The seven companies of the Twenty-first Ohio Volunteer Infantry were superbly armed with the five-shot, cylinder-fed Colt Revolving Rifle, while the men of Union Col. John T. Wilder's "Lightning Brigade" were armed with seven-shot, magazine-fed Spencer repeaters. But Wilder was not initially in immediate support of Thomas, though he always later believed he *could* have fought his way in—and that he could have crushed Longstreet in counterattack. To be sure technology was significant, but it nevertheless was not technology that produced the decisive result: *that* was achieved by good leadership and by exemplary use of available resources.

Thomas, beyond doubt, here truly earned his new appellation, "the Rock of Chickamauga." Nearly every soldier who had been in this phase of the battle and later left a record of his experiences mentions having seen Thomas and asserts how much of an uplifting effect on morale Thomas infused with his stolid conduct. Among the many other things that Thomas did was to find a way to offset the potency of Confederate sharpshooting, the Civil War equivalent of sniper fire. The Confederates had developed sharpshooting to a high art: many Rebel brigades contained whole battalions of sharpshooters who advanced ahead of the main attack as skirmishers. This kind of irregular advance—by rushes of well-dispersed elements—would, of course, in a later era become one of the main ways to cope with defensive potency, and here too it showed its value. When the advance against Thomas's perimeter finally stalled and static fighting ensued, the sharpshooters climbed trees or snuck close and picked off officers. Thomas perceived a way to neutralize them. He approached a Kentucky regiment and asked if it had any good squirrel hunters. A detail of six men was formed. It crept forward. One Rebel sharpshooter was spotted in a tall oak. The detail fired, the sharpshooter fell dead to the ground, and some dozen or more other Rebels scrambled down from the trees and ran off.

Conclusion

Various students tend to select different battles or episodes of the war as their favorite candidates for the status of "turning point," while some others conversely discard the concept altogether. Among those who do espouse the concept, Vicksburg and Gettysburg make almost every list of "turning points": unquestionably they were great benchmarks. The Confederacy thereafter was divided into two parts, the Union held the Mississippi River, and never again would the Army of Northern Virginia be able to take the initiative offensively. Rather more significant (especially after Thomas's performance at Chicka-mauga is added to that of the key figures in the Vicksburg and Gettysburg campaigns), the Union's key generals who perhaps could fashion the eventual victory had been identified: Grant, Meade, Sheridan, Sherman, and Thomas.

But top command is only one thing; in a conflict like the Civil War, it was not enough. When a nation such as the United States, with only a small Regular Army, finds itself in a large war, it necessarily has to rely heavily on volunteer officers. The mass of these will, to be sure, remain at company-grade levels; but the better (or luckier) of them may rise to field- and sometimes even general-grade ranks. Both sides made much use of volunteer officers. Sometimes, particularly when their appointment had been motivated merely by political considerations, they were a hindrance to military success. Other times some of the amateur generals managed to excel—either because they possessed a streak of natural gift for making war or because they possessed some military managerial merit upon which they could build and they diligently studied the tactical manuals and the good performances of others.

It is even possible, of course, for an amateur officer or militiaman to trans-form into a professional. The Civil War's quintessential example of one who did is the North's Alfred H. Terry. He entered the war as a militia colonel, in command of a ninety-day regiment at First Bull Run, and subsequently recruited the Seventh Connecticut, which was committed to serve for three years or the war's duration. Terry helped with the capture of Port Royal, South Carolina (in November 1861), served in the siege of Fort Pulaski, Georgia (concluded in April 1862), and in various operations against Charleston. In the autumn of 1863 he took command of the X Corps in Benjamin F. Butler's Army of the James. The high point of Terry's service came in January 1865 when he was given charge of repeating (but this time doing it right) an operation first attempted the preceding month by Butler that had then been an abysmal failure. This was to take Fort Fisher, guarding the mouth of the Cape Fear River. For this achievement, Terry was given a brigadier general's commission in the Regular Army. He remained on duty as a career officer after the Civil War, served well in various assignments, was promoted to major general in 1886, and retired in 1888. He proved that a non–West Pointer (and even someone who possessed no formal military education) could become an exemplary professional.

If, however, it is fair to assert that two quintessential representative samples of the better true-volunteer generals (those who would *not* become professional officers) that each side possessed—say, Joshua Lawrence Chamberlain and

Alfred H. Terry. The war's best example of a talented amateur who transformed himself into a professional soldier. (courtesy the Civil War Library and Museum MOLLUS, Philadelphia, Penn.)

Rutherford B. Hayes for the North, and Nathan Bedford Forrest and J. J. Pettigrew for the South—we see illustrated a significant contrast. The South's tended more to be eccentric geniuses and brooding intellectuals, often with an aristocratic bent; the North's were more likely to be professional men with more universally applicable managerial skills. This is speculative and interpolative, open to argument, but much material in the superb biographical studies of these four individuals undergirds the point.

The professional officers and their volunteer compatriots had, however, a large task remaining in late 1863. Coming only about two and one-half months after the enormous disasters of midyear, the Confederate achievement at Chickamauga provided a major morale boost and a genuine cause for renewed Southern hope. To be sure, the Confederates had lost the greater number of men in the battle, as almost always was the case for the attacker: 18,454 Southern casualties to 16,179 for the Union. The true "turning point" aspect of Chickamauga was not perceived until long thereafter. *That* was the Confederacy's failure to follow up on its achievement, to retake and hold Chattanooga.

There were foreign observers at the Battle of Chickamauga, and they were deeply impressed by the carnage. A reporter for *Le Figaro* (Paris) said of this battle: "These Americans are fighting on a military system inaugurated by the Kilkenny cats. The two armies meet and fight and slaughter each other with the utmost fury. Then they fall back and reorganize for another general massacre. Positively, the war will end when the last man is killed." Although Grant's response to this was that "our cat has the longer tail," an obviously still-extant Southern will to continue, war weariness, and internal controversy in the North that well might increase, coupled with all the other realities—the raiders, guerrillas, technologic experimentation, and manifest military viability, even after the decisiveness of Gettysburg and Vicksburg—suggested that the Civil War might last a long time yet indeed.

SUGGESTED READINGS

Special Studies of Note

Civil War Prisons: A Study in War Psychology, by William B. Hesseltine (New York: Frederick Ungar, 1964). Hesseltine, my mentor's mentor, was a historian of towering importance.

The Guns at Gettysburg, by Fairfax Downey (New York: Davis McKay, 1958). While all of Downey's works are a bit too "popular" in style, this is a good account of U.S. and C.S.A. artillery tactics, technology, and organization.

Hayes of the 23rd: The Civil War Volunteer Officer, by T. Harry Williams (New York: Knopf, 1965). Frank Vandiver has proclaimed, perhaps rightly, that this was Williams's best.

History of Andersonville Prison, by Ovid L. Futch (Gainesville: University of Florida Press, 1968), is solid and factual—unlike the novel by MacKinlay Kantor, which *isn't.* Also, there is a newer, more colorfully written work by William Marvel that many buffs treasure.

Infernal Machines: The Story of Confederate Submarine and Mine Warfare, by Milton F. Perry (Baton Rouge: Louisiana State University Press, 1965), is a true classic.

Inside War: The Guerrilla Conflict in Missouri during the American Civil War, by Norman Fellman (New York: Oxford University Press, 1989), is kaleidoscopic and stimulating.

Jennison's Jayhawkers, by Stephen Z. Starr (Baton Rouge: Louisiana State University Press, 1973). Starr, a gifted amateur historian, was much admired by T. Harry Williams.

The Marble Man: Robert E. Lee and His Image in American Society, by Thomas L. Connelly (New York: Knopf, 1977), is controversial but readable, impressive, and provocative.

The New York City Draft Riots: Their Significance for American Society and Politics in the Age of the Civil War, by Iver Bernstein (New York: Oxford University Press, 1990), is mainly not military history, and at least two-thirds of the book are hard to read, but the treatment of the riots is superb.

The Night the War Was Lost, by Charles Dufour (Garden City, N.Y.: Doubleday, 1960). Dufour exaggerates the importance of the fall of New Orleans, but the story is well told.

Tennessee's Forgotten Warriors: Frank Cheatham and His Confederate Division, by Christopher Losson (Knoxville: University of Tennessee Press, 1989), is a superb (revised) master's thesis.

Two Great Rebel Armies: An Essay in Confederate Military History, by Richard M. McMurry (Chapel Hill: University of North Carolina Press, 1989), is quintessential, a "must not miss" book.

U. S. Grant and the American Military Tradition, by Bruce Catton (Boston: Little, Brown, 1954). This brief, concise, too often underrated "sleeper" is a very good and important work.

The Union Cavalry in the Civil War, by Stephen Z. Starr, 3 vols. (Baton Rouge: Louisiana State University Press, 1979–1986).

Weapons of the Civil War, by Ian V. Hogg (New York: Military Press, 1987), is the best of its genre.

Battle and Campaign Studies

The Campaign of Chancellorsville, by John Bigelow (1910; reprint, New York: Morningside Press, 1991), is a great classic in military historical writing. Any student of campaigns needs to know about this one.

The Chickamauga Campaign, December 1862–November 1863, by Patrick Abbazia (Bryn Mawr, Pa.: Combined Books, 1988), is a fine work that is too unheralded.

The Gettysburg Campaign: A Study in Command, by Edwin P. Coddington (New York: Charles Scribner's Sons, 1968), is "deep" to "wade through," but it is important.

Pickett's Charge: A Microhistory of the Final Attack at Gettysburg, July 3, 1863, by George R. Stewart (Boston: Houghton Mifflin, 1959), is detailed and documented, with maps and photographs.

This Terrible Sound: The Battle of Chickamauga, by Peter Cozzens (Urbana: University of Illinois Press, 1992), is a good campaign study by a nonacademic historian.

The Vicksburg Campaign, by Edwin C. Bearss, 3 vols. (Dayton: Morningside Press, 1991). Bearss tells more than most people really want to know, but his monumental campaign study stands as the best that has yet been done on Vicksburg. Michael Ballard is at work on one, which doubtless will be up to *his* high standards.

Women

Civil Wars: Women and the Crisis of Southern Nationalism, by George Rable (Urbana: University of Illinois Press, 1989). Rable—the *last* of the thirty-six "wee Harrys" and one of the best—is a young master with a golden touch.

My Story of the War, by Mary Livermore (Hartford: A. D. Worthington, 1888), is a valuable firsthand account—replete with numerous well-told anecdotes—that tells much about Civil War hospitals and nursing.

Patriots in Disguise: Women Warriors of the Civil War, by Richard Hall (New York: Paragon House, 1993), documents the stories of fifty-six who comprise his "Honor Roll of Female Soldiers," but he includes some who were not disguised as men, such as "Michigan Bridget" Deavers, and others who were not soldiers at all, but scouts or spies. Given this, it is egregious that he failed to mention Emma Sanson, the fourteen-year-old girl who guided Forrest and his men to a ford across the Black Creek, near Gadsden, Alabama, making possible a spectacular Confederate victory. Lauren Cook Burgess's forthcoming book doubtless will be eminently superior.

An Uncommon Soldier: The Civil War Letters of Sarah Rosetta Wakeman, alias Pvt. Lyons Wakeman, 153rd Regiment, New York Volunteers, edited by Lauren Cook Burgess (New York: Oxford University Press, 1994). What made this soldier "uncommon" was, of course, that "he" was in truth a "she." This is *really* good stuff, and probably only the harbinger of more on the fascinating topic of women who served as Civil War soldiers.

When Sherman Came: Southern Women and the "Great March," by Katherine M. Jones (Indianapolis: Bobbs-Merrill, 1964).

Memoirs

The Battle of Gettysburg, by Frank Aretas Haskell, edited by Bruce Catton (Boston: Houghton Mifflin, 1957). Lieutenant Haskell wrote this forty-thousand-word letter to his brother, the most vivid and detailed eyewitness account of Pickett's Charge.

Berry Benson's Civil War Book, by Berry Benson (Athens: University of Georgia Press, 1992). This new edition has an introduction by Herman Hattaway. It is an interesting firsthand account by a Rebel who "never surrendered."

Dancing along the Deadline: The Andersonville Memoir of a Prisoner of the Confederacy, by Ezra Ripple, edited by Mark A. Snell (Hoyt Novato, Calif.: Presidio Press, 1966). Bruce Catton thought this memoir revealed much about why so much suffering took place and how much it "was a matter of agony and death and bleak hopelessness for the people who were actually involved in it."

Memoirs: Historical and Personal, by Ephraim McD. Anderson (St. Louis: Times Printing, 1868). Anderson was an upper-class and well-educated Southerner. Beyond the insightful observations he made about things military, his memoir reveals much about social conditions in the Confederacy. He had a masterful command of language, and thus his book is a true treasure for the modern reader.

Three Months in the Southern States, April–June 1863, by Arthur James Lyon Freemantle (Lincoln: University of Nebraska Press, 1992), is a classic and charmingly interesting firsthand account—including the Battle of Gettysburg—by a British officer; the new edition has an introduction by Gary Gallagher.

Three Years with Quantrill, by John McCorkle (Norman: University of Oklahoma Press, 1992). This new edition, with notes by Albert Castel and commentary by Herman Hattaway, is the best of the western guerrilla memoirs. It is a "must read" for folk who have some personal interest in the Kansas-Missouri border.

Biographies

A Battle from the Start: The Life of Nathan Bedford Forrest, by Brian Steel Wills (New York: Harper Collins, 1992), is a very good book that misses being a great book for an unfortunate and ironic reason: this is Wills's revised dissertation. Forrest is too complex a subject for a young scholar to handle adequately. In the spirit of Douglas Southall Freeman's urging for the would-be biographer, Wills *should* have worked on it another ten or twenty years, but that is suggesting the impossible. Perhaps eventually he *will* write a better book on Forrest.

Carolina Cavalier: The Life and Mind of James Johnston Pettigrew, by Clyde N. Wilson (Athens: University of Georgia Press, 1990), is a wonderfully interesting book, which has been egregiously underrecognized.

General Sterling Price and the Civil War in the West, by Albert Castel (Baton Rouge: Louisiana State University Press, 1968). Castel proved himself to have a master's touch.

Grant Moves South, by Bruce Catton (Boston: Little, Brown, 1960). Everyone needs to have read at least a little of Catton's work.

Grant Takes Command, by Bruce Catton (Boston: Little, Brown, 1968).

In the Hands of Providence: Joshua L. Chamberlain and the American Civil War, by Alice Rains Trulock (Chapel Hill: University of North Carolina Press, 1992). Trulock was an amateur historian, but this truly is a labor of love; she found some good, previously unused sources.

Jubal: The Life and Times of General Jubal A. Early, CSA, by Charles C. Osborne (Chapel Hill: Algonquin Books, 1992). Gary Gallagher, who is also working on Early, said of this work: "It's not as good as I feared, but it's awfully good!"

Meade of Gettysburg, by Freeman Cleaves (1960; reprint, with a foreword by Herman Hattaway, Norman: University of Oklahoma Press, 1991), suggests, to a considerably convincing degree, that Grant was unfair to Meade.

Nathan Bedford Forrest: A Biography, by Jack Hurst (New York: Knopf, 1993), is more readable than Wills's biography of Forrest but considerably less solidly underpinned by scholarship. This is an interesting book by a good writer, who here was attempting something beyond his capabilities.

Pemberton, by Michael Ballard (Jackson: University of Mississippi Press, 1991), does justice to "the pariah of the Confederacy," the Northerner who ill-served the South's cause.

Rebel Raider: The Life of General John Hunt Morgan, by James A. Ramage (Lexington: University of Kentucky Press, 1986), is a very fine study of "the thunderbolt of the Confederacy."

William Clarke Quantrill, by Albert Castel (New York: Fell, 1962). In Castel's distinguished career, he made many innovative contributions to scholarship; this is among his best.

Especially about Blacks

Army Life in a Black Regiment, by Thomas Wentworth Higginson (New York: W. W. Norton, 1984), is the insightful commentary by the very famous white colonel who led the first Regular Army regiment of black troops.

Forged in Battle: The Civil War Alliance of Black Soldiers and White Officers, by Joseph T. Glatthaar (New York: Free Press, 1990), is fine, inspiring work by a young master.

The Sable Arm: Black Troops in the Union Army, 1861–1865, by Dudley Taylor Cornish (1956; reprint, with a foreword by Herman Hattaway, Lawrence: University Press of Kansas, 1987), is the pioneering work on a crucial topic.

Fiction

Aide to Glory, by Louis Devon (New York: Dial Press, 1952), is an interesting fictional character study of John Rawlins, General Grant's aide-de-camp and later secretary of war.

Andersonville, by MacKinlay Kantor (New York: World Publishing, 1955), is a Pulitzer Prize–winning, best-selling novel about the misery and despair in this infamous prison.

The Bugles of Gettysburg, by La Salle Corbell Pickett (Chicago: F. G. Browne, 1913), is an interesting and even-handed novel by General Pickett's wife, observing the battle's fiftieth anniversary.

The Horse Soldiers, by Harold Augustus Sinclair (New York: Harper, 1956), is a well-executed novel about Union Col. Benjamin Grierson's raid. It was made into a memorable movie starring John Wayne.

The Killer Angels, by Michael Shaara (New York: McKay, 1974), is a Pulitzer Prize–winning fictional account of Gettysburg. Many readers have asserted that this is the best of all the Civil War novels that deal primarily with combat. It was the work upon which the recent movie *Gettysburg* was based. The historical narrative is sound; the situations and personality characterizations are fictional.

Mosby's Night Hawk, by Clarke Venable (Chicago: Reilly and Lee, 1931), is a dashing adventure tale about Mosby's irregulars.

My Enemy, My Brother: Men and Days at Gettysburg, by Joseph E. Persico (New York: Viking Press, 1977), is raw-edged fiction.

The Richmond Raid, by John Brick (New York: Doubleday, 1963), is a good novel by the author of several popular Civil War works of fiction, this one about Col. Ulrich Dahlgren's notorious and controversial raid to try to liberate Union prisoners of war held in Richmond and possibly to assassinate President Davis.

PART IV

Endgame Phases

❧

The more conventional military operations of late 1863 and early 1864 made undeniable—if indeed not *already* all too clear—several crucial facts. Both sides desperately needed to make some command changes in the West. But R. E. Lee and his eastern army remained viable and dangerous, and if the Union could not defeat Lee, then at least it would have to *pin him down.* This, of course, would be the fulfillment of Lincoln's long-cherished strategy of simultaneous advances. The president would be delighted when he found the idea embedded in Grant's proposed plan for bringing an end to the war and picturesquely declared that "Those not skinning can hold a leg." Some of the intended leg-holders eventually botched their assignments, but it was not practicable to get rid of them until after the 1864 election because of their political prominence. The question was how *could* the job be accomplished in *spite* of having to retain officers such as Nathaniel P. Banks and Benjamin F. Butler?

CHAPTER 13

No End in Sight

Late 1863–Early 1864

Early in October 1863 the Confederates came close to scoring an achievement of note in the Atlantic coastal waters. Thoughtful Southerners had long pondered the problem of transcending the passive nature of torpedoes, dependant upon the happenstance of being triggered by a passing horse, wagon, person, or boat: they searched for more positive means of delivery. Of all the high-ranking Southern generals, none showed more interest in technical innovation than Beauregard. From the conclusion of the Shiloh campaign until near the war's end, he was in command of the defenses at Charleston, South Carolina; hence, that city was the scene of more experimentation than any other place. There, the idea for direct delivery of torpedoes was developed.

A small attack boat, with a torpedo placed on the end of a long spar projecting from the bow, would approach a target at high speed. The spar, which could be raised and lowered by windlass, would be lowered at the critical moment and the torpedo rammed against the target hull a few feet below the waterline. It was believed that the attack vessel itself would escape damage, being armored and sufficiently far away from the explosion. Some of these vessels were fabricated but never used in combat because they were superseded by a much more viable class of torpedo rams, called "Davids." So named because these relatively small vessels were intended to be used against Goliath-sized targets, the cigar-shaped Davids had water ballast tanks that could be filled (or emptied) by pumps, lowering most of the hull to just below the waterline.

In the waters off Charleston on the night of October 5, 1863, the CSS *David* attacked the USS *New Ironsides*. A torpedo was smashed into the iron hull and exploded. The huge ship was jolted, rigging came crashing down, cannon were knocked loose, and an enormous stream of water shot into the air. The little *David* was deluged and the crew abandoned ship, but two of the officers later climbed back aboard, relit her fires, and brought her home. Injury to the *New Ironsides* at first appeared insignificant, but an inspection late in November revealed that very serious damage had indeed occurred. Information about the damage was kept secret, and the Confederates never learned the extent of their accomplishment, although the vessel remained out of action for more than a year. Meanwhile, other somewhat more conventional events on land demonstrated the reality of the military situation: no apparent end of the war was yet in sight.

The Bristoe Station Campaign

Following the Gettysburg campaign, a lull of nearly three months' duration prevailed in the East. Both armies needed time to regain strength. Lee concentrated east of the Blue Ridge Mountains, near Culpeper, while Meade deployed north of the Rappahannock River. Both had detached a portion of their force for temporary duty elsewhere.

When October arrived, Lee hoped to take advantage of Meade's diminished strength and inflict some damage, perhaps even to threaten Washington. On October 9, 1863, A. P. Hill's and Richard S. Ewell's corps, screened by Stuart's cavalry, marched first west and then north, closing toward the Federal lines at Culpeper. For two days the armies skirmished. Gradually, Meade withdrew and Lee advanced. On October 11 the Confederates occupied Culpeper. Lee then dispatched Hill's corps on a wide and circuitous westward swing, while Ewell's corps continued to pursue the Federals along the line of the Orange and Alexandria Railroad. For another two days Meade's rear guards skirmished with the oncoming Rebels. But the numerically superior Federal army remained relatively safe, for Meade conducted his retrograde very skillfully.

Early on October 14, Hill's lead division approached New Baltimore, five miles north of Warrenton. Hill's scouts learned that the Federals were marching northward, strung out along the tracks of the Orange and Alexandria Railroad, so Hill ordered a division to hurry eastward to Bristoe Station. Himself riding rapidly toward this railroad stop, as he neared, Hill saw a Yankee column crossing Broad Run, east of the station. Without reconnoitering, Hill ordered an attack. His two leading brigades slammed into the obtuse angle formed by the railroad and the stream. To their enormous surprise they were suddenly subjected to a punishing fire, delivered by the Federal II Corps, which had been carefully concealed behind the railroad embankment. Hill had fallen into a trap, and his men paid dearly for his impetuosity. The encounter cost the Confederates 1,300 casualties; the Union lost 548.

The engagement gave Meade time to assemble and solidify his forces in the vicinity of Centreville. For another two days, along the banks of Bull Run, the armies probed each other's positions. Finding the Northerners well entrenched, and knowing he hardly could afford to remain long in the vicinity, on October 17 Lee began a retreat. During the next three days, there occurred something of a mirror-image reversal of the campaign's first phase: the Confederates withdrew, constantly fending off attacks upon their rear.

The final action of the campaign occurred on October 19, at Buckland Mills, where Stuart's cavalry routed a Union cavalry division. By October 20 the bulk of Lee's army was safely south of the Rappahannock. The campaign had resulted in Lee inducing Meade to move his army some forty miles to the north. But, unable to do anything more, as Bruce Catton pointed out, *this* really was Lee's last offensive. It cost the Confederates 1,381 men, nearly all of them lost in the battle at Bristoe Station; Meade numbered his losses at 2,292. As far as the overall war effort was concerned, if decisive battle could not be produced in the East late in 1863, a somewhat more ominous development did come in the West.

Chattanooga and Missionary Ridge

The Confederacy's failure to capitalize meaningfully on its victory at Chickamauga proved to be a quite significant shortcoming. Bragg had not realized how much of a victory he had won. Shortly after the battle, unsure even that the Yankees were in full retreat to Chattanooga, Bragg interviewed a Rebel private who had been captured and then had escaped. "Do you know what a retreat looks like?" Bragg sternly inquired of the man. "I ought to, General," he allegedly replied. "I've been with you during your whole campaign." Bragg secured the heights around Chattanooga, Missionary Ridge, and Lookout Mountain and hoped that he could capture Chattanooga without another hard fight, simply by investing the place—a vain hope, indeed.

The Army of the Cumberland was momentarily hurt, but soon it recovered. In immediate response to Chickamauga, the Federal high command decided to send the XI and XII Corps from the Army of the Potomac, combined under the command of Joe Hooker, west to Rosecrans. Some skeptics thought this would take a month or more, but Secretary of War Edwin M. Stanton predicted it could be done in the incredibly short span of seven days. Telegrams were dispatched to the railroad officials and to the army, rail lines were commandeered, red tape was broken, and the job was done. The first troops moved on September 25, and by October 2 the last of them arrived in Alabama, from there to march to Chattanooga. It was a brilliant and superlative logistical operation. Some twenty-five thousand troops—four infantry divisions and ten batteries of artillery with all their weapons and equipment and three thousand draft animals—were transported twelve hundred miles in the fastest overland movement of so large a body of combat troops to that time in the history of warfare.

Meanwhile, crucial changes in command assignments occurred. On October 16 the Federals created the Military Division of the Mississippi, combining the Departments of the Ohio, the Cumberland, and the Tennessee. U. S. Grant was given the new command, and one of his first acts was to relieve Rosecrans, elevating Maj. Gen. George H. Thomas as his replacement. In Grant's former position, Sherman took over the Department of the Tennessee, and Burnside would continue in command of the Department of the Ohio. Grant himself turned his personal attentions to attenuating the problems at Chattanooga.

The so-called Confederate siege of Chattanooga proved an easy thing to lift, because the investment was so tenuous. Some of Hooker's units cleared the Rebels from Cummings Gap, which divides Raccoon Mountain. Then the Union troops thrust straight to the Tennessee River and seized Kelly's Ferry. On October 27, in a daring operation, a pontoon bridge was thrown across the Tennessee River at Brown's Ferry and thus a line of supply was opened— soon dubbed "the Cracker line"—from Lookout Valley to Bridgeport. Within a few days full complements of supplies were coming through. The Confederates failed to make any significant response.

During the night of October 28–29, Longstreet's corps attacked John W. Geary's Second division of Hooker's corps, at Wauhatchie Station, a stop in Lookout Valley along the Nashville and Chattanooga Railroad. If the Confederates could have taken that place, they would thus have cut off Hooker's rear. Although it was one of the few important night engagements of the war, Wauhatchie Station was a piecemeal and ill-conducted encounter. Capturing Union pickets and killing the sentries, the Rebels achieved initial surprise. Kicking out their campfires, the Yankees formed a V-shaped battle line, supported in the rear by one battery of artillery. A squad of Confederate sharpshooters managed to work around behind, firing on the cannoneers throughout the night. But because the moon was periodically covered over by heavy clouds, visibility was impaired, and often the only targets anyone saw to shoot at were muzzle flashes. When Hooker heard the sound of firing he ordered out

Nashville and Chattanooga Railroad depot. Railroads played crucial roles in the conduct of the war; veritably, "Victory Rode the Rails." (courtesy Leib Image Archives, York, Penn.)

reinforcements, and later still more Federal troops bolstered the positions. The Rebels elected to retire to Lookout Mountain, and the confused engagement ended at 4:00 A.M. with the Cracker line still secure.

In the ensuing weeks, Grant directed an operation aimed at driving the Confederates from the high ground around Chattanooga. On November 24 Lookout Mountain was secured. Although no fighting occurred on the mountaintop, the engagement became known as "the Battle above the Clouds," a misnomer caused by fog banks that nearly filled the valley below. The operation cleared the way for the primary effort against Missionary Ridge. The main role in that attack went to Sherman's men, the Army of the Tennessee. They were to assail the northern spur of Missionary Ridge, and then drive south, along the main ridgeline, rolling up the Rebel flanks. Hooker's men were to hit the opposite end, while Thomas's were to assault at the center (though only the forward positions in a trench at the base of the ridgeline), thus preventing significant Rebel redeployments. Elsewhere the Union attack did not fare so well. Hooker's men encountered stiff resistance. After hard fighting, however, they did manage to drive in Bragg's left flank slightly. Sherman's men, the main assault force, floundered and were compelled by rough terrain and stubborn fire to halt their advance.

Missionary Ridge was a steep series of hills running roughly north-south, linked by deep, broken gullies and strewn with brush, rocks, and fallen trees. At midafternoon on November 25, Thomas's men stepped across the valley in front of their objective. Before them was about one mile of open ground, but it was not well swept by the defending artillery because the Confederate guns at the tops of the hills were ill-placed and the gunners could not sufficiently depress the muzzles of their pieces. Defending fire was neither heavy nor accurate, although it was enough to induce Thomas's leading elements to break into a forward run. The Rebel riflemen were easily engulfed: some of them scampered up the slope, but most threw down their arms and surrendered.

Then, spontaneously, and to the astonishment of most of the watching Federal officers, some of Thomas's men—notably the division led by young Maj. Gen. Philip H. Sheridan—began to scale the ridge, straight into the Rebel center. The last thing Sheridan had said to the men before they moved forward was "Remember Chickamauga." Over and over as they trudged forward every one of the men kept shouting the name of that battle now to be revenged. The Rebel artillery belched canister, but the guns were too near the topographical crest and not properly located at the military crest, so in many cases the tubes could not be sufficiently depressed. Lowering their bayonets, Sheridan's men broke into a dead run, the young general himself riding at the head of Col. Charles Harker's brigade.

Grant was appalled, indeed angry; all logic dictated that no frontal assault could succeed. But Bragg's thinly manned lines were not well emplaced, and, most significant, the Rebels were diminished in determination. Their morale and esprit were low, their confidence in each other lacking, and their ability to mutually support each other, in many instances, nil. The Rebel resistance began to melt. Sheridan grabbed a flask from an orderly and raised it to a group of Rebel officers he could see at the ridge crest. "Here's to you!" he shouted, but just then a shell exploded nearby and sprayed him with dirt. "That's damn ungenerous!" he hollered out. "I shall take those guns for that!"

By 4:30 P.M. some numbers of the Federals had secured positions atop the ridge. Frantic Confederates tried lighting shell fuses and rolling cannonballs down the slope, while other Rebel gunners tried to drag their pieces rearward.

Philip H. Sheridan. He was short, foul mouthed, and so pugnacious that he once thrashed a Southern train conductor whom he thought had treated him rudely, but he was a soldier's soldier. Much favored by both U. S. Grant and William T. Sherman, Sheridan was destined to succeed Sherman as commanding general of the army. (courtesy Leib Image Archives, York, Penn.)

Sheridan rode his horse up a winding dirt path, right through some of the vacated Rebel entrenchments and to the crest that by then was swarming with blue-clad troops. With their line cut in several places, the last Confederates were now hastily taking flight.

"My God," cried one Indiana private, "come and see them run!" Sheridan leaped astride one of the cannon barrels that had sprayed him with dirt. Wrapping his short legs around it, he waved his hat and cheered. Grant took notice and was much impressed; he would be much inclined to call on Sheridan again in the future. The unfortunate brigade commander, Colonel Harker, however, had a more unhappy experience on the ridge crest than did Sheridan. Harker decided to jump up on a gun and cheer, too: but he mistakenly chose a piece that only shortly before had been fired, and he scorched his behind so badly that he was unable to ride a horse for more than a week.

Bragg's army staggered back toward Chickamauga Creek, and crossed that stream during the night. Despite the desperate fighting, casualties were relatively low for a major battle: the Federals had engaged some 56,000 men, with 753 killed, 4,722 wounded, and 349 missing for a total of 5,824; Confederates engaged numbered about 46,000, with 361 killed, 2,160 wounded, and 4,146 missing for a total of 6,667, many of these taken prisoner. The route for a Yankee invasion of Georgia was thus partially opened. The defeat at Chattanooga precipitated Bragg's resignation from field command, at long last—for it was quite overdue.

Perhaps most important of all, Missionary Ridge was the final catalyst in ensuring Grant's elevation, early in 1864, to the rank of lieutenant general and his assuming the overall command of all the armies of the United States. In the meantime, Sherman, under Grant's direction, conducted an operation that proved to be something of a dress rehearsal for the larger operations that would come later, in the fall of 1864: his Meridian campaign.

Sherman's Meridian Campaign

By now, Sherman's attitude had become a hard one. In 1862 he had written to his brother, Sen. John Sherman of Ohio: "It is about time the North understood the truth, that the entire South, man, woman, and child is against us." And, as he had indicated in 1862 to Grant, "we cannot change the hearts of the people of the South but we can make war so terrible that they will realize" its folly, "however brave and gallant and devoted to their country" they may be. In 1863, to a Southern woman who complained about his soldiers' stealing, he answered, "Madam, . . . War is cruelty. There is no use trying to reform it; the crueler it is, the sooner it will be over." Later, during the Atlanta campaign, he explained to his wife: "To realize what war is, one should follow our tracks."

Sherman's campaign to Meridian early in 1864 was one of the most significant raids of that winter, one that combined almost all of the elements in Grant's intended new strategy. This was both a test of the concept and a dress rehearsal for the subsequent 1864 campaigns in the West. Mark Grimsley in *The Hard Hand of War* points out that "Grant had approved the Meridian expedition, and it formed a good example of the sort of war he expected to conduct against the South." And, Grimsley strictures, one needs to know "something of Grant's overall design," if one is to understand "the hard war policy as it was implemented in 1864–65." Grant saw the war as a whole: he was less interested in taking objectives than in destroying enemy main forces; he wanted the 1864

William T. Sherman.
Perhaps, as some rate him,
the second-greatest general
of the war; he certainly was
one of the most interesting.
(courtesy Leib Image
Archives, York, Penn.)

spring offensive to be maximally strong; and he wanted to combine destruction of Rebel forces with destruction of their war resources.

Sherman's thrust was meant to be the infantry arm to operate in conjunction with a long-planned cavalry raid into Mississippi, which Maj. Gen. W. Sooy Smith conducted from Memphis. The overall objective was to cripple western Confederate rail support, eliminate an area supplying Southern troops with staples, and so hamper further enemy operations in the region as to reduce the number of Union troops needed to protect the Federal navigation of the Mississippi River.

Sherman departed Vicksburg on February 3 with twenty thousand men traveling in two columns, one arching north of the city, the other going directly east toward Jackson. At the same time, diversions and feints were ordered against Mobile and Selma, Alabama, and the Mississippi Gulf coast. The Confederate commanders were confused; they had no way of determining just what *was* being threatened and so had difficulty in choosing an appropriate response. Lt. Gen. Leonidas Polk, commanding the Department of Alabama, Mississippi, and East Louisiana, received word on February 4 of Sherman's initial movements. Polk began a series of deployments and, in a frenzy, made decisions and counterdecisions designed to stave off the invasion into the Confederacy's "breadbasket."

Polk asked his cavalry chieftain, S. D. Lee, to "detain the enemy as long as possible from getting into Jackson," and Polk rapidly shifted some of his Mobile garrison northward. Lee initially had only twenty-five hundred men facing Sherman; and in the first encounter, on February 4, Sherman's men easily pushed Lee rearward. At Jackson, Lee received one thousand reinforcements, but even this proved inadequate to impede Sherman's continuing advance. On the morning of February 6, Lee retreated eastward, and the Federals occupied Jackson. Sherman crossed the Pearl River on February 7, and Lee hit him again, scattering the Yankee foraging parties.

Sherman then tightened his command into a single heavy column, one that Lee's much inferior force found impossible to harass. The Confederates hastily ordered more reinforcements, this time from Johnston's army in north Georgia, but, before they arrived, Sherman had reached Meridian. On February 14 one of his columns entered the town, and, as he put it, "for five days 10,000 men worked hard and with a will in that work of destruction. . . . Meridian, with its depots, store-houses, arsenals, hospitals, offices, hotels, cantonments no longer exists." The Federals also destroyed about 115 miles of railroad, sixty-one bridges, and twenty locomotives.

Sherman had conducted this campaign by employing his later famous destructive techniques: his men lived off the country through which they moved, saving their own supplies, consuming food and fodder meant for the Rebels, and destroying what lay in their path, leaving burned buildings and desolation to the rear. Stephen D. Lee, named this "the Sherman Torch," and Lee contended vehemently for the rest of his life that Sherman had acted in a wantonly vindictive manner. "Was this the civilized warfare of the nineteenth century?" Lee asked, asserting that more than three-fourths of what Sherman destroyed was private property. True, it was private property, Sherman reasoned, but most of it was quite beneficial to the Southern war effort. And much of it conversely was now to be used in a manner beneficial to the Northern war effort. But Sherman was to be disappointed in his hoped-for juncture at Meridian with troops under William Sooy Smith, so Sherman then returned to Vicksburg.

For the Sooy Smith expedition, February 11–26, 1864, Sherman had ordered Smith to leave Collierville, Tennessee, just west of Memphis, on February 1 and to raid southward through Okolona, Mississippi, to unite with Sherman at Meridian on February 10. Sherman had intended for Smith to follow that schedule, even if it meant coming with a smaller force, but Smith ignored the schedule, and did not even leave Collierville until February 11, when he had at last gathered all of his seven thousand cavalry, twenty artillery pieces, one pack train, and one ambulance train.

Smith's column did achieve some impressive initial accomplishments: it burned much corn and cotton, tore up part of the Memphis and Ohio Railroad track, easily vanquished the six hundred Mississippi militiamen who tried to block it, and attracted more than one thousand slaves who joined the column seeking protection. But Smith was destined to soon have an inglorious encounter with Nathan Bedford Forrest.

The Confederate cavalry force of twenty-five hundred men, which was scattered north of Meridian, had numerous encounters with Smith's dispersed raiding troopers over the course of the ensuing seven days. Then on February 20 Smith's main column skirmished with some of Forrest's men, at Prairie Station, fifteen miles north of West Point. Another skirmish occurred at Aberdeen, just northeast of West Point. Smith, perhaps intimidated by Forrest's reputation and uncertain of the Rebel numbers, grew fearful for the safety of the slaves in his company, and so he ordered a concentration of all his men at Prairie Station. Then at dawn on February 21 they commenced riding toward West Point.

Some of Forrest's advanced elements clashed with Smith's spearhead and steadily—while exchanging fire—drew the Federals into a swampy area four miles south of West Point, delineated by the Tombigbee River, Okatibee Creek, and Sakatonchee Creek. There Forrest elected to force a general engagement. Before it could develop into that, however, Smith became fearful that he was being entrapped and ordered a retrograde. After a two-hour fight, the Yankees managed to disengage. Forrest ordered a pursuit.

Throughout the night, along a twenty-five-mile route, the Union and Confederate forces engaged in several clashes. At dawn on February 22, four miles south of Okolona, Forrest's advanced units attacked Smith's men in an open area called "the prairie." More and more Rebel horsemen came up. The Unionists suddenly broke ranks and ran, and an eleven-mile running skirmish ensued. Twice the Northerners tried to make a stand: at one mile and at two miles north of Okolona. Finally, after having lost six artillery pieces, Smith's men managed to stiffen their defense: they arrayed in wooded hills and around the buildings of Ivey's Farm, a plantation seven miles northwest of Okolona. Forrest's men charged twice but were repulsed; Smith's men countercharged twice and were likewise repulsed. The Federals then broke off the engagement and continued their retreat to Pontotoc. Mississippi militia took over trailing and harassing Smith's force, which got back to Collierville, Tennessee, on February 26.

The Meridian campaign had produced mixed results for both sides. Sherman had attained many, but by no means all, of his goals. He had swooped through Mississippi and destroyed much therein, but S. D. Lee and Bedford Forrest had accomplished quite a bit in warding off superior forces. Sherman had done a tremendous amount of damage, but he had withdrawn before doing as much as he might have. The Confederates could take some small comfort in having forced the termination of a raid, while the Federals, in sum, had successfully tested the concept of army-sized raids and, somewhat less successfully, the concept of concerted advance.

The Confederacy's Submarine Scores Its Only Kill

Many thinkers around the globe had long since begun to probe the problem of making undersea boats. Much had been written about the concept, quite a bit of it in the United States. The Union planned several submarines, and actually built one, at the Washington Navy Yard, but it was never put into service. The trouble with all of the pioneering submarines was that they were terribly dangerous and unreliable: once submerged all manner of things could go wrong and often did. The Confederates were more desperate, and therefore more daring. No accurate records survive to indicate how many Confederate submarines were lost, nor how many crews perished, but the latter number is substantial. The last of the vessels alone sank a total of five times, killing a crew each time.

The first Confederate experiments with submarines took place in the fall of 1861, at Richmond and in the James River, but the first meaningful success occurred in New Orleans. There, at the Leeds Foundry, several models were fabricated. One of the financial backers, Horace L. Hunley, a well-to-do sugar broker, took an intense interest in the project and himself became unquestionably the greatest expert of his time on submarine design, construction, and operation. The *Pioneer* became operational in March 1862 and destroyed a target barge in Lake Pontchartrain, but after New Orleans fell, in April 1862, Hunley and the other submariners moved—first to Mobile, Alabama, and subsequently to Charleston, South Carolina.

All of the Confederate submarines were screw driven, powered by cranks turned by men inside. This never gave as much motive power as was desired, and experiments were conducted using primitive electric motors, but in the end the best the Southerners could do was to figure a way to increase the number of crank operators. What submersed the boat were pump-operated water ballast tanks and iron diving vanes (which projected like wings from each side) that could be controlled from within. The course had to be followed mostly by dead reckoning, because the magnetic compass swung crazily when the boat was submerged. The final model of a Confederate submarine set an endurance record of two hours and thirty-five minutes below the surface before coming up safely, but most runs were short and consisted of serial dives, periodically coming up to check direction. A candle provided the only light inside, as well as a visible sign if the air supply was growing dangerously low: when the flame burned to a pinpoint, it was time to surface.

Experiments at Mobile also convinced the builders that some better method had to be found for delivering the torpedo. All the early submarines towed their warhead, allowing it to come up against the target's bottom after the submarine had passed beneath. But in rapidly moving water the lighter-weight torpedo had the tendency to move faster than the submarine itself. And so the decision was reached to employ the same principle for torpedo delivery as used by surface boats. A twenty-foot spar was attached to the submarine's bow. The sub would submerge only to hatch depth and ram the enemy boat. In August 1863 the submariners were transferred from Mobile to Charleston, the sub being hauled on a couple of railroad flatcars. A reward of one hundred thousand dollars had been promised to anyone who could sink either the *New Ironsides* or the USS *Wabash,* and fifty thousand dollars was offered for every *Monitor* sunk.

After a few successful practice dives, a fatal accident occurred on August 29, 1863. The sub was fished from the bottom, refitted, and Hunley now decided to pilot it himself. Hunley was truly a good submariner, but he too perished in a freak fatal accident, on October 15, 1863. A diver found the boat at nine fathoms, and once again it was raised. Still dedicated to the enterprise, the other builders supervised the cleaning and repair, rechristened the sub in honor of its late skipper as the CSS *Hunley,* and meticulously trained a new crew—at Mount Pleasant, on the north side of Charleston Harbor, where the builders established the world's first submarine school.

The *Hunley* made several successful practice dives and commenced regular cruising, gradually increasing the length of the trips from four to seven miles each way. To attack, however, many conditions had to be just right: an ebb tide was needed to set out and a flood tide to return, the wind had to be scant, and the moon must be dark. Finally there came a night when nearly everything seemed promising, and at dusk on February 17, 1864, the *Hunley* cast off on its last, but also a history-making, voyage. Its prey—the USS *Housatonic*—lay at anchor a few miles south of the entrance to Charleston Harbor. The *Housatonic* was a 207-foot-long screw-driven sloop armed with a one hundred–pound Parrott rifle, three thirty-pound Parrott rifles, an eleven-inch Dahlgren smoothbore, two thirty-two-pounder smoothbores, and three howitzers; it displaced 1,240 tons. A warning sounded at the last minute, but too late: the torpedo exploded, and the *Housatonic* sank. Most of its crew were picked up by nearby boats, but five sailors were never seen again.

Meanwhile, what of the *Hunley*? The Federals assumed it had escaped, and the Confederates fervently hoped that it had, and there is some suspicion that the vessel did surface after the explosion and that the crew sent a signal to the shore, but the submarine did not come back.

And here we have a bit of a mystery. Late in the nineteenth century, divers reported that they had found the *Hunley*'s wreckage under that of its victim: the *Housatonic* had overridden the submarine and had sunk on top of it. But in 1995 reports began to circulate concerning the modern finding of the *Hunley*—more than one thousand yards from the *Housatonic*'s remains. There is clear evidence that the *Hunley* had started to return and then some disaster occurred: possibly a rivet jarred loose by the explosion. At the time of this book's going to press there was much talk, and expressions of hope, about possibly raising the *Hunley* wreckage and putting it on display. But what did those late-nineteenth-century divers see underneath the *Housatonic*? Is it possible that there was more than one submarine? Probably not.

But the Rebels at various times did have more than one submarine, and we do not know—and probably never can know—precisely how many there were. In 1879 one Confederate submarine was found near New Orleans by a channel-dredging crew that pulled it ashore. The submarine lay in mud for a generation, and then on April 10, 1909, it was put on display at the Louisiana Home for Confederate Veterans. After all the veterans had died, the submarine was moved to Jackson Square, New Orleans, where it has been on display ever since.

The sinking of the *Hunley* marked the end of Confederate submarining. But it was the beginning of a revolution in naval warfare.

Red River Campaign

Grant preferred that the next major objective in the West be Mobile, Alabama, but political pressures suggested to President Lincoln that a higher priority should be given to clearing and securing the Red River line, as far as Shreveport, Louisiana. This would placate certain nominally loyal planters; further, it would facilitate the purchasing of their cotton by the army, eliminate a major Rebel supply depot at Shreveport, and open the way to further Union incursion into Texas. Maj. Gen. Nathaniel P. Banks was just the kind of man that such a scheme appealed to because he had been commissioned mainly in consideration for his political importance.

It was a dicey venture, however, because the level of the river had been falling recently. The plan called for a large combined naval and military force: Adm. David Dixon Porter—with a river flotilla of twelve ironclad gunboats, two large wooden steamers, and four smaller steamers—would support Banks's infantry force of twenty-eight thousand men. To defend against this, the Confederates could muster but fourteen thousand men, under President Davis's former brother-in-law, the capable Maj. Gen. Richard Taylor.

As the campaign got under way, the Federals enjoyed several successes. Obstructions that the Confederates had emplaced were cleared. Fort DeRussy near Simsport was captured easily. The fleet proceeded to Alexandria, which the Unionists occupied on March 19. But then confusion commenced: impatient orders arrived from the high command, Banks indulged in a series of delays, and when the flotilla at last did venture above Alexandria it encountered rapids— the hospital ship was lost, smashed against the rocks. Meanwhile, Banks's main infantry force, which was marching overland separately toward Shreveport, encountered stiff resistance at Sabine Crossroads, near Mansfield, forty miles below Shreveport.

The Battle of Mansfield (also called Pleasant Grove or Sabine Crossroads) on April 8, 1864, marked Banks's deepest thrust into Louisiana. It developed in haste, neither side managing to get anywhere near all of its available forces engaged: the Confederates committed some nine thousand men to the fight, while some twelve thousand Unionists eventually entered into it. Banks's men were strung out in a long file. The Confederates opened by sending several preliminary harassing waves forward and then late in the afternoon struck with their main force. The Rebels charged like "infuriated demons" and smashed one, then another, of Banks's divisions. There was brief, full-scale, but disjointed, fighting before Banks's men fled in panic-stricken rout. They went, however, only as far as Pleasant Grove. There a stout defense held until the Southern assault petered out.

In the pursuit Taylor's men captured twenty cannon, scores of wagons, and hundreds of prisoners; 2,235 Federals were killed, wounded, or captured, while

Taylor lost about 1,000 men. On the next day, Taylor assaulted at Pleasant Hill. The fighting increased in intensity as the day wore on, but the power of the defense was once again amply demonstrated. Despite Banks's inept handling of the tactical direction, the assaults were fended off, and the Federals lost only 1,369 to the Confederates' 1,626 casualties. Banks now decided to terminate the campaign.

The gunboats began retracing their course down the Red River, with Rebel artillery pieces and riflemen following them along the banks and firing upon them. At Blair's Landing, on April 12, a detachment of Confederate cavalry, with artillery support, discovered several transports and gunboats, some grounded and others severely damaged, so they tried an attack. The Confederate cavalry commander was inebriated, however, and this induced him to unleash an overly bold charge against the gunboats. The Federals on board coolly fired from behind the protection of cotton bales, hay, and sacks of oats, inflicting some three hundred casualties, while suffering none themselves. A few of the damaged transports had to be abandoned, but the remainder of the flotilla recommenced its journey downriver.

The Confederates pursued as far as Alexandria, where another major battle almost developed. Low water delayed Banks's ships; the depth of the water over the rapids had fallen to three feet. The navy's ironclads drew seven feet. For a time it looked like they might not be able to get through at all, but a lieutenant colonel, an engineer and former lumberman from Wisconsin, solved the problem. Three thousand men and three hundred wagons set to work building jetties to narrow the channel, thus deepening the water and enabling each heavy ironclad under a full head of steam to shoot the rapids. It was an almost comical venture, while army bands stood and played on the riverbanks and troops cheered it along, but it succeeded. Banks returned to New Orleans, late in May, too late to conduct the Mobile expedition that Grant had wanted in concert with the opening of the major simultaneous advances in the East and West.

The Battle of Brice's Crossroads

The Battle of Brice's Crossroads is of much interest to the serious military historian because it so well illustrates the innate grasp of war making that Nathan Bedford Forrest possessed. While he did not know the modern terminology, he applied the nine principles of war: objective, offensive, mass, maneuver, economy of force, unity of command, security, simplicity, and surprise; the optimum characteristics of modern army operations: initiative, agility, depth, synchronization, and versatility; and the four elements of combat power: maneuver, firepower, protection, and leadership. He was a master of mission, enemy, troops, terrain, and time available. And, last, he had an abundant appreciation of logistics.

On June 1, 1864, Federal Brig. Gen. Samuel D. Sturgis led a column of forty-eight hundred infantrymen and thirty-three hundred cavalrymen equipped with new rifles and carbines and augmented by four hundred artillerymen with twenty-two pieces of artillery out of Memphis; the mission: to find and destroy Forrest and his men. Sturgis's command, which had been specially selected for known fitness and fighting ability, was fully twice as large as Forrest's and was accompanied by supply wagons carrying eighteen days' rations and numerous ambulances and medical wagons.

The Federals moved slowly into northern Mississippi and on June 6 destroyed several miles of railroad track at Rienzi. Forrest's command was widely dispersed. The first clash occurred on June 7, a small skirmish at Ripley, Mississippi. By June 9 Sturgis had his command encamped nine miles from Brice's Crossroads on the road leading from Ripley. Forrest himself was at Booneville, eighteen miles away, and that night had a council of war with his superior, Maj. Gen. Stephen D. Lee, and several top subordinates.

Forrest decided to attack and gave orders that his vanguard should commence marching at 4:00 A.M. One battery of artillery was to move with this lead element, and even though there were eighteen miles of muddy road to be traversed, Forrest implicitly trusted that he could count on its commander, Capt. John C. Morton, to have the guns where they would be most needed. The countryside surrounding the crossroads was densely wooded with heavy undergrowth. Forrest consciously made note of the expected weather and terrain, as he said to one of his brigade commanders:

> I know they greatly outnumber the troops I have at hand, but the road along which they will march is narrow and muddy; they will make slow progress. The country is densely wooded, and the undergrowth so heavy that when we strike them they will not know how few men we have. . . . It is going to be hot as hell, and coming on a run for five or six miles over such roads, their infantry will be so tired that we will ride right over them. . . . I want everything to move up as fast as possible.

The amazing reality is, however, that Forrest was correct in assessing that his own men could travel more than twice the distance that the Federals would cover and still be fit to fight.

The Federal advance guard made first contact with a Confederate mounted patrol about two miles northwest of Brice's Crossroads. The blue-clads drove the Rebels away and pursued them toward the crossroads. The Southerners turned left at the crossroads and galloped in the direction of Baldwyn. The Federals came up in main force, and the Confederates immediately charged. The gray-clads were driven back but quickly reformed in the blackjack and scrub-oak thickets and along the rail fences that bordered the eastern side of the field on both sides of the road.

The undergrowth hampered the Federal commanders from making accurate estimates of enemy strength, but they concluded that they did indeed face a formidable array so they posted two brigades in battle line. By 10:00 A.M. Forrest was up with the rest of the advance brigade. There still trailed to the rear a vital 700-man brigade of horsemen, and another infantry brigade of 2,787 men was still further back toward Booneville. Eventually the battle would pit 3,300 Federal cavalry, 4,800 infantry, and twenty-two pieces of artillery—8,100 men in all—against 4,865 Confederates with eight pieces of artillery. The initial moments of engagement were critical, for Forrest perceived that he must not allow the superior-in-numbers enemy to take the offensive.

Forrest, believing that one man in motion was worth two standing to receive an attack, elected to feign an offensive move. He had his men tear down alternate panels of the fence behind which they were arrayed while at the same time actually strengthening the position with brush and logs. One Rebel brigade executed a feint, advancing into the open field. The Federals failed to see the disparity of numbers and allowed the fake "attack" to continue for nearly one hour: precisely the time that Forrest was trying to buy. Suddenly, up came the additional 700 Rebel troopers. Forrest quickly had them dismounted and arrayed into battle line. The Confederates now had 1,635 men on the field. Forrest again feigned an attack, buying still more vital time. Some of the Rebels, however, advanced too far, failing to realize the necessity of merely feinting, and encountered an enfilade fire that forced them to fall back in confusion, but they quickly rallied.

When Forrest had first arrived on the field, he had dispatched a staff officer toward Booneville with the order that the last brigade commander should "move up fast and fetch all he's got." When the final forces were still not up by 11:00 A.M., Forrest realized that he had better close with the dismounted enemy cavalry he was facing before the Federal infantry arrived.

Forrest rode up and down the line shouting encouragement and assuring the troops that this time it was no feint. The bugle sounded, and the Rebels calmly walked in formation toward the Federal lines, some four hundred yards away when they came into sight. The Union forces opened a furious fusillade, but word passed down the Rebel line to "Hold your fire, and at the flash of their guns every man fall to his face, and then up and with a yell and a volley, and over that fence go!" The Union volley killed seventy-five Rebels and wounded many more, but the line raised up and charged before the surprised Yankees could fire again. Rifles were used as clubs. The fighting, which lasted a bit less than one and one-half hours, was bitter. Finally, the Federal cavalry was beaten and driven back all along the line.

Forrest had obtained his first objective. It was 12:30 P.M. The Federal infantry, meanwhile, had been double-timing for six miles and even attempted a dead run for the final mile. The heat and uphill run dropped many men, either from exhaustion or sunstroke. Those who could then strung out in a fan-shaped double line.

For half an hour there was a lull, and at 2:00 P.M. Forrest began an attack. The Confederates immediately encountered stiff opposition. When a gap opened in one part of the Rebel line, Forrest himself and his staff dismounted and, brandishing pistols, ran forward to fill the breech. Then one Rebel bugler rode up and down the line sounding "charge" at various points, deceiving the Yankees as to the Rebel strength. This induced the Federals to make time-consuming redeployments. The fighting continued. Time dragged by. Finally, at 4:00 P.M. Forrest decided that the critical moment had come: the battle would be won or lost *now*. Both sides had about depleted their stamina and men were lying in the rills, the lucky ones drinking rainwater.

Forrest rode up and down the line yelling, "Get up men. I have ordered Bell to charge on the left. When you hear his guns, and the bugle sounds, every man must charge, and we will give them hell." Forrest ordered all his artillery to the front and personally saw to its placement. When one of his brigade commanders warned that the guns were precariously far forward without support, Forrest retorted: "Support hell, let it support itself, all the damn Yankees in the country can't take it."

A few cannon blasts were followed by blaring bugles: the Rebels charged all along the line. Smoke quickly grew thick and combined with the underbrush and blackjack thickets to greatly hinder vision. Sometimes the firefights were between soldiers in lines no more than thirty paces apart. Four Rebel guns were pushed forward by hand, and then they blasted the Federals with $1\frac{1}{2}$-inch iron balls at point-blank range. The Federals began scampering down the Baldwyn Road. The Rebels pursued, with their guns, too, going all the way to the crossroads, forcing the blue-clads toward Tishomingo Creek. Captain Morton captured six enemy cannon at the crossroads and turned them on the now panic-stricken Yankees.

The fleeing Federals had more bad luck: a supply wagon turned over on the bridge across Tishomingo Creek, blocking the retreat and cutting off a major portion of the train. Some terrified Federals crawled over the wagon and continued their run; others swam the creek or drowned in it. Forrest pushed on vigorously in pursuit. The Federals tried making a desperate stand along a ridgeline two miles northwest of the crossroads. They could only hold a little while before giving way again. Then they formed another defensive line behind a fence in a skirt of woods.

Forrest was not finished. He rode up to scan the front, and then he sat down beside a tree and spent some time in deep thought. Suddenly he spoke to the artillerist, Captain Morton: "Captain, as soon as you hear me open on the right and flank on the enemy over yonder, charge with your artillery down that land and across the branch." One of the other Rebel captains whispered to Morton, "Be-God, who ever heard of artillery charging?" Well, the natural military genius Forrest may not have *heard* of it, but he *thought* of it.

Forrest led the cavalry through the woods and across the fields, on approach to the enemy right, which the Rebels slashed into in a column of fours. Then the artillery moved forward as it had been ordered. The Federals resorted to their bayonets, trying to contend with the charging horsemen as well as the double-shotted advancing guns. Hand-to-hand fighting ensued, but the Rebel gunners stood fast. And another Confederate infantry brigade suddenly came up. It was the crucial moment. All Union resistance crumbled.

But Forrest allowed only a brief rest. At about 1:00 A.M. on the morning of June 11, the pursuit resumed. Sturgis and his panicked men fled through Ripley, and onward another fifty or more miles, with Forrest's men chewing at them all the way. Finally the Federals stopped late the next night at Salem, Forrest's boyhood home. The Federal army had taken almost ten days to march from their assembly area near Memphis to Brice's Crossroads, but they covered the same route in their harried retreat in one day and two nights.

Forrest had quickly established a clear and meaningful objective by aiming at destruction of the Union force by defeating it in detail. His aggressive attacks with minimum preparation had kept the Union force on the defensive. Outnumbered two-to-one Forrest used his escort of one hundred men as a tactical reserve, and he committed it to battle to stem a precarious threat. He also used the artillery audaciously, by double-shotting the guns and sending them forward—thus achieving shock action. He personally intervened in the action to bring about a more complete engagement. He constantly kept the enemy guessing. He intimately knew his subordinates and their capabilities and what he could count on them to do; but at the same time he was personally present at critical points and times. He always ensured that his principal subordinates clearly knew what he expected of them. He well used scouts and information supplied by local citizens. He had a degree of insight into his enemy's capabilities. He achieved surprise on first contact, and he never relinquished the initiative. He was a master of simplicity; his orders were simple, and his plans were simple.

The Federals had lost 223 killed, 394 wounded, and 1,623 missing—a total of 2,240. The Confederates lost 96 killed and 396 wounded—a total of 492. Forrest's men had also snatched almost all of the Federal artillery and 176 wagons. It was one of Forrest's greatest moments, and the affair was a classic of its kind.

So, as spring began to draw to a close, even more so in the western theater than in the East, rather little seemed to indicate that the war might be anything but a stalemate. But, already, at this point in time, things had begun to change.

CHAPTER 14

Grant and Sherman in Grand
Simultaneous Advance

By the start of the 1864 spring campaigns, the armies on both sides were composed of veterans led by men of experience; staffs had been perfected, and food, forage, and ordnance now were well managed. The two main armies on each side exemplified the best that West Point–leavened citizen-armies could achieve in that era. R. E. Lee was well supported by his principal corps commander, the extremely capable James Longstreet, while the other two corps were nominally well led, by A. P. Hill and Richard S. Ewell, although the latter two men were handicapped by poor health. Grant chose to accompany the Army of the Potomac, nevertheless leaving General Meade in command. The Army of the Potomac was reorganized into three large corps under Winfield Scott Hancock, John Sedgwick, and Gouverneur K. Warren. In addition to Meade's army, Grant had ordered into Virginia a separate corps, the IX, led by Ambrose P. Burnside. The Federals now opposed Lee on the Rapidan, outnumbering him by about 120,000 to 65,000.

Meade worked harmoniously with Grant, but perhaps more important the lieutenant general enjoyed more flexibility in relations with Lincoln than had any of his predecessors. This is not at all, however, to say that the president gave Grant free rein. The political generals Banks, Butler, and Sigel still had to be retained not only in service but also in positions of responsibility and prestige. It would be highly desirable if the war could be won by the fall, before the November election. And last, Grant should be cognizant of his losses, for battle deaths too were a politically sensitive issue.

Grant's plan was that these two main forces should wrestle and fully occupy each other, even if in stalemate, while the western armies fought it out. Key supporting elements in the plan called for Banks to move against Mobile and for Butler to move from Bermuda Hundred to cut the Petersburg-Richmond Railroad. The Confederacy would now be unable to redeploy, as typically it previously had done, and strengthen its most threatened defenses. Grant intended to make maximal use of the road network, railroads, rivers, ports, and telegraph lines that either already existed or would be constructed; indeed, these things were crucial to his plans. Further, Grant himself injected a kind of management and leadership that theretofore had been lacking.

What Grant proved able to do, which none of the predecessor generals succeeded adequately in accomplishing, was handle effectively—and coordinate— the vast array of forces that the Union had assembled. As the popular historian James R. Arnold observed in *The Armies of U. S. Grant:* "Although he had a West Pointer's skepticism about the ability of civilian officers, he showed greater flexibility than any other army leader in letting competent civilians rise to their level." Thus, Grant promoted Maj. Gen. John A. Logan, Col. Marcellus Monroe Crocker, Col. John E. Smith, Brig. Gen. Morgan L. Smith, and Col. Thomas E. E. Ransom—civilians all (save that Logan had fought in the Mexican War and Crocker had matriculated but been expelled from West Point)—to high rank because their performance merited it.

"We all regard Gen'l Grant as fate," one of his subordinate generals had written during the Vicksburg siege. "We feel that he knows everything about the situation and everything that is to happen about it." If anything, now in the supreme field command, this trait seemed to be further magnified. He kept his subordinate commanders well informed, writing or telegraphing them often. He frequently visited them personally—traveling via horseback, boat, or rail— and provided them firmly with either direction or guidance. Meade's chief of staff observed that "there is one striking feature of Grant's orders; no matter how hurriedly he may write them on the field, no one ever has the slightest doubt as to their meaning." That was true, however, only if the recipient of the order was a professional soldier or a civilian soldier with a cooperative and receptive attitude—some of the political generals, most notable is Ben Butler, either would *not* fully understand Grant's orders or would blatantly choose to do something else. Thus, Banks eschewed attacking Mobile in favor of the Red River campaign instead, and Butler became entrapped ("corked" into a bottle, as Grant put it in his memoirs).

But there were not, as has been implied by many previous historians, *two Grants* (the good soldier and the inept politician). Brooks Simpson has made a good argument that Grant consistently understood the political implications of the Civil War. That Grant tailored his military strategy according to political realities and used it to achieve political goals is what set Grant apart from other Union generals. He perceived the delicate problem: on the one hand he had to protect, and ultimately use in the war effort, the freed slaves; and on the other hand he had to avoid driving the white Southerners to desperation, wherein they might have resorted to guerrilla warfare.

The Crucial 1864 Campaigns Commence

The Army of the Potomac crossed the Rapidan at Germana Ford, and on May 5 the Battle of the Wilderness began. The Federals detected some enemy activity along the road from Orange Court House, where Lee had placed Ewell's corps. Both armies seemed unaware of their mutual proximity. Early in the morning the Federals struck Ewell, incorrectly thinking his corps was only a smaller fragment, and in the dense, undergrown labyrinth, the fight escalated. (The woods later caught fire, lending an added element of terror.)

The Union attack drove Ewell's lead division backward, and with vision impaired those Southerners who bore the brunt of the onslaught broke and fled. For a moment the Union seemed on the brink of stunning achievement, but a successful counterattack by a just arrived brigade under Brig. Gen. John B. Gordon overlapped both Union flanks. Two additional blue divisions on the Union left tried unsuccessfully to find the flank they had been told to support and were driven eastward. In confusion, some of their numbers ran into Confederate lines. Ewell then halted and dug in because he knew Lee wished to avoid a general engagement until Longstreet's corps, far to the southwest, could come up.

Meanwhile A. P. Hill advanced on the Orange Plank Road, where he threatened to thrust between Warren and Hancock. Meade had ordered Hancock with his four divisions to attack before Longstreet could join Lee. Hancock, however, was apprehensive about facing the aggressive Hill and delayed while improvising crude log breastworks along the road in his rear. At 3:30 P.M. Hancock advanced on the Confederates, finding them dug in amid the tangled mass of Wilderness growth. The twenty-five thousand Union troops at first seemed likely to overwhelm the scant seventy-five hundred entrenched Confederates. Withering and blind firing followed. Four times the blue infantry was thrust toward the gray defenders. Four times they stalled, and at last night fell.

During the previous day Hill's two divisions had barely held against six Federal divisions: five from Hancock's corps and one from Warren's. At 5:00 A.M. the Federals struck again, with Hancock's corps hitting Hill simultaneously on three sides. Exhausted and low on ammunition, the Confederate position crumbled. Longstreet's corps arrived as Hill's streamed to the rear. These fresh troops blunted Hancock's attack and by 10:00 A.M. had stabilized the Rebel right. Reconnoitering, Longstreet's scouts discovered an exposed flank in the Federal line. With Lee's permission, Longstreet executed a turning movement into the exposed division and began rolling up Hancock's entire corps from south to north. Only the personal exhortations of Hancock himself stopped a total rout of his corps. They fell back to their starting positions behind the breastworks erected the day before along the Brock Road. There they resolutely held against further Confederate attacks.

The next day the two armies remained in their positions, both still digging. Neither commander could perceive a weak spot, and so the Battle of the Wilderness ended. The Federals had suffered 17,666 casualties, while the Confederates lost somewhat more than 10,000 men. The bloody and inconclusive two-day struggle did not dampen Grant's optimism.

Unlike the results of the battles in previous years presided over by generals such as McClellan, Pope, Burnside, and Hooker, Grant's tactical failure did not precipitate a retreat. Grant well understood his need to keep Lee from reinforcing General Johnston, and that necessitated an unabated offensive in Virginia. Grant intended to base his army on the Virginia rivers, permitting successive movements to pass around Lee's eastern flank. The enlisted men, surprised and pleased that they were not going to retreat, soon dubbed these maneuvers "the jug-handle movement." The campaigns ahead might be bitter and hard, but they were ready. When the Federal column turned not northward but instead to the south—toward Spotsylvania Court House—one private quite typical of them all recalled, "Our spirits rose, . . . we began to sing. . . . That night we were happy."

Grant now launched a raid with his strong cavalry corps, hoping to break Lee's railroads. Early in April, to impart vitality to his cavalry, Grant had brought from the West a young infantry officer, Philip H. Sheridan. Short and cocky, Sheridan possessed a demeanor that fit his aggressive nature. He had been suspended for a year from West Point for "boisterous" behavior—chasing a fellow cadet with a bayonet—but had returned and graduated in 1853, thirty-fourth in a class of forty-nine. Somewhat consciously flamboyant, Sheridan rode his rounds on "Rienzi," a great black horse, at a pounding gallop. Confident, capable, and always energetic, Sheridan seemed to Grant just the man he wanted. Unfamiliar at first with mounted troops, Sheridan had turned in an initial lackluster performance. Nevertheless, he improved rapidly. Sheridan recognized in himself, and thus consciously attempted to cultivate, two noteworthy traits. He was willing to seize the offensive whenever possible and as aggressively as possible, and he was willing to exploit to the maximum any vulnerability that an opponent might expose.

On May 9 Sheridan commenced his gigantic cavalry raid toward Richmond, a venture that stretched over sixteen days. Drawing Stuart with them, Sheridan's men fought engagements at Davenport, Beaver Dam Station, North Anna, Davenport Ford, and, most significant, on May 11, some six miles north of Richmond at a place called Yellow Tavern. There, after a sharp and helter-skelter cavalry encounter, Stuart, the famed "Cavalier of Dixie," fell mortally wounded. Otherwise, however, the encounter gave the Southerners the required time to make more formidable additions to Richmond's strength, and they successfully forced Sheridan's raiders rearward toward the James River. The Federals ultimately accomplished rather little as a result of the Richmond raid, save perhaps to demonstrate—to themselves as much as to anyone—that their cavalry was now growing in superiority.

Grant and Sherman in Concerted Offensive:
The Atlanta Campaign Begins

In the West, well served by his principal subordinates Thomas and McPherson, Sherman and his team were perhaps even sharper than the team in the East. Sherman's subordinates and the rank and file respected him and were fiercely loyal to him. He was almost two years older than Grant and had once been Grant's military superior. While certainly not from the start, Sherman humbly came to sense a greater genius in Grant and gladly thereafter served as his second. Heading the Military Division of the Mississippi, Sherman now commanded an army group. Its largest unit was the Army of the Cumberland, sixty thousand men commanded by George H. Thomas. Next in size was Grant's old Army of the Tennessee, now led by the brilliant young James B. McPherson. First in his 1853 West Point class, McPherson had been Grant's engineer officer at Fort Donelson and Shiloh. The smallest unit, Burnside's old Army of the Ohio, was now under John M. Schofield. Experienced in departmental command, Schofield lacked background with an army in the field. He would learn, however, under an able tutor, William T. Sherman.

Sherman's opponent, Joseph E. Johnston, had participated in virtually no combat since the Battle of Fair Oaks and did not enjoy the full confidence of his more combat-seasoned corps commanders, nor that of Jefferson Davis. Warm in manner, however, Johnston elicited affection from those around him. He was unpretentious, and his magnetism evoked intense loyalty. Johnston communicated to his men his care for them, and he remained ever popular with the army. In addition to Joe Wheeler, his able young cavalry leader, Johnston enjoyed the services of the best corps commander in the West, the veteran William J. Hardee. The other corps was headed by a newcomer transferred from the Army of Northern Virginia, John B. Hood. Brave, aggressive, and capable, Hood had been previously wounded twice, both times severely, and he now had lost the use of one arm *and* he was missing one leg. He had performed very well at the brigade and division levels, but in his new position he now stood a bit beyond the level at which he could perform. (Disastrous for the Confederacy, Hood was destined later to receive one more promotion, to full general and command of the army.)

While Grant was engaged in the Battle of the Wilderness, Sherman began his thrust. With almost one hundred thousand men, Sherman rather considerably outnumbered Johnston (though not by the two-to-one measure that Johnston later claimed). The Confederates, however, occupied a craggy site so naturally formidable and so well fortified by skill and care that Sherman picturesquely called it "the terrible door of death." To turn Johnston's position Sherman planned to throw McPherson rapidly on Johnston's communications while Sherman's other two armies occupied Johnston's whole attention, both attacking cautiously in front.

McPherson's mission was to reach the enemy's rear at Resaca and break the railroad to deprive Johnston of rations. Sherman was worried that Johnston might turn on and crush McPherson's small army, so McPherson was to exercise extreme caution and, if need be, fall back to the mouth of Snake Creek Gap where the rough terrain would render him safe. But Resaca was appealingly vulnerable; the town was guarded by only one brigade. On May 9 McPherson reached Resaca and assailed it. The place, however, did not fall, and so McPherson withdrew. Johnston himself then began to withdraw, to cover Resaca.

In Richmond, the Confederates had already taken a measure to counter Sherman's offensive. At the first inkling of Sherman's advance, they had ordered troops from Alabama and Mississippi. General Polk left his department to command them himself. Polk marched with alacrity, and while he did not reach Sherman's flank, he did reach Resaca in time to cover Johnston's retreat. Further,

Polk brought fourteen thousand men with him: thus, in the West, despite still being outnumbered, the Confederates effected a meaningful concentration against Sherman.

Spotsylvania

Meanwhile, Grant encountered difficulty in Virginia. He tried to reach Lee's communications near Spotsylvania Court House, a strategically important crossroads; and as the huge Union army marched southeastward, Lee, receiving timely reports, dispatched troops to block the way. Confederate cavalry slowed the Federal advance, and Lee's men succeeded in beating Grant's army to the site. On May 8 the Federals assaulted. Although the general attack failed, a fluid situation developed as various fights erupted at Todd's Tavern, Corbin's Bridge, Alsop's Farm, and Laurel Hill. Lee did as best he could with the weakened command that fate had forced upon him: substitutes now led two of his three corps, for A. P. Hill had fallen sick and Longstreet was away suffering from a wound.

On the next day, May 9, widespread skirmishes continued; and a far-away Rebel sharpshooter instantly killed John Sedgwick—one of Grant's most beloved subordinates. Sedgwick had been trying to reassure his men. They shouldn't worry, he had just said, for "they couldn't hit an elephant at this distance," when a bullet struck him just under the left eye. Grant later told his staff that to lose Sedgwick was worse than to lose a whole division. He was the highest-ranking general of the Union Regular Army to lose his life in the Civil War.

After much readjustment of battle lines, Lee's army stretched out in an irregular position. On the right side of the line's center a salient jutted quite far to the front: "the Mule Shoe," which was later better known as "the Bloody Angle." Grant issued orders for an assault. Doggedly, he said he was prepared to continue indefinitely, even though it might be "necessary to fight it out on this line if it takes all summer."

This brought the supreme moment of the Civil War for a young officer, a May 1861 West Point graduate, now a colonel in command of the 121st New York Infantry Regiment, Emory Upton. Ever since participating in his first infantry fight, in the spring of 1863, Upton had been pondering the problems posed by the powerful weaponry in use and the need for modifications in tactics. Having given the matter much meditative thought, he had concluded that linear attack against strong defensive emplacements was not a wise approach. Rather, and

Emory Upton. Also a fresh West Point graduate just when the war commenced, not only he was to play a big role in the war, but his thinking and his writings had tremendous impact on the U.S. military in the postwar years as well. (courtesy the Civil War Library and Museum MOLLUS, Philadelphia, Penn.)

particularly when there was open ground between the opposing forces, it might be more productive to close quickly with the enemy than to achieve maximum firepower. But he prescribed that the assault column should be launched only from up close, thus reducing the number of volleys that the defenders could fire off. If the weight of the column forced a breach, this would offer flanks to roll up. Grant and Meade gave ear to young Upton and agreed to allow him a chance to test his method. On the afternoon of May 10 they assigned him twelve picked infantry regiments to make the attempt. The assault commenced at 6:00 P.M.

The spot that had been selected, the western side of the Mule Shoe, was not a promising one. In front of Upton's force was a heavy abatis. The main trench, solidly bolstered with logs and banked-up earth, was several dozen paces beyond. Along the top was a head log, blocked up a few inches above the earth, allowing Confederate riflemen to stand, aim, and fire through a narrow slit. Upton arrayed his men into four lines, which he instructed to advance in "waves." All would go with fixed bayonets, but the rearward line would not cap its muskets, hence not fire, until they actually reached the trench.

The men rushed forward. A sharp fire greeted them. But the solid column kept going. At the trench there was brief, and desperate, hand-to-hand fighting. Everything worked as Upton had hoped. But now, however, his men were too few for the task they faced, supporting units failed to appear, and Confederate reinforcements quickly began to move to seal the breach in their line. Upton had to bring his men back, in the darkness, to their original departure point, leaving one thousand dead and wounded behind. But Upton had inflicted at least equal casualties upon his foe and had captured twelve hundred prisoners.

Grant was pleased. Attacking with a column in "wave" could succeed, if such charges were well supported on the flanks. Surprise was important, and reserves needed to be ready to exploit any breakthrough. "A brigade today," Grant said, "we'll try a corps tomorrow." On May 12, commencing at 4:30 A.M. and lasting until past midnight, twenty-four Federal brigades attacked a few hundred yards of enemy entrenchments. The assault proved one of the most terrible fights of the whole war. Lee's line eventually did break under the furious onslaught, and an entire infantry division, along with twenty guns, fell captive; but Lee rallied his men, and by the next day the Rebels had mended their line. The two armies stood very near where they had when it all began. Only the salient was abandoned. One Southern man wrote of Grant, "We have met a man this time, who either does not know when he is whipped, or who cares not if he loses his whole Army."

The three-day attempt to break through the Confederate defenses had failed. The entrenchments were too strong, and the tactical skill and the counterattacks of the very maneuverable Confederate formations proved too formidable. Grant now ordered from Washington the reserves he had held back to reinforce any success in the East—though certainly he had failed to attain the success he had wanted. In heavy rain, which rendered the roads almost impassable, Grant spent the next week looking for a weak spot and seeking unsuccessfully first to slip by the enemy's right flank and then attempting a surprise assault on his left. Small engagements occurred every day, but nothing decisive developed.

The Simultaneous Advances Continue

In Georgia, Sherman faced Johnston's recently strengthened force. Rather than attacking, Sherman turned, a comparatively easy task because Johnston's front ran perpendicular to his railroad communications. Johnston hoped to counterattack but could not: each time Sherman halted, he fortified, making any assault upon his superior forces too hazardous. On May 16 Johnston retreated again, falling back to Cassville. Here at last he found the opportunity for which he had been wishing. He planned to fall upon Schofield's small army of thirteen thousand men with two of the three corps of his army of sixty thousand; but mistaken apprehensions by Hood (most ironic, in view of events later to occur!) induced the Rebels to abandon the attack and retreat to Allatoona Pass.

Sherman on May 22 was prepared to thrust his whole army around Johnston's left flank, aiming at Marietta or even for the Chattahoochee River. Nonetheless, he found himself unable to reach Johnston's rear. On May 26 he discovered the Confederates across his path, and well protected, so he too entrenched. Again a stalemate resulted. Sherman tried to entice the enemy to attack, but beyond probes and occasional assaults, Johnston would not oblige him. Sherman called it "a big Indian war." In wooded country the enterprising Rebels used spades and axes to build new works as rapidly as they were dislodged from old ones. Always protected by barricades, and so concealed by branches and underbrush, Sherman explained that "we cannot see them until we receive a sudden and deadly fire."

While Sherman successfully turned Johnston almost forty miles back from his Resaca position, Grant, by May 18, abandoned trying to force a battle with Lee in the vicinity of Spotsylvania. In fact, the experience of those ten days of intermittent battle caused Grant to halt attacks and seek to catch Lee in a mistake by additional turning movements. Grant began a dual-purpose turning movement on the night of May 20–21. Taking advantage of Hancock's keen competence and the intrinsic invulnerability of large Civil War infantry units, Grant in essence dared Lee to try hitting his detached force. If Lee were lured into attacking the separated element, Grant could come upon his rear and assault him where he was unprotected by entrenchments.

Instead of attacking Hancock, however, Lee moved southward. When Grant's army arrived on the North Anna, it found Lee's men well entrenched in another V-shaped position. In the Battle of the North Anna on May 23–25, Grant managed to cut a gap in the railroad north and west of Hanover Junction. Otherwise, Grant chose not to press another attack when Lee was ready for him. Grant quickly moved around Lee's eastern flank and by May 29 was near the site where the 1862 Seven Days campaign had begun.

Grant was beginning to wrestle with the unwelcome reality that again he would have to move around Lee's eastern flank to a base on the Peninsula, very close to where McClellan had been two years before. Both Lincoln and Halleck regarded such a scheme as not only futile but also dangerous for the safety of Washington. Furthermore, a siege, as it was beginning to be apparent was likely, would damage public morale and might even adversely affect the 1864 presidential election. Thus, Grant delayed his long-planned move south of the James River until raids in the Shenandoah valley under the direction of Gens. David Hunter and Phil Sheridan were well started.

Grant made one more effort to attack Lee, but he blundered badly on June 1–3 at Cold Harbor. Thinking he had discovered a weak spot, Grant instead found a powerful and well-entrenched enemy. It was Grant's poorest showing, one that nearly equated with Lee's decision to unleash Pickett's Charge at Gettysburg: in the first two days of fighting the Union lost five thousand men, and on the third day another seven thousand fell in a single hour. "I have always regretted that the last assault at Cold Harbor was ever made," Grant later wrote in his memoirs. "At Cold Harbor no advantage whatever was gained to compensate for the heavy loss we sustained. Indeed, the advantages, other than those of relative losses, were on the Confederate side. . . . [because] This charge seemed to revive their hopes."

Sliding eastward, on June 12 the Army of the Potomac began moving toward the James River and commenced to cross on January 14, aiming toward the vital railroad center, Petersburg, situated twenty miles south of Richmond. A first and unsuccessful attack was made on Petersburg on June 15; and other assaults on the next three days all failed. The four days of fighting before Petersburg cost about 8,150 Federal killed and wounded. So, on June 18, what proved to be the longest sustained operation of the Civil War began. It was punctuated, spectacularly, on July 30 by an explosion in a tunnel dug underneath the Rebel lines and an unsuccessful assault called the Battle of the Crater, but in essence it was a conventional siege lasting nine and one-half months.

Trench warfare and maneuvers aimed at securing limited objectives now became the norm. Throughout, whenever possible the Union army sidled toward the west, stretching the lines longer and ever longer. Miles of elaborate trenches, forts, redans, and abatis were constructed. The key to the siege lay in severing the roads and railroads that supplied both Petersburg and Richmond. In the initial investment Grant's men severed the Norfolk and Petersburg rail line, and subsequently between August 18 and 21 the Federals fought viciously and severed the Weldon Railroad.

But as long as a single supply artery remained in Rebel hands, and if Lee's sorely tested troops still held their lines, the siege could continue. Indeed, the static situation even rendered it possible to dispatch some of the Confederate defenders to bolster their forces in the Shenandoah valley. This Lee did in mid-September. Learning of this, Grant decided to threaten Richmond's defenses to induce Lee to shift troops northward, thus weakening some sector of the Petersburg lines that Grant then perhaps could penetrate. This ambitious two-pronged drive commenced on September 29.

Richmond was surrounded by three rings of permanent defenses, plus two forward water batteries on the James River at Chaffin's Farm and Drewry's bluffs. Two corps of Benjamin Butler's Army of the James were to cross the army's namesake river and attack, while some eight hundred infantry under Maj. Gen. Edward O. C. Ord crossed on a pontoon bridge opposite Varina Landing. The Rebels dug a trench eastward from Chaffin's to New Market Heights and contained Butler's main force, but Ord and his men scored a triumph in successfully storming Fort Harrison, a major Confederate bastion, and nearby works. Ord was badly wounded in the assault, but his gallant conduct added to his reputation (and earmarked him for succession to the command of Butler's army when he became able to return to duty in January 1865). The Rebels' loss of Fort Harrison was dear, because it rendered much of the exterior line of Richmond's permanent defenses untenable. Lee counteracted vigorously the next day, but the Federals now (more effectively than their enemy had been able) manned the formidable earthworks and fended off three attempts by the Southerners to retain their fort.

The Southerners were, however, able to hold on to all of their inner defenses and shift troops to restore stalemate both at Richmond and at Petersburg. For fifty-one miles the Confederate lines eventually stretched—from west of Richmond on around and below Petersburg. The Northern front line was thirty miles long, a series of redoubts connected by trenches and parapets. The Northerners named most of their forts after officers who had been killed since the beginning of the Wilderness campaign, while the Southerners named theirs after living commanders, including one for Lee himself. Behind some of the fortifications many soldiers were able to camp in relative safety and ease. But in the hot sector just east of Petersburg shelling and sniping continued daily, and there the men knew no rest or comfort.

CHAPTER 15

The War Draws to a Conclusion

During the summer of 1864 the Northern populace's morale and will to continue the contest reached its lowest ebb; despite that, on June 19, 1864, off the coast of Cherbourg, France, the USS *Kearsarge* sank the vexatious commerce raider, the CSS *Alabama,* and obviously other progress was being made. Nevertheless, long casualty lists were appalling. More and more, to many people victory seemed so distant and so costly that it truly was not worth striving for. It looked very much as if the Republicans could not win reelection in November, Abraham Lincoln would be turned out of office, and his place filled by the Democratic candidate—General McClellan—who was running on a peace platform. McClellan was adamant that there could be no peace without reunion, but many Unionists feared that McClellan would terminate the war with some sort of negotiated capitulation.

Even though the Federal army continued its slow advance into Georgia, Atlanta stubbornly refused to fall before Sherman's vastly superior numbers. Moreover, in Virginia, on June 23 Gen. Jubal Early led fourteen thousand Confederates down the Shenandoah valley, and they raided as far as the outer defenses of Washington, D.C., which they reached on the afternoon of July 11. Lincoln even briefly came under enemy fire at Fort Stevens, where he had gone to view some of the action.

With the summer's end and the beginning of autumn, things suddenly changed. General Early, after all, had not succeeded in entering the capital. He and his men had gotten as close as they were going to get, on July 11 and 12 and then were obliged to withdraw during the night of July 12. And Atlanta did at last fall, perhaps the final catalyst in ensuring Lincoln's victory at the polls in November. (It may even be fair to assert that this reelection was the point of no return for the South, for it meant that the war would be continued and it would be pressed vigorously toward an end.) Finally, Phillip Sheridan achieved some spirit-boosting triumphs in the Shenandoah valley.

The Confederacy still had some military potency, and even some new tricks up its sleeve, but the time finally was soon to come when the South's chances began to wane completely. One harbinger of that fact came on September 4 at Greenville, Tennessee, when the fearsome Confederate raider and cavalry leader John Hunt Morgan—"the Thunderbolt of the Confederacy"—was surprised and killed.

A Clear and Perceptible Turning of the Tide: The Battle of Mobile Bay

In the vicinity of Mobile, Alabama, things were beginning to look ever better for the Federals, and equally more dismal for the South's hopes. Federal Rear Adm. David G. Farragut had begun making plans as early as January 1864 for the capture of Mobile Bay. By August he was ready: he had a fleet of fourteen wooden ships and four Monitors (a new class of vessels) to contend against the defending Confederate Adm. Franklin Buchanan's three gunboats and the ironclad *Tennessee*. "I am going into Mobile Bay in the morning if 'God is my leader' as I hope he is," Farragut wrote to his wife on August 4. They entered the main channel at dawn. Despite an underwater minefield that sank one of the Monitors, and the punishing guns of Fort Morgan, the Federal vessels showed superior speed and handling. "Damn the torpedoes, full speed ahead," Farragut is said to have bellowed, thus coining one of the several most famous naval phrases of all time. In the end Buchanan was compelled to surrender, and the fort fell. The city itself would hold out against siege, until mid-March 1865, but because of Farragut's success on August 5, the Federals had snatched control of Mobile Bay. The Confederates were now down to but one last major port: Wilmington, North Carolina (which would hold out until February 23, 1865).

The Explosion at City Point

On August 9, 1864, the Confederacy scored a spectacular—but isolated and uncapitalized-upon—success: a tremendous explosion occurred at City Point, Virginia, where the Union had established a huge supply depot. The explosion killed 58 people, wounded another 126, did property damage in excess of $4 million, and even came close to killing General Grant, who was present. It was one of the greatest explosive eruptions of the Civil War, a blast so powerful that a McClellan saddle loaded with equipment was hurled from a canal boat into a crowd on the banks, like a gigantic bowling ball, knocking people askew, and instantly killing one man who was struck in the stomach.

Not until after the war had ended was the cause of the explosion made known: it had been the result of a hand-delivered clockwork torpedo, containing twelve pounds of explosives, disguised as a wooden box of candles. Confederate Secret Serviceman Capt. John Maxwell had perfected the device, and on July 16, 1864, in company with a companion he left Richmond with it, arriving near City Point before dawn on August 9. The two men crawled through picket lines, and Maxwell nonchalantly walked down to the wharf, carrying his box. Pretending to doze, at last he saw a barge captain come ashore. Maxwell bluffed his way past a sentry, a guard who spoke but little English whom Maxwell was able further to befog by speaking rapidly in a Scottish dialect. Aboard, Maxwell handed his box to a black laborer and told him the captain wanted it stowed below.

The explosion—accompanied by an unknown number of sympathetic detonations of ammunition and powder stores—was so loud that it permanently deafened Maxwell's companion, and considerably shook Maxwell himself, but the two escaped. The venture was an enormous success, by far the greatest of its kind achieved during the war. But again, typical of all the unorthodox Southern technological achievements, the explosion produced no long-term impact on the struggle.

The Fall of Atlanta

Confederate Gen. Joseph E. Johnston believed—and many apologetic historians later would assert—that he had been effectively employing a Fabian strategy of delay, trading real estate for time, but Johnston failed adequately to impress or please President Jefferson Davis. Still, the condition of the army, while Johnston remained in command, was as sound as possible. If Atlanta were to be held, Johnston probably had a better chance to do it than anyone. Yet, it indeed seemed probable that Johnston would have soon abandoned Atlanta, for by early July he had retreated to the Chattahoochee River, and subsequently he appeared to have no inclination to do anything other than that which he long already had been doing: retreat. The ultimate problem was that Davis and Johnston did not trust each other, and Johnston was unduly taciturn about communicating his plans. So the president at last lost his patience, and on

July 17, 1864, Johnston was replaced by John Bell Hood, known for his aggressive and combative spirit.

Hood ordered immediate offensives: on July 20 the Battle of Peachtree Creek, on July 22 the engagement that the Confederates officially named the Battle of Decatur, which the Federals (and most historians) called the Battle of Atlanta (more properly according to Albert Castel, but less commonly known as the Battle of Bald Hill), and on July 28 the Battle of Ezra Church. All were costly disasters.

In the first, Hood tried to replicate a performance of his beau ideal, Robert E. Lee. But not only was Hood no Lee, worse, he did not have the same kind of smooth and flexible functioning within his second echelon of command as was the case in the Army of Northern Virginia. The blame was not all Hood's, for parts of his plan were executed blindly, in an uncoordinated fashion, and in a half-hearted manner. As the noted scholar Castel has put it, "where the Confederates had the advantage in strength, they did not fight well; and where they fought well, they were too weak."

Bald Hill offered Hood the best chance for achieving one of the most spectacular victories of the Civil War, but it fizzled as only a near miss. Why? Because Hood tried to do too much with too little in too short a time, and as the battle unfolded he managed poorly, making unwise or inadequate responses to the developing situation. As Castel has observed, it "could be used as a classic example of a commander's not making sufficient allowance for the factors of time, distance, fatigue, and what is called [by Clausewitz] the 'friction of battle.'"

Bald Hill, while not high, dominates the surrounding countryside, and possession of it opened a way for harassing Atlanta just one and one-half miles away. On July 21 a Federal force seized the hill and moved a howitzer battery to the crest, which began lobbing shells into the city. The citizens grew frantic, women and children ran in various directions, and many persons scrambled aboard outbound trains while others proceeded to crowd the saloons and get drunk, or drunker than they already were.

Hood learned from his cavalry that the two wings of Sherman's army were separated and furthermore that McPherson's left flank was unprotected. During the night Hood would withdraw Stewart's and Cheatham's corps into Atlanta's inner defenses. Stewart's would remain to occupy the Union forces north and northeast of Atlanta, but Cheatham's would move to strike McPherson frontally, while Hardee's corps and Wheeler's cavalry circled around McPherson's left in

John Bell Hood. An able and brave fighter who rose above his level of competence; by the time he became an (acting) full general of the Confederate army he had lost the use of one arm and one leg had been amputated. (courtesy Leib Image Archives, York, Penn.)

a fifteen-mile night march to strike his wagon train at Decatur and the rear of his troops nearby.

It was a bold and daring plan, and if it had worked as Hood conceived it, he would have achieved a spectacular victory. Richard McMurry, in his fine and sensitively insightful biography of Hood, offers much to illustrate that Hood was not an utterly unfit simpleton, but rather that historians and students of the war have been too harsh in their assessments of him. But things did not proceed during the night as Hood had hoped they would, and he was forced to make various modifications to his plans. Various units failed to cover the distances in the time spans Hood had prescribed. The movements of Hardee's corps and Wheeler's cavalry touched off further panic among Atlanta's citizens, who assumed that Hood was evacuating the city. Luckily for Hood, Sherman reacted poorly and failed to take effective countermeasures.

The attacks commenced, belatedly and disjointedly, and there was hot and hard fighting. McPherson, himself precariously close to the engagement, ran out of luck. A band of Rebels emerged from nearby underbrush, ordered him to halt; he did not, trying instead to ride off into nearby woods. A bullet pierced his lungs and ended his life. But his loss to the Union did not ensure Confederate success. Shortly before sustaining his mortal wound he had ordered up a reserve brigade, and this unit slammed into the advancing Rebels, forcing them rearward.

Too late, in midafternoon Hood ordered Cheatham's frontal attack to commence. He had flubbed his chance for a coordinated assault to destroy a major portion of the Federal army. Once he knew of the delayed but crucial movements of his elements he should have canceled rather than modified his plan. Indeed, he was fortunate that Sherman did not accede to the proposals made both by Schofield and by Howard to counterattack against Cheatham's exposed left flank. If Sherman had, that corps would have been cut off from Atlanta. It probably would have brought not only immediate Federal possession of Atlanta but also the virtual destruction of Hood's army.

Ezra Church was, rather, a repetition of disappointment for Hood. Here, however, his subordinates—as well as the absence of the extraordinarily good fortune for which Hood now believed it was reasonable to gamble for—were more to blame for the disaster than Hood himself. The Federals possessed great numerical and material superiority, and this was the primary key to the recent series of Union victories.

Indeed, too, the results were not due—as many historians have wrongly asserted—to great generalship on Sherman's part. Nor were they matters of good fortune, for Sherman was place-oriented, methodical, and disinclined to take risk. He missed several opportunities to demolish Hood's force. And, it was the ongoing viability of armies in the field, not the security of Atlanta, upon which the ultimate Confederate victory depended. The fact is, Castel asserts, Sherman had it within his power to make a stunningly huge contribution toward bringing the war's end sooner, and in that he failed, because he simply passed up the chances.

But now, at least, Federal morale was high while Confederate spirits were low. This rendered Hood's forces less likely to be able to cope effectively against Sherman's host, and especially so if the Federals enjoyed the tactical defensive. Indeed, the crucial truth is that the Army of Tennessee now had lost confidence in *its* offensive potential.

The outcome of the Battle of Jonesboro on August 31 sealed the fate of Atlanta. Again Hood expected and attempted too much with the meager resources he possessed, but by this point the only thing that could truly have helped would have been a miracle. On September 1 the Confederates evacuated the city and the Federal army occupied it the next day. "Atlanta is ours, and fairly won," Sherman telegraphed to Halleck in Washington.

Sheridan in the Valley

On September 19 at the Third Battle of Winchester and on September 22 at the Battle of Fisher's Hill, Sheridan scored major triumphs in the Shenandoah valley, demolishing General Early's army. These victories won Sheridan promotion to brigadier general in the Regular Army. He then proceeded to subdue rife guerrilla activity with a "scorched earth" policy that induced him to boast that thenceforth a crow flying over that valley would have to carry its own provender.

It is a mistake made by many students, however, to conclude that the Federal hard-war policy of 1864–1865 was really the beginning of twentieth-century "total war" or—even more morally questionable—that they introduced an American way of war that led eventually to atrocity, such as the 1968 My Lai massacre in Vietnam. Mark Grimsley argues in *The Hard Hand of War* that "subordinate commanders tried to prevent excesses"; and, for a specific example, "Sheridan's razing of the Valley, for an operation of its scale, was probably one of the more controlled acts of destruction during the war's final year." What the Federals truly were trying to do was to force a change in behavior: they wished to compel Southerners to cease aiding the Rebel war effort. "Sheridan's operations concentrated on crops, livestock, mills, and barns, not entire communities," and not masses of innocent civilians.

Price's Missouri Raid

In the Far West, another ambitious Confederate scheme came to an ignominious end. Maj. Gen. Sterling Price, who had led twelve thousand men into Missouri and for some weeks wreaked much havoc and attracted much attention, on October 23 fought a fruitless and costly draw in the Battle of Westport. Compelled to retreat, on October 25 Price lost heavily in the rearguard action at Mine Creek near the Marais des Cygnes River in Kansas.

The March to the Sea

After the fall of Atlanta, Hood's army withdrew into northern Alabama. Subsequently, it attempted an invasion of Tennessee, while Sherman's army, after occupying Atlanta for two and one-half months, commenced the famous March to the Sea on November 16. The venture had long been contemplated by Grant and Sherman, and now with troops that had been earmarked for Mobile having been drawn into Missouri to cope with Price's operations, it seemed propitious to make the march through Georgia.

It was to be an integrated part of Grant's grand strategy, aimed at overcoming a significant twofold advantage theretofore enjoyed by the Confederacy: of being on the defensive and being able to use interior lines. Grant envisioned army-sized raids (rather than penetrations, that is, invasions and occupations) of enemy territory. Concomitantly, in order to preclude the South's ability to redeploy to meet and counter any significant threat of the moment (as it had managed to do, rather spectacularly on several previous occasions), Grant prescribed something that Abraham Lincoln had long advocated: simultaneous advance along several fronts. Any, or even all but one, of such simultaneous advances could in effect become holding actions—in favor of the one advance that would become the Union's principal hammer-blow against the South's will to continue making war. *This* one advance, this will-breaking venture, became Sherman's march.

Sherman's "grand raid" had a military objective of breaking railroads to isolate the Rebel armies from their sources of supply and to damage these sources by destroying mills, foundries, and critical agricultural resources. It also had the political goal of demoralizing the Confederates by showing them how vulnerable they were. And indeed it did produce a profound psychological impact on the Southern people. The famed Civil War historian Frank E. Vandiver once said tongue in cheek that "communities from Texas to Virginia swear that Sherman's army marched through them." Resolved to "make the march and make Georgia howl," Sherman's objective was not only to destroy resources but also to induce fear into the hearts and minds of the Southern populace. "They don't know what war means," Sherman proclaimed, "but when the rich planters of the Oconee and Savannah see their fences, and corn, and hogs, and sheep vanish before their eyes, they will have something more than a mean opinion of the 'Yanks.' "

It was a march conducted by a seasoned army of selected and hardened veterans. Sherman wisely realized that burdens were going to shift markedly from headquarters to lower-grade officers. Indeed, much reliance was to be entrusted even on the initiative that might be shown by enlisted men. That they measured well to the challenge was a key element in the success of his army. A second key was the quality of the troops. Sherman carefully limited

Ruins of a roundhouse. The South, much more so than the North, had grave difficulty in maintaining or repairing damaged railroad equipment and structures. They were favorite targets for destruction. (courtesy Leib Image Archives, York, Penn.)

the *kind* of men who could go on the expedition. He had his senior officers and medical staff conduct "a rigorous weeding-out process," so that, as he put it, "only the best fighting material" would remain. On the campaign the army averaged less than 2 percent unfit for duty on any given day. (Compared with all other Union forces, during campaigning periods, this was a 46 percent–lower illness rate.) Not only were the men tough but they were feisty as well: as one of them put it, "all the boys are ready for a meal or a fight and don't seem to care which it is." They were men who *wanted* to go on the march! "I wouldn't miss going on this expedition for 6 months pay," one officer noted in his diary.

Sherman had no communications to protect. Hood's army was much too far away to threaten. As Sherman moved through the heart of Georgia, ultimately toward Savannah, he created such ambiguity about his route that he had no difficulty avoiding the meager forces available to oppose him. The Federal force lived off the country and destroyed in its path anything of value to the

Confederate war effort. The army concentrated on destroying the major east-west railroads; a specially equipped engineer regiment wrought irreparable damage on the rail emplacements. The earlier "Sherman's neckties," or "Sherman's hairpins" (rails that had been heated in bonfires built from the cross ties and then bent around trees), could sometimes be rebent into useable shape; now special tools were used to put a twist into the iron, thoroughly ensuring against their ever again being employed for rail lines.

Sherman made a deeper thrust into the heartland of the Confederate interior than the South had yet experienced. It marked a complete change from only two months earlier, when the Confederate interior had still seemed virtually invulnerable to large-scale Union operations. It had a corresponding effect upon the people's will, and, in the end, it devastated the Southern logistical infrastructure. The impact was enormous: both in actual devastation and in the inducement of fears into the hearts and minds of the civilian populace. The fears were intensified by the "bummers"—Sherman's foragers who ranged wide of the main columns.

But, contrary to popular myth, Mark Grimsley asserts in *The Hard Hand of War*, "for the most part . . . Georgia whites suffered primarily the loss of crops and livestock." They were left with enough provisions to make it through the winter but with none to share with friends or to feed Rebel troops. Some of the "bummers" found slim pickings, but most found a lot, destroyed a lot, and themselves ate a lot: one German-born private exulted to his family, "we lived like God in France." But, Grimsley asserts, "the extent to which houses and towns were burned during Sherman's March to the Sea . . . turns out to be much exaggerated."

Sherman's army reached the Atlantic coast near Savannah on December 13, enabling him to make contact with the Union navy's South Atlantic Blockading Squadron and to establish a new supply line. He took the city just in time to present it to President Lincoln as a "Christmas present." Sherman wrote Union chief of staff Maj. Gen. Henry W. Halleck, "We are not only fighting hostile armies, but a hostile people, and must make old and young, rich and poor, feel the hard hand of war, as well as their organized armies. I know that this recent movement of mine through Georgia has had a wonderful effect in this respect." And indeed Sherman was correct, for as President Davis succinctly summed up the nonmaterial impact of the march: the "campaign has produced [a] bad effect on our people. Success against his future operations is needed to reanimate public confidence." Those "future operations" would soon commence. Earlier, General Grant had wanted Sherman to base himself on the Savannah River and to advance toward Augusta, Georgia, but by now Grant and Sherman had come to envision a second thrust to be made by Sherman's army: northward, through the Carolinas.

Hood's Mad Gamble: The Nashville Campaign

Instead of opposing Sherman, Hood decided to march into middle Tennessee. This odd spectacle of two armies marching away from each other into the other's territory had occurred during the American Revolution and had more than once characterized operations during earlier wars. Hood, however, unlike Sherman, planned not a raid but a reconquest of middle Tennessee; and the two regions, Sherman's area of operations and Hood's, did not have equal value. Middle Tennessee could not possibly contribute as much to sustain the Confederate armies as did the railways in Georgia. Further, as a raider Sherman had the goal and the opportunity to avoid the enemy forces; but Hood, aiming to conquer territory, *had* to engage Union troops in his path. The advantage of the strategic defensive thus accrued, and continued to belong, to the Union. Sherman had counted on this when he left in Tennessee a large but motley contingent under the command of the careful Maj. Gen. George H. Thomas.

On November 21, 1864, Hood moved his army out from Florence, Alabama; various constituent elements, dispersed and traveling along several different routes, headed for Tennessee. Remnants of Thomas's scattered forces clashed lightly, from time to time, with the moving Rebel army: on November 22 at Lawrenceburg, Tennessee, and on November 23 at Henryville, Fouche Springs, and Mount Pleasant. There was a rather spirited cavalry skirmish on November 24 near Columbia, but the Confederates were driven away, and the Federals secured a strong position just south of the Duck River. On the night of November 29 "the Spring Hill Affair" occurred, which later would be one of the war's most controversial nonfighting events, for a myth would grow that Hood just barely missed a golden opportunity to ambush and cut off a major portion of the Federal troops moving northward. In fact, Hood was probably unaware of the presence of Federal troops in Nashville, and he hoped to pass around Schofield so the Rebels could continue northward. In any case Hood was tired, confused, likely in pain from wounds he had suffered in previous battles, and not in control of the situation.

The next day, November 30, 1864, witnessed one of the most spectacular as well as costly and tragic encounters that the Army of Tennessee ever experienced: the Battle of Franklin. Even many years thereafter, Confederate survivors recalled this "five tragic hours" of battle with horror. "My flesh trembles and creeps and crawls when I think of it today," wrote Sam Watkins, author of a readable memoir, *Company Aytch*. "My heart almost ceases to beat at the horrid recollection. Would to God that I had never witnessed such a scene!"

After first turning back the Federal force opposing him—a portion of Thomas's army, two corps under Maj. Gen. John M. Schofield—almost as far as Nashville, Hood made a costly frontal attack against the entrenched Federals. Hood's army was approximately the same size that his opponent had assembled, but Schofield's men were secure within formidable fieldworks. A frontal assault was most unwise, but Hood was rash, and he was angry at his men for not showing a sufficiently spunky attitude and willingness. Hood lost 15 percent of his force, including six generals killed or mortally wounded. Schofield, even though he had resisted Hood's attacks quite successfully and his casualties numbered barely one-third of Hood's, withdrew to Nashville, where he joined General Thomas in well-entrenched positions protected from turning movements by the Cumberland River, that waterway being protected by patrolling Union gunboats.

On December 15 and 16, 1864, in freezing weather, Thomas, in an essentially frontal battle, easily defeated Hood's shivering and demoralized minions. This was a well-planned and methodical operation; it was neither the result of accidental collision nor was there any surprise. Thomas delayed the attack, waiting for more propitious weather and nearly exhausted the patience of Grant, who actually took the steps to replace Thomas, which, of course, proved unnecessary.

The Battle of Nashville was fought, bizarrely, within the sight of a huge array of civilian and noncombatant military spectators. One of the participants recalled that "citizens of Nashville, nearly all of whom were in sympathy with the Confederacy, came out of the city in droves. All the hills in our rear were black with human beings watching the battle, but silent. No army on the continent ever played on any field to so large and so sullen an audience." They would see a dispirited and hapless Southern force be vanquished. On the first day the main thrust smashed against the Confederate left. The redoubts were carried, and Hood's beaten forces fell back about a mile to the rear, to reform in a new position. On the next day, in mixed rain and snow, the attacks resumed. There were hours of desperate fighting, but at last, as Thomas reported, the Confederate lines were "hopelessly broken," and the Rebels "fled in confusion."

Superior in numbers, morale, and cavalry, Thomas's army conducted a damaging pursuit. Only the well-managed efforts of Lt. Gen. Stephen D. Lee's corps prevented total demolition of the Confederate army, the remnants of which were driven into northern Mississippi, where they subsequently suffered much from the ravages of winter and poor supply. Discredited and disgraced, Hood resigned. His army had lost so heavily in numbers and fighting fitness that it had effectively ceased to exist.

Sherman's March through the Carolinas

As Sherman's army continued its history-making campaign, now into its second phase, a winter sojourn through the Carolinas, he and his army continued to bring about the de facto emancipation from slavery of many thousands of blacks. On one occasion Sherman measured *in miles* the blacks who trailed behind the raiding infantry. An estimated ten thousand slaves followed the army to Savannah, and in the Carolinas another seven thousand reached safety at Fayetteville, North Carolina. For some of the Union soldiers, this was a welcome and rewarding experience, a chance to assist blacks in their struggle for freedom. Others, however, found blacks a nuisance and vented their prejudices and wartime frustrations.

Surprisingly, Sherman's troops on the march had only infrequent contact with Southern *whites*. Rumors of gross mistreatment, whether or not they had any basis of truth, induced many thousands of citizens, particularly in South Carolina, to evacuate to "safer" areas. Only in the larger cities and towns did Sherman's men encounter whites in sizeable numbers. *In general,* Sherman's army treated Southern civilians well; but, some few of Sherman's men perpetrated violent crimes. In several instances members of Sherman's command hanged Southerners to the point of death in an attempt to find where the citizens had hidden their valuables.

On February 17, 1865, Sherman's men entered Columbia, South Carolina, the state capital. Many buildings in Columbia had long been put to use as makeshift warehouses for massive amounts of accumulating cotton, and this made the place a veritable fire trap. Before the invaders left, about one-third of the city burned. Much of the destruction was accidental, and some Union soldiers attempted to help put the fires out, but the conflagration has symbolically come to be equated with Sherman's harsh policies of war-making. Unique among the spectators observing Sherman's triumphal entry were numerous recently liberated prisoners of war. One of them, Samuel H. M. Byers, slipped up to Sherman and handed him a copy of a poem he had composed while incarcerated, called "Sherman's March to the Sea." It pleased Sherman so much that he elevated Byers to a position on his staff, and the two men remained friends for life. (The poem, however, was the inspiration for the words and music later penned by Henry Clay Work, the nationally famous "Marching through Georgia." This song was played so often whenever Sherman appeared in public that he came to hate it passionately!)

Because Confederates were now gathering fragments of forces—mostly remnants of the bedraggled and battered Confederate Army of Tennessee, recently restored to the command of Joseph E. Johnston—Grant prepared for their probable attempt at exploiting interior lines to achieve dangerous concentration against Sherman. If Sherman were attacked, Grant wanted him to have a supply line so he could remain stationary and hold his ground. Grant therefore sent General Schofield with a part of General Thomas's army by rail and water to land on the North Carolina coast, take Wilmington, and establish a line of communications with which Sherman could connect if necessary. Fort Fisher— the principal Confederate defensive emplacement at Wilmington—fell to a combined assault in the middle of January 1865. Schofield's XXIII Corps reached the North Carolina coast on February 9 and, along with the X Corps of the Army of the James under Maj. Gen. Alfred Terry, occupied Wilmington on February 22. The Union force, some thirty thousand effectives, then prepared to move up the Cape Fear River and secure Fayetteville, North Carolina.

Sheridan's Shenandoah Valley Raid

By the winter of 1865, Federal efforts to improve their cavalry had at last created a well-led force, numerically superior and better armed than its Confederate counterpart. Grant used the cavalry to make several minor and two major raids. The first major raid (February 27–March 24, 1865) under Philip Sheridan, went from Winchester, Virginia, through that state to the Federal army at Petersburg.

Leaving Winchester, Sheridan led his ten thousand cavalrymen southward through the Shenandoah valley toward Staunton and Lynchburg. Near Staunton he encountered his only significant opposition, eighteen hundred men under General Early. Securing some bridges and burning others above Staunton, as the Yankees steadily progressed they consumed Rebel supplies and easily fended off Early's cavalry. On March 1 Sheridan occupied Staunton, forcing Early to relocate to Waynesboro about twelve miles to the east. There the Rebels attempted to make a stand, holding a position at the Rockfish Gap in the Blue Ridge Mountains with two infantry brigades and an artillery battalion.

Advanced units under Bvt. Maj. Gen. George A. Custer, reconnoitering during the rainy morning of March 2, discovered that there was a wide distance between Early's left flank and the South River. Custer dismounted three of his regiments and had them move under the cover provided by heavily wooded terrain. At 3:30 P.M. they struck in this vulnerable sector, while at the same time Sheridan's cannon and the rest of his force blasted away at Early's center and right. The Rebels quickly quailed and began to run. Sheridan's men captured sixteen hundred troops, twelve cannon, and two hundred supply wagons, while Early and the few remaining Confederates escaped, fleeing in several directions.

Sheridan then moved through Rockfish Gap into previously unspoiled territory north of the James River. His men then spent the ensuing four weeks burning barns, destroying mills, and badly damaging the Virginia Central Railroad and the James River Canal. Thus, the raid successfully disrupted both Richmond's rail and its canal communications. Too, it materially hurt the enemy and depressed Rebel spirits.

Forrest Meets His Match at Last: James Wilson's Raid

The other major raid was conducted under the command of an 1860 West Point graduate, quite mature beyond his years and now deservedly a brevet major general, James H. Wilson. With the remarkably able Bvt. Brig. Gen. Emory Upton as his principal subordinate, Wilson moved his force from Tennessee into Alabama aiming to capture Selma. This city, an important center of Confederate war industry, was situated on a rail route that ran between Georgia and Mississippi. The raid was not a spur-of-the-minute concept. Indeed, Wilson later credited his success to the benefits produced by an extensive training program for both officers and men during winter encampment late in 1864 and early in 1865. The command was a "veteran outfit," nearly all units having served more than two years and many being in their fourth year of combat. Wilson's aim was to travel fast, confuse the enemy with speed and maneuverability, and seize crucial momentary opportunities to concentrate and smash any forces sent against him.

Forrest prepared to fend off the raiders, as he had previously been able to do so many times, but now he was outgunned. Thanks to Wilson's insistence and perseverance in the matter, almost all of the Federal cavalrymen were armed principally with Spencer seven-shot, magazine-fed, metal-case-cartridge-using

James Harrison Wilson. One of the best of the young West Pointers who graduated just as the war began, he deservedly rose to the rank of brevet major general and conducted the war's most devastating raid. (courtesy the Civil War Library and Museum MOLLUS, Philadelphia, Penn.)

repeating carbines. In addition, the men also carried a six-shot revolver and a light cavalry saber. Each division was equipped with a battery of horse artillery. Also, Wilson had become convinced that the Alabama terrain made it essential that he have a pontoon train. His battalion of *pontonniers* were outfitted with enough equipment to build a four-hundred-foot bridge.

Forrest also would be outmaneuvered and outfought. In Wilson and Upton, Forrest at last met his match, as they acted superbly together. The force left its encampments along the Tennessee River and moved into northern Alabama on March 18, 1865. A compact column, 13,480 strong, it moved with a swiftness not achieved by any of Forrest's previous foes. Not dependant on the land for food or forage, the troopers each carried on their mounts five days' worth of light rations, twenty-four pounds of grain, one hundred rounds of ammunition, and a pair of extra horseshoes.

On March 29 Wilson crossed the Black Warrior River and by March 30 was in Elyton, where he destroyed several factories. Then, in a fourteen-mile running fight on March 31, inflicting about one hundred casualties while sustaining less than one-half that number, they drove through hapless Confederates who were unable to slow them down, much less halt them, and wrecked the iron furnaces and collieries between that town and Montevallo. Eleven hundred men were dispatched to Tuscaloosa, to burn all of military value—the bridge, factories, mills, and even the University of Alabama (which was then a military school).

On April 1 good fortune smiled on the Federals; one of Upton's cavalrymen captured a Confederate courier. The dispatches he was carrying revealed vital data concerning Forrest's plans and the positions then occupied by his troops. Forrest made a game stand, in the Battle near Ebenezer Church, where he was trounced by about nine thousand of Wilson's men, losing three hundred men to Wilson's twelve killed and forty wounded.

The next day, April 2, 1865, Wilson's men assailed Selma. The place was well fortified, but there were inadequate numbers of combat-ready defenders; and, from a captured engineer, Upton's division had obtained a complete sketch of the defensive works. Forrest tried desperately to defend the place, mainly with hastily assembled militiamen who were terrified and distracted by the rapid fire from the Federal's Spencers. Although the fighting grew hot, heavy, and desperate, degenerating into hundreds of individual combats, by the end of the day Wilson had secured the place and all of its machinery and captured twenty-seven hundred prisoners, forty guns, and large stores of supplies.

On April 8 Wilson and Forrest met together in conference. "Well, General," Forrest said glumly, "you have beaten me badly, and for the first time I am compelled to make such an acknowledgment." Wilson replied, "Our victory was not without cost. You put up a stout fight, but we were too many and too fast for you." The military professionals had prevailed at last, even against the great Bedford Forrest.

Wilson now added to his advantage, organizing numerous freed slaves into regiments, assigning one regiment to each of his divisions. While these untrained new black soldiers did not add to Wilson's combat capability, their availability allowed Wilson to keep more of his main force concentrated and not be bothered with logistical or security details. Wilson's raiders soon proceeded eastward to take Montgomery, Alabama. Continuing onward, in a dramatic night attack on April 16, 1865, they captured Columbus, Georgia, which was but weakly defended by scanty numbers of Confederates, for the Georgia governor had delayed calling out the state militia, having underestimated the speed with which the Federals could move. Too, in the darkness, the Confederate defenders tended to waste many of their shots by firing too high. Capturing Columbus was a stunning capstone to the taking of Selma and Montgomery, because much of the material which had formerly been stored in those two cities had been moved to Columbus.

Wilson's command slashed toward Macon, which they seized on April 20. That same day Wilson received a telegram from Sherman announcing a cease-fire, but Wilson also learned that President Jefferson Davis was fleeing southward from North Carolina and now through Georgia. On May 10 Wilson's men wound up their spectacular campaign with the capture of the Confederate president, near Irwinville (*not* in women's garb as the story grew in myth, but with his wife's similar cloak mistakenly thrown over his shoulders).

Wilson's stellar campaign, often overlooked—because it happened so late in the war and because it was overshadowed by zestful interest in Sherman's final march and the endgame in Virginia—destroyed the military and economic productivity of the final area in the South that could have supported a continuation of the war. In addition to the 288 pieces of artillery taken by Wilson, the destruction was formidable: seven iron works, seven foundries, seven machine shops, two rolling mills, five collieries, thirteen factories, four niter works, three arsenals, one navy yard, one powder magazine, five steamboats, thirty-five locomotives, 565 railroad cars, and untold quantities of quartermaster, commissary, and ordnance stores.

The Concluding Episodes

All the while, Sherman's army continued its march, though not without danger and difficulty. The invaders had to deal with an increasingly larger and highly mobile opposing Confederate force. They made one near-spectacular attempt, in the Battle of Bentonville, March 19–21, 1865. After reaching Fayetteville in mid-March, Sherman's men moved forward in two columns. The right under Oliver O. Howard marched toward Goldsborough where it was intended that it should unite with a column under John M. Schofield coming inland from the coast; the left under Henry W. Slocum moved toward Raleigh. On March 16 Slocum encountered a few Confederates near Averasborough. Easily fending off these Rebels, Slocum then turned east toward Goldsborough. Joseph E. Johnston, now possessing about twenty-one thousand men, decided to strike Slocum in force, perhaps to delay or even to prevent the Federal unification at Goldsborough.

Early on March 19 a Confederate cavalry force struck Slocum's leading units just south of Bentonville. The Southerners were easily forced back, but soon

Johnston counterattacked. Slocum was induced to draw his men into a strong concentration and make a stand. Johnston's men charged several times but could neither penetrate Slocum's lines nor force them to move. So Johnston then fell back and tried to establish a strong defensive position.

. On March 20 little fighting occurred, but Sherman brought up more and more troops. The Southerners enjoyed scant success, delaying Sherman's army with gunfire. They did, however, impede the march by felling trees across roads, lighting fires in barrels of turpentine, or setting pine trees ablaze to block roads and frighten horses and mules, and emplacing land mines (which Sherman declared to be a violation of civilized warfare).

On March 21 Sherman attacked Johnston's front, while one division of the XVII Corps tried to sidle around the Confederate left. Johnston was able to block the flanking movement as well as hold his position frontally during the remainder of the day. That night, however, he fell back toward Smithfield.

On March 23 Sherman's and Schofield's forces united at Goldsborough, swelling the Union force to 80,000 men. Johnston, having lost 2,606 men in the Bentonville operations, clearly felt the end was approaching. Nevertheless, dutifully, Johnston continued in the field, and trailed Sherman's army when on April 10 it resumed a northward march. Soon, however, Johnston concluded that his numbers were far too few to continue offering effective resistance, and so he opened surrender negotiations.

Suffering in the Petersburg trenches, bad from the beginning, had grown much worse when winter came. Reid Mitchell found a letter from a New Jersey soldier in which he claimed that some soldiers in the trenches were literally dying from homesickness.

Conditions were even worse on the Rebel side: huge numbers of Confederates succumbed to hunger and hardship each night and crossed over to the Union lines to surrender. After the war Col. Walter H. Taylor, Lee's adjutant general, confessed that during the final months, "hundreds of letters addressed to soldiers were intercepted and sent to army headquarters, in which mothers, wives and sisters, told of their inability to respond to the appeals of hungry children for bread, or to provide proper care and remedies for the sick; and in the name of all that was dear, appealed to the men to come home and rescue them from the ills which they suffered and the starvation that threatened them." Any soldier who did get such a letter was sure to have been morbidly depressed.

Whenever opportunity opened, the Federals stretched the lines still more, and there was little that the Rebel force could do to counter the situation. Early in February as Union troops moved toward the Boydton Plank Road to sever it, Lee counterattacked (this was known as the Battle of Hatcher's Run), and though the Southerners suffered heavy losses, the road continued for a time to yet remain in Rebel hands. Lee struck back at his enemy whenever he could. On March 25, 1865, the Confederates unleashed a daring strike and stormed Fort Steadman just east of Petersburg. They could not, however, exploit their breakthrough, and a subsequent Federal counterattack drove them out.

The fall of Petersburg came a week later. On April 1, 1865, Grant launched another thrust toward the Southern right, threatening Five Forks, a vital road junction to Lee's rear. Lee countered by moving nineteen thousand men, one-third of all that he had left, to oppose nearly fifty thousand Federals. For the preceding three days Sheridan's three cavalry divisions and two infantry corps had been fighting and pressing toward that point. Now they stormed forth hard, and the Confederate defense shattered. The Yankees swooped into the works, seized eleven flags and four cannon, and captured more than one thousand men. Thousands more Rebels surrendered. When it was over, about eleven hundred Confederates had been killed or wounded and another fifty-two hundred were prisoners.

The next day, April 2, at 4:30 A.M., Grant hurled a massive onslaught against the Petersburg trenches, and the main defenses crumbled. Lee was able to extricate his remaining remnant, but Union troops occupied Petersburg by nightfall. The Confederate government was compelled to evacuate Richmond. Thus, on April 3 Union troops occupied not only Petersburg but Richmond as well, and on April 4 President Lincoln visited the erstwhile Confederate capitol, as the Appomattox campaign commenced.

Robert E. Lee's sorely depleted army tried to swing around and elude the Federals, hoping to travel to Danville, Virginia, where Lee vainly hoped they might have been able to unite with what was left of Joseph E. Johnston's army. Lee hoped to use the still-operational Richmond and Danville Railroad, but when he reached Amelia Court House, he had to wait for twenty-four hours before trains brought him badly needed supplies. But to Lee's bitter dismay, logistics men—incorrectly thinking that ammunition would be the Rebels' first needs—had sent no food. Meanwhile, Federal cavalry cut the railroad at Jetersville, forcing Lee to abandon his hopes of using the railroad and his hungry men to try scurrying across the rolling countryside toward Lynchburg.

On April 6 nearly one-fourth of Lee's army was entrapped and captured at Sayler's Creek—the last major engagement between the Army of Northern Virginia and the Army of the Potomac. Lee received news of this disaster at Farmville, where he and the rest of his men had been able to secure rations.

The next day Grant opened correspondence with Lee, proposing that the Rebels surrender. President Lincoln wired Grant that "Gen. Sheridan says 'If the thing is pressed I think Lee will surrender.' Let the *thing* be pressed."

Lee then commenced to lead his remaining thirty thousand men in a north-by-west arc across the Appomattox River. But Sheridan's cavalry and most of two infantry corps hurried to block the way into Lynchburg and seized the Confederate supply trains at Appomattox Station. Beginning at dawn on the morning of April 9, units of the Confederate corps now commanded by Maj. Gen. John B. Gordon and Fitzhugh Lee's cavalry desperately probed at the Union lines and made some encouraging progress for a time, but they soon found the powerful Union infantrymen to be strongly emplaced in lines that were too formidable. Now the Yankees began to drive forward, and at the same time other Federals attacked the Confederate rear guard.

After listening to all reports of the situation Lee took final action and then declared, "It would be useless and therefore cruel to provoke the further effusion of blood, and I have arranged to meet with General Grant with a view to surrender." Truce flags fluttered, and couriers arranged a meeting between Lee and Grant. Early that afternoon, in the parlor of the house belonging to Wilmer McClean, Lee surrendered.

Elsewhere, other Confederate surrenders soon followed. Mobile capitulated on April 12. The U.S. flag was raised above Fort Sumter on April 14, the same unfortunate day on which President Lincoln was assassinated. Sherman and Johnston reached a tentative agreement on April 18. Although the Washington government rejected the terms, Johnston and Sherman subsequently met again and made a new agreement, on April 26, at Durham Station, North Carolina, where a final agreement of capitulation was reached.

So, Grant's grand strategy of large-scale raids, in the end, had proved to be a satisfactory antidote to the military stalemate. A broken stalemate dictates, however, *only* that military activity, if continued, become more fluid; a broken stalemate *does not* dictate the defeat of one side. Even when the Union armies accepted the surrender of the Confederate armies, the latter side still had other open alternatives, most notably a protracted guerrilla effort. Indeed, Sherman firmly believed that certain Confederate chieftains would definitely continue fighting. Sherman wrote to Grant, opining that the organized resistance would dissolve into "numberless bands of desperadoes, headed by such men as Mosby, Forrest, Red Jackson, and others, who know not and care not for danger and its consequences." But this did not happen.

Conclusion

Many years after the Civil War was over, former Confederate Lt. Gen. Stephen D. Lee said that the reason the Confederacy held out as long as it did was because the women of the South would not allow surrender until the very end had been reached. He doubtless overstated and romanticized the point, but he touched nevertheless upon a key factor: support from the home front was crucial and necessary, and when it finally crumbled so too did the would-be nation. (This is the essential thesis of Beringer, Hattaway, Jones, and Still in *Why the South Lost the Civil War.*)

The capitulation of the Confederacy was but a symptom of *defeatism* that had by this time permeated the South. Few—indeed, *very few*—Southerners wished to continue the fight. Those on the home front grew ready to capitulate before the soldiers at the battle front did. It was pathetic letters from wives, sweethearts, and mothers that induced many a tired Rebel soldier to give it up and desert—and far many more of them were delivered than were intercepted by zealous Confederate staff officers. "Before God, Edward," one soldier's wife lamented. "Unless you come home we must die. Last night I was aroused by little Eddie's crying. . . . He said 'Oh, mamma, I'm so hungry!' And Lucy, Edward, your darling Lucy, she never complains, but she is growing thinner and thinner every day." In January 1865 another wretchedly suffering and barely literate North Carolina woman penned this to her son in the ranks: "Tell theam all to s[t]op fiting and come home to live if you all wod put down you gouns and come home and let the Big men stae the fiting wod Soon Stop if you all Stae theaire you all will bee kild I want you all to come home."

And the war itself had made some of its own conditions, for somewhere along the way, just as the Union had officially added to its original war aim, so too had the Confederate leadership altered the concept of the political goal of the war. Now, even if the Confederacy did continue, slavery was gone. Preserving that institution had been only a part—but certainly a large part—of what the Confederacy came into being to protect in the first place. Beyond the loss of slavery, much else previously dear to Confederates seemed now to have been demolished. State rights appeared to be gone. Soul-searing casualty lists painfully proclaimed the loss of a staggeringly large number of young men. Confederate nationalism had been too romantic and too flimsy. The supposedly different form of government for which the people of the Southern Confederacy might have been willing to endure unending struggle in order to maintain was too murky and beclouded in its difference.

Even God seemed to be turned against the South. Indeed, a peculiar brand of theology suffused throughout many of the Southern churches, which more and more tugged at people's hearts and consciences, suggesting to them that they had violated God's will. A true depression settled into the psyches of the Southern people. They had long been praying for peace, but gradually the prayers shifted from being entreaties for peace with some tinge of satisfaction—peace at least in part on the South's own terms—to more and more being pining prayers for unadulterated peace, peace on any terms. Something had happened during the final winter of the war; something by early 1865 had rendered Southern morale beyond recovery, and even before the armies surrendered, the people were beaten.

SUGGESTED READINGS

Special Studies of Note

April '65: Confederate Covert Action in the American Civil War, by William A. Tidwell (Kent: Kent State University Press, 1995). Tidwell does some prodigious interpolation from the sources to arrive at his conclusions and has failed to convince a good many modern scholars, but it is patently certain that there *was* a Confederate Secret Service and there *indeed was* some Confederate covert action.

The Armies of U. S. Grant, by James R. Arnold (London: Arms and Armour Press, 1995), is very popularly written and bizarrely underpinned (even to the point of quoting and citing in footnotes material from markers in historical parks). Nonetheless, this is a respectable and insightful synthesis—perhaps even a brilliant one.

The Captain Departs: Ulysses S. Grant's Last Campaign, by Thomas M. Pitkin (Carbondale: Southern Illinois University Press, 1973), is a "must-read" for die-hard Grant buffs.

Civil War Command and Strategy: The Process of Victory and Defeat, by Archer Jones (New York: Free Press, 1992). This stream-of-consciousness extraction is a little hard to read.

Let Us Have Peace: U. S. Grant and the Politics of War and Reconstruction, 1861–1868, by Brooks D. Simpson (Chapel Hill: University of North Carolina Press, 1991). Simpson is the most insightful recent Grant scholar and will someday write a much better biography than the Pulitzer Prize–winning—but very inferior, especially from the military perspective—one by William S. McFeely.

Lincoln under Enemy Fire, by John H. Cramer (Baton Rouge: Louisiana State University Press, 1948), is short and great.

A Stillness at Appomattox, by Bruce Catton (Garden City, N.Y.: Doubleday, 1953). Though he had a slight pro-Northern bias, all of Catton's many books are readable, and most of them are useful to the military scholar. For this, the third volume of a history of the Federal army of the Potomac, he won a Pulitzer Prize.

A Study in Warfighting: Nathan Bedford Forrest and the Battle of Brice's Crossroads, by Parker Hills (Danville, Va.: Blue and Gray Education Society, 1996), is second in a series issued by the Blue and Gray Society, an outstanding new organization that conducts tours, seminars, and archival projects and works in support of battlefield preservation efforts as well as underwrites the series of scholarly monographs that includes this sparkling piece of work by a career National Guardsman.

Battle and Campaign Studies

Decision in the West: The Atlanta Campaign of 1864, by Albert Castel (Lawrence: University Press of Kansas, 1992), is a very long (and not easy) read but is well presented and important. Sprightly written in the first person—to convey a sense of immediacy—this prize-winning work is spectacularly revisionist and a "must" for correctly understanding the Atlanta campaign.

Into the Wilderness with the Army of the Potomac, by Robert Garth Scott (Bloomington: Indiana University Press, 1985), is a nice piece of work by a talented amateur historian.

Jubal Early's Raid on Washington: 1864, by B. Franklin Cooling (Baltimore: Nautical and Aviation Publishing, 1989). Civil War enthusiasts too often underestimate Cooling's keen abilities; his works deserve to be read much more than they are.

October 25th and the Battle of Mine Creek, by Lumir F. Buresh (Kansas City: Lowell Press, 1987), is a fine battle history by an able, dedicated, and unpretentious amateur historian.

Richmond Redeemed: The Siege at Petersburg, by Richard J. Sommers (Garden City, N.Y.: Doubleday, 1981). Like Castel on Atlanta, this is very long and not easy to read—but, also like Castel's work, this is a spectacular contribution to our understanding of the Civil War and is highly recommended for the truly serious.

The Road to Bristoe Station: Campaigning with Lee and Meade, August 1–October 20, 1863, by William D. Henderson (Lynchburg: Howard, 1987), is a good book on this little known campaign that was of more significance than is often realized.

Yankee Blitzkrieg: Wilson's Raid through Alabama and Georgia, by James P. Jones (Athens: University of Georgia Press, 1976), is a very important and underappreciated work.

Memoirs

"Co. Aytch," Maury Grays, First Tennessee Regiment; or, A Side Show of the Big Show, by Samuel R. Watkins (Chattanooga: Times Printing, 1900), is one of the greatest war narratives, marred only by an occasional tall tale inserted to enhance its humorous appeal. An absolutely marvelous tour de force in modern living history based on this memoir is available; a seventy-five-minute video featuring the acting of Bob

Funk and music of Bobby Horton can be purchased from Walkala Home Videos, P.O. Box 191, Parrish, AL 35580.

Four Years with General Lee, by Walter H. Taylor (1877; reprint, with an introduction by James I. Robertson Jr., Bloomington: Indiana University Press, 1962).

The Passing of the Armies, by Joshua Lawrence Chamberlain (Dayton: Morningside, 1974), is great on the war's ending.

Sherman and His Marches

Citizen Sherman, by Michael Fellman (New York: Random House, 1995). Fellman attempts to articulate the psychological nuances that caused Sherman to act the way he did. At times Fellman twists and squeezes too hard, trying to wring more out of his sources, but it is an admirable study and goes well with John Marszalek's more conventional biography.

The March to the Sea and Beyond: Sherman's Troops in the Savannah and Carolinas Campaigns, by Joseph T. Glatthaar (New York: New York University Press, 1985). Glatthaar is among the finest of younger Civil War historians, and his works shimmer.

Sherman: A Soldier's Passion for Order, by John F. Marszalek (New York: Free Press, 1993). If this is not the last word that needs to be written on Sherman, it is because Marszalek is a master historian but lacks the "poet's touch" perhaps needed.

Sherman's Forgotten Campaign: The Meridian Expedition, by Margie Riddle Bearss (Baltimore: Gateway Press, 1987), is a very fine book by the wife of the famous scholar Edwin C. Bearss.

Sherman's March through the Carolinas, by John G. Barrett (Chapel Hill: University of North Carolina Press, 1956), is an old, but distinguished, piece of work that is well worth reading.

When Sherman Came: Southern Women and the "Great March," by Katherine M. Jones (Indianapolis: Bobbs-Merrill, 1964).

Other Biographies

Braxton Bragg and Confederate Defeat, by Judith Lee Hallock, vol. 2 (Tuscaloosa: University of Alabama Press, 1991).

John Bell Hood and the War for Southern Independence, by Richard M. McMurry (Lexington: University Press of Kentucky, 1982).

Fiction

The Crater, by Richard Slotkin (New York: Athenaeum, 1980), is the fictional retelling of the Battle of the Crater on July 30, 1864, and has a great account of efforts by a regiment of ex-slaves.

The Gun-Bearer, by Edward A. Robinson and George A. Wall (New York: Robert Bonner, 1894), is the vivid fictional account of a young Union recruit in the Battles of Franklin and Nashville, offering excellent insight into the daily life of the average soldier.

The History of Rome Hanks and Kindred Matters, by Joseph Stanley Pennell (New York: Scribner, 1944), is a classic novel. Reviewers raved, some comparing it to work by Thomas Wolfe; it has a racy and ribald style.

Picture Books

George N. Barnard: Photographer of Sherman's Campaign, by Keith F. Davis (Kansas City: Hallmark Cards, 1990), is a beautiful as well as informative picture book. The original material for this work was put on display at a number of selected art museums around the country.

Grant and Lee: The Virginia Campaigns, 1864–1865, by William A. Frassanito (New York: Charles Scribner's, 1983). Frassanito's works are always stimulating and unusual.

The Full Embodiment of Military Professionalism

 ∽

Abraham Lincoln proved to be the last president to directly exercise military functions. (That is, Lincoln sometimes controlled the "how" as well as the "what." In World War II, to illustrate contrast, Franklin D. Roosevelt left the "hows" to the military men.) After the Civil War, but not until after, consistent heed was given in the United States to a real distinction between political competence and military competence. Only during the last two years of the Civil War did merit consistently outweigh political considerations for appointments to the higher army positions. Because there had previously been no generally accepted criteria for judging professional competence, it had thus been impossible to develop consistent standards for promotion based on merit. So true military professionalism, in its fullest sense, was not really possible in the United States until late in the Civil War.

While the U.S. Constitution contains a number of significant passages pertinent to the military, the document itself is somewhat vague concerning the nature of the military establishment. For example, the president's function as commander in chief is not precisely delineated. The framers mixed political and military matters and certainly expected that the president would exercise specific military functions. But, within the purely military sphere, this *could not* work well if professionalism were to flower.

The Work of the Army: 1865–1898

The nation demobilized very rapidly; the peacetime army was, however, maintained at levels significantly higher than ever before. The first postwar authorization established an army of slightly less than sixty thousand officers and men—nearly four times the size of the pre–Civil War army. It allocated for one full general (Grant), one lieutenant general (Sherman), five major generals (Halleck, Meade, Sheridan, Thomas, and Hancock), and ten brigadier generals (McDowell, Cooke, Pope, Hooker, Schofield, Howard, Terry, Ord, Canby, and Rosecrans). All of these post–Civil War Regular Army general officers were West Point graduates, save for Terry (who, of course, by this time had come to shine as a self-made professional); and almost all of them had been reasonably distinguished as students, save for Canby (who had graduated next to last in his class), but his long and successful career had well redeemed his lowly status as a completed cadet. As the years passed, however, the strength of the army diminished until it reached an average of around twenty-five thousand total personnel. Steadily, army expenditures declined from their Civil War peak of more than $1 billion per year to $35 million in 1871, and thereafter they hovered around that figure for the ensuing twenty-five years.

The Regular Army forces for the most part redeployed westward to participate in the Indian wars. Nearly all army personnel were stationed at one of the many scattered and far-flung posts, which had quite small garrisons. While the army was thus physically much isolated from the rest of society, the railroad and the telegraph kept it in meaningful touch nevertheless. Most notable, and especially in the carefully nurturing hands of some remarkable reform-minded officers, the prevailing atmosphere was a favorable one for further development of military professionalism.

Some blacks were retained in active service: not nearly as many as wished to continue, but nevertheless some. This was the first time in American history that blacks remained in the Regular Army during peace. These men would attain distinction in the West—where Indians gave them their distinctive nickname, meant to be a connotation of respect, "the Buffalo Soldiers." Eventually, blacks also won commissions in the new Regular Army—although slowly at first. Between 1870 and 1889 twenty-two black cadets won appointment to the U.S. Military Academy. In 1877 Henry O. Flipper became the Academy's first black graduate, to be followed by John H. Alexander in 1887 and Charles Young in 1889. (No other blacks graduated from West Point until 1936. Black troops, and officers, remained in racially segregated units until after World War II.)

Removing racial obstacles within the officer corps was not totally unakin to doing away with aristocratic privilege—hence, a crucial step toward achieving full professionalism.

The army's main duty, for the first twelve years following the Civil War, was occupation of the defeated South during Reconstruction—a difficult and trying duty. As long as martial law prevailed, the commanding generals of the five military districts into which the South was divided held sweeping power. Protecting the civil rights of the newly freed slaves was an ongoing and vexatious problem. Race relations were frequently a sticky matter. During the last half of 1865 and for the first months of 1866, the proportion of black troops to white troops in some parts of the South was three-to-one or even higher. There was scant precedent, and none at all of a precise nature, in the army's previous experience for the tasks it was now required to do: maintaining civil order, coping with property-ownership disputes, administering voter registration and election procedures, protecting federal tax officials, even—albeit only partially—suppressing the Ku Klux Klan, and helping with the apprehension of other criminals.

If the number of occupation troops was small, this did not mean that their legal power or influence was small. As states gradually gained readmission to the Union—that is, as their senators and representatives were reseated in Congress—the army lost its special authority. But the troops that remained in the readmitted states continued to be a significant symbol of federal authority and power. As Reconstruction came to a gradual end, and a formal end in 1877, the troops were not (nor were they ever) *fully* withdrawn from the South; some posts continued to be maintained.

The Indian wars of 1865–1890 differed from previous struggles, which dated from the earliest colonial times, mainly in scope and intensity. They constituted a final struggle by the Indians; there was nowhere left for them to be pushed. The Indians were faced with a fundamental choice: to surrender or fight; many chose to fight. Over all manner of terrain—which included plains, mountains, and deserts—and in all manner of drastically variant climates, there ensued much violent activity, ranging from guerrilla actions, skirmishes, pursuits, massacres, raids, campaigns, and battles. The ultimate key turned out to be logistics. The Indians were dependent on wild grass to feed their horses and were greatly limited in ability to campaign during winter. The Americans had grain and could continue relentlessly. Perhaps most significant of all, the buffalo were nearly rendered totally extinct. The process was speeded up after ever more extensive train tracks were completed. Sometimes trains stopped, to allow travelers to engage in a "recreation" that was nothing more than wanton slaughter.

The Indians' military viability was already sorely on the wane, when on June 25, 1876, between twelve and fifteen thousand of them did manage to achieve the spectacular annihilation of Lt. Col. George A. Custer's force of 230 men at the Battle of the Little Bighorn. News of the disaster shocked the nation, but it was the climax of the Indian wars. While the army before had been hampered by inadequate numbers of troops, thereafter huge numbers of soldiers were poured into the arena, and the Indians scattered. It was all downhill after that, until the final episode at the December 1890 Battle of Wounded Knee.

The Indian wars were very different from the Civil War. The Indians proved to be some of the world's best light cavalry, but the army's challenge was equally one of environment. The theater of war was either uninhabited or only sparsely settled. The distances were immense, causing much difficulty with supply, movement, and communication. Only those officers who approached their problems with a flexible and open mind were able to achieve noteworthy success. Too, those officers who had some respect for the Indians and who learned something of their ways, rather than those who regarded them as mere savages, became the best Indian fighters.

The Fuller Emergence of Military Professionalism in the Western World

In the early spring of 1992 the German American History Institute in Washington, D.C., sponsored a three-day symposium where a gathering of scholars from France, Germany, and the United States presented papers comparing and contrasting the American Civil War with the wars of German unification. Their conclusions suggested more contrast than comparison, but the four wars all did produce great lethality, were fought by huge and rapidly mobilized nonprofessional armies that were well managed by professional officers, and were characterized by efficient staff functioning.

During the later part of the nineteenth century, conditions grew propitious in several European countries as well as in the United States for refining military professionalism. Nowhere was this more so than in Germany—which emerged as the world's most thoroughly professional military power, and an immensely potent one. The last of the three so-called wars of German unification, the Franco-Prussian War, was an especially striking illustration that Prussia had achieved a new—and one that was desirable to emulate—standard.

Everywhere there appeared some variation on the general staff. In 1878 France at last established a true war academy, the Ecole Militaire Supérieure. The French also, along with the Italians, the Austrians, and to a certain extent the Russians, copied Germany's system of short-time active service for large numbers of citizens, with everyone spending a long period in the reserves. The United States was finally lured away from its historical reverence for and emulation of French military institutions; thenceforth, the Americans focused more interest on other countries, especially Prussia. Visibly reflecting this change, the Prussian-style spiked helmet actually became a part of the American soldier's dress uniform.

Near midcentury, a renewed wave of major military reform had commenced in Prussia, a state uniquely needful of having a strong military force, as she had no natural boundaries and her territories were widely scattered. But she was an economically poor state, so a permanent and very large army would have been prohibitively expensive. Nurturing capability of responding to emergency was the answer, and Prussia became the first country to introduce permanent universal service by a huge reserve force.

During the third, fourth, and fifth decades of the century, the Prussians achieved important improvements in training programs, basic equipment, artillery, and small arms. Indeed, Prussia led the world in the development and adaptation of modern and superior shoulder weaponry. In 1827 Johann Nikolaus von Dreyse had invented the muzzle-loading, and in 1836 the breech-loading, needle guns—so named because of their long slender firing pin.

Then, at midcentury the unification of Germany, and a subsequent stunning defeat of France, crowned all of Prussia's military achievement. In essence, the Prussian government and the Prussian military system became one and the same. A not totally off-the-mark joke illustrates: Prussia was not a country with an army, but an army with a country. German scientific experimentation proliferated, business prosperity flourished, and industry—which theretofore had lagged behind that of Britain and France—rapidly expanded. Banks, factories, railways, and modern cities sprang into existence.

In 1857 the regent, Prince William (who in 1861 would become King William I), named Helmuth von Moltke as chief of staff and Albrecht von Roon as minister of war. During the summer of 1858 Roon outlined the details for a general military-reform project. A number of political officeholders unleashed heated attacks on the military reforms, but in 1862 William found in Otto von Bismarck the civilian minister who would defy popular opinion, overthrow the parliament, and implement the military reforms.

The general staff rose to a new preeminence; and it would soon prove itself: in applying to the conduct of war a continuous intelligent study, providing commanders in the field with a constant flow of valid information and good advice. When the first major test came, Roon was able to put into the field a total of 1,183,389 officers and men—a force, as one French historian ruefully opined, unheard of since the legendary armies of Xerxes.

What might be termed the *Prussian system* was now in place. Huge Prussian armies could be mobilized rapidly, swiftly take the field, and operate with deadly precision. Railroads made an immense difference: Prussia's Central European location that had previously made her very vulnerable to more powerful and united neighbors now became an exploitable asset of interior lines. "Not by speeches and majority votes, are the great questions of the day decided," Bismarck asserted in an oft-quoted (and oft-misquoted) statement, "but by iron and blood." The German Empire was forged in the flame of the three wars that followed (in 1864, 1866, and 1870). Only the third one, the Franco-Prussian War, deserves some mention here.

A new age in warfare had dawned, and *this* the French had not perceived. The French continued to believe that a truly superior military officer was one who relied on his natural inherent gifts and did not need the advice and help of a staff. As a consequence, the French staff corps had actually regressed during the forty years preceding the Franco-Prussian War. By a tragic combination of bad luck, stupidity, and ignorance, France blundered into a war against what no one quite realized was the greatest military power that Europe had yet seen.

On August 6, 1870, the Germans achieved two victories: in the somewhat irrelevant Battle of Sprichern and in the Battle of Froeschwiller. In the first battle, the overly aggressive Gen. Karl Friedrich von Steinmetz attacked the French at Sprichern, where the enemy had not only a strong position but also greater numbers in supporting distance. The nearly daylong Prussian assaults failed conclusively, but the French inefficiently maneuvered their reserves, and those at hand became exhausted. A Prussian turning column then forced the French to withdraw. Meanwhile, at Froeschwiller, a much more spectacular— and significant—battle had been unfolding.

At the outset the French forces occupied a position so strong that their commander, Field Marshal Count Marie Edme Patrice Maurice de MacMahon, was fully confident that the Prussians would not attack at all. But they did. Officers proved unable to keep large masses of men in formation, and the fighting grew fragmented. Company-grade and noncommissioned officers played unprecedented roles in tactical direction. The French were at last threatened with envelopment and were forced to retreat, doing so only with great difficulty. MacMahon lost 11,000 killed and wounded and 9,000 prisoners—almost one-half of his command—while the Prussians lost 10,500.

This battle has impressed military historians as a landmark illustration of several significant lessons concerning evolving warfare. Cavalry on each side played little role. The French cuirassiers charged repeatedly but were stopped by bullets fired by assailants they could not see; not one French horseman got within a sabre's reach of any Prussian. The rifle dominated the battlefield; the era of shock action in the traditional sense was over. As in the American Civil War, the infantrymen's firepower was so potent that there seemed to be little or no use for the bayonet—close-quarter combat had been rendered a rarity. Last, the Prussian artillery proved of major, if not decisive, importance. This day, August 6, 1870, is said (by European-oriented military scholars) to have heralded the advent of a new age of applied technology in warfare.

The defeats of August 6 were not singularly catastrophic in determining the war's outcome, but they had far-ranging results. The two main French field armies were still quite strong, and had the Germans required say two or three months to recuperate from their costly victories—as indeed had been usual in earlier wars—the French might have been able to cope effectively with their situation. But the Germans did not require this interval of time: it took them only three days to recover. Further, the August 6 defeats were something of a final blow to Napoleon III. He was ill, and now he completely lost his nerve. He gave inconsistent commands and vacillated. The armies sluggishly commenced moving back toward the fortress of Metz. Napoleon—growing weary, and perhaps in panic—decided to turn control of operations over to Field Marshal François Achille Bazaine, who proceeded to prove that he had already risen quite above his level of competence. Bazaine ignored his staff, depriving himself of their help; and so both operational and supply arrangements for the tightly concentrated force promptly fell into great confusion.

Napoleon and Bazaine played into Moltke's hands. Bazaine, inefficient and slow, got trapped near Metz. To ensure that he remain sealed inside that place, on August 18 the Prussians fought the costly Battle of Gravelotte–St. Privat, where one elite Prussian unit of 30,000 infantrymen rashly charged frontally in formation and paid the price: 8,000 fell in approximately twenty minutes. But the result was just as the Prussian commanders intended: Bazaine, and his 173,000 men, were now bottled up. Napoleon, meanwhile, had made his way by railroad to Chalons to join the other French field army, 130,000 strong with 423 guns, under MacMahon. Moltke, learning of the enemy's route of march, jumped at the opportunity to exploit his interior lines and rapidly sent a force to engulf MacMahon's men near the Belgian frontier.

The September 2, 1870, debacle of Sedan resulted—the greatest disaster that French arms had *ever* suffered. "We have them in a mousetrap," Moltke exulted on the evening before the battle. MacMahon's second in command, Gen. Auguste Alexandre Ducrot, summed up the feelings of all the French generals who by now could perceive what lay in store for them. "We are," he ruefully said, "in a chamber pot, and we are about to be shat upon." U.S. Gen. Phil Sheridan, William Howard Russell (the *Times* correspondent from London), and a host of dignitaries and officers from Britain, Russia, and all over Germany joined the Prussian king to view the spectacular battle.

As Sheridan watched German troops storm over French positions on a far ridgeline, he was reminded of his own similar experience at Missionary Ridge seven years previous. He later wrote in his memoirs that the sight was one "of unsurpassed magnificence and sublimity." Sheridan made his own contribution to the Prussians' war effort: He noticed that French troops were moving to the German flank, and he predicted that French artillery would soon open up in support of the advance—Sheridan, the king, and the other dignitaries had best retire to a safer place. He was right! The Prussian officers were much impressed.

Remaining with the Prussians for six weeks, Sheridan got along well with them because his own predilections harmonized with their professionalism and attention to detail. If he had heard of Chief of Staff Helmuth von Moltke's previous assertion that the American Civil War had been a mere disorganized melee between armed mobs wandering through the woods, he did not speak of it. He was, however, not overawed by the Prussians and wrote home to President Grant that he did not think there was much there for Americans to learn. The Prussian infantry "was as fine as I ever saw," Sheridan wrote, but he felt that they had an easy time campaigning in the rich farmlands of France. How well might they have done in the much rougher conditions of northern Virginia, eastern Tennessee, and central Georgia, he perhaps mused to himself—and was not so sure of the answer. And, Sheridan thought that the Prussians inadequately hewed to the hard-war philosophy that he espoused. He suggested that the Prussians were "too humanitarian" in their treatment of the French population and coldly asserted to his European acquaintances that "Nothing should be left to the people but eyes, to lament the war!"

∾

Never, before Sedan, had gunfire been used with such precision; the French army dissolved. The Germans took 21,000 prisoners during the battle, and the remaining 83,000 at its conclusion—as well as Napoleon III himself. Two days later, in Paris, Napoleon III's regime was overthrown. (The Germans kept him prisoner until 1871, and then he joined his wife and son who had escaped to England; he died there in 1873.)

The war's outcome, in essence, had already been decided. Bazaine, still shut up in Metz, surrendered the Second French Army of 173,000 men on October 27, 1870. The Prussians laid siege to Paris, and when its food supplies became exhausted the city government surrendered on January 28, 1871. The fighting, however, continued until late May, while the "commune" was besieged. The formal end came with the Treaty of Frankfurt. France surrendered Alsace and Lorraine to Germany and agreed to pay an indemnity of 5 billion francs (about $1 billion dollars).

The war made Germany an empire and France a republic. France had necessarily withdrawn troops from Rome to fight in the war against Prussia, and this allowed the Italians to occupy Rome and complete formation of the Kingdom of Italy. Italy and Germany emerged as great powers, joining France, Austria-Hungary, and Russia in a five-way contest for European dominance. Britain attempted to maintain a balance of power among the countries. The remainder of the century—although there *were* ongoing international tensions—was the most peaceful period in modern European history.

Seven years later, as part of his world tour that he began shortly after leaving the presidency, U. S. Grant paid a visit to Germany and was received by Bismarck. Resplendent in dress uniform, Bismarck chatted at length with Grant about a general whom they both admired: Sheridan. Grant proclaimed that he believed Sheridan was as great a general as any who had ever lived. Bismarck praised Grant's wonderfully keen insight (and perhaps recalled Sedan when Sheridan had demonstrated his quick eye for military detail).

The next day Grant agreed—the only time he did so on the tour—to review a detachment of troops. During the review, Grant and Bismarck had a revealing conversation, the gist of which was reported by John Russell Young, a reporter for the *New York Herald,* who was one of Grant's traveling companions.

> "What always seemed so sad to me about your last great war was that you were fighting your own people," Bismarck opined. "That is always so terrible in wars, so very hard."
> "But it had to be done," replied Grant.
> "Yes," said Bismarck, "you had to save the Union just as we had to save Germany."

"Not only save the Union," responded Grant, "but destroy slavery."

"I suppose, however, the Union was the real sentiment, the dominant sentiment," inquired Bismarck.

"In the beginning, yes," said Grant, "but as soon as slavery fired upon the flag it was felt, we all felt, even those who did not object to slaves, that slavery must be destroyed."

Bismarck then said, "I suppose if you had had a large army at the beginning of the war it would have ended in a much shorter time."

Grant responded that "We might have had no war at all, but we cannot tell. . . . If we had had a large regular army, as it was then constituted, it might have gone with the South. . . . A great commander like Sherman or Sheridan even then might have organized an army and put down the rebellion in six months or a year, or, at the farthest, two years. But that would have saved slavery, perhaps, and slavery meant the germs of new rebellion. There had to be an end of slavery. Then we were fighting an enemy with whom we could not make a peace. We had to destroy him. No convention, no treaty was possible—only destruction."

"It was a long war," said Bismarck, "and a great work well done—and I suppose it means a long peace."

"I believe so," said Grant.

The U.S. Military Establishment in Late Century

After Reconstruction, and aside from the Indian wars, in other activities prior to the Spanish-American War, the U.S. Army became involved in a wide variety of noncombatant duties. It quelled several domestic disturbances. It was called upon to put down strikes by disgruntled workers in 1877 and in 1894. Army personnel occupied and administered affairs in Alaska, after its purchase in 1867 until Congress provided civil government, and later the army supported exploration expeditions in Alaska. The army also took primary responsibility for two of the four great geographic surveys conducted in the United States during the late nineteenth century.

There followed a number of technological and engineering achievements. The army organized and operated, from 1870 to 1891, the nation's first modern weather service. A number of construction projects occupied army personnel; most notable was the completion of the Washington Monument. Much work was done on rivers and harbors by the Army Corps of Engineers, and work also was done by army personnel on construction of coastal fortifications. The Signal Corps perfected field telegraphy. Army use of telephones was introduced experimentally in the late 1870s, and a field telephone was developed by 1889. The heliograph was introduced for use in the Southwest. The use of balloons by the army, which had been terminated during the Civil War, recommenced in the early 1890s, and there has been an unbroken continuance of army aviation ever since. And, last, the army medical department built the Army Medical Library into one of the great such institutions in the world.

After an army board examined more than one hundred weapons, the Model 1873 Springfield breech-loader was adopted as standard. This single-shot weapon used a .45-caliber cartridge. Then, in 1890, another board recommended adoption of the Danish .30-caliber bolt-action Krag Jorgensen rifle, which had a box magazine that held five cartridges. This was done in 1892, and the piece was issued throughout the Regular Army by 1897, though the reserves continued to use the 1873 Springfield. Automatic weapons and much more potent artillery pieces combined with the new shoulder weaponry to enhance firepower far beyond Civil War standards. All this made the tactical task of "crossing the deadly ground" in attacks even more of an impenetrable problem. Much thought and effort went into devising an efficacious tactical system, but essentially the problem remained unsolved.

Following the end of the Civil War, a virtually institutionalized "business pacifism" prevailed in the United States, fostering a potent hostility toward the military establishment. A number of states even denied the right to vote to those who served in the Regular Army. Despite all of this, the officer corps came to be more and more a quintessential reflection of middle-class America, for they were a true cross section thereof. Representative of everyone, the officer corps was affiliated with no one; it was a diminutive mirror image of the nation itself, and it collectively manifested a potent inclination to develop professionally.

These years proved to be quite fertile, creative, and formative ones for the armed forces. A crucial key was that the process of nurturing professionalism did not require a great outlay of money. William T. Sherman cautiously and scrupulously avoided contact with Congress when in 1881 he set up the School of Application for Infantry and Cavalry at Fort Leavenworth, asserting it required no additional funding beyond "ordinary garrison expenses." Hence, Sherman avoided political interference. Although it took some time for the school to develop as Sherman desired, it eventually did fulfill his hopes.

William T. Sherman as Commanding General

Sherman served as commanding general of the army for almost fifteen years, from 1869 to 1883, longer than anyone other than Winfield Scott. The historian Charles Royster has suggested that Sherman was "perhaps the most widely known, most durably famous, most often applauded American of his time."

Beyond doubt, Sherman was the leading American military personality for the post–Civil War generation. Committed to preserving the lessons of the Civil War, he was among the first of the leading generals to publish his memoirs, a two-volume work written in 1873 and 1874 that contains much thoughtful commentary about the future of warfare. Although John F. Marszalek, Sherman's most thorough biographer, has opined that "there is little to indicate that *reform* was his purpose," Sherman nonetheless "had a firm commitment to military professionalism," and he facilitated its development, perhaps mainly by supporting the work of other younger, reform-minded officers.

In Sherman's most passionate post–Civil War involvement, he became a great champion of military education at all levels. He carefully nourished and defended the Artillery School at Fort Monroe, which had been reestablished in 1868. Treasuring West Point for its stress upon discipline and training, he watched paternally over the U.S. Military Academy—which he regarded as being most significant as a repository of military memory and as a source of military ambition, rather more so than for its technical instruction in engineering. He loved West Point and went back there for nostalgic visits whenever he could, and he insisted that it was "the best Military College in the civilized world." But he feared that the enemies of the Academy might still someday prevail in Congress and abolish the school. If that happened then, all the more, the army would have to depend on its own schools, such as his favorite "pet," the School of Application for Infantry and Cavalry at Fort Leavenworth. Last, Sherman approved of and encouraged various professional institutions that could supplement the army's school system. These included a professional association (the Military Service Institution of the United States, which had as its primary purpose the promotion of writing and discussion about military science and military history) and numerous professional military journals.

Most important was the tone that Sherman set for the army. Sherman was thoroughly imbued with the professional military ideal and ethic. He had deplored the use of the army to support Republican state administrations in the South during Reconstruction, and he would object to the notion, as it arose several times later in the century, that the army should be used as a police force. This, he assiduously asserted, was not within the true soldierly vocation. Also, Sherman steadfastly rejected his own involvement in politics. Indeed, after 1856 and for the rest of his life, he never even voted. Aside from "War is hell," which is not quite one of his precise quotes, Sherman's most famous utterance concerned the U.S. presidency: "I will not accept if nominated, and will not serve if elected." Sherman believed the office destroyed those who held it, but ultimately it was his total espousal of military professionalism that explained his mind-set. Sherman felt that to exchange being commanding general for being president would have been a demotion!

Emory Upton—Military Reformer

One of Sherman's protégés, and the most influential officer working in behalf of army reform during the post–Civil War years, was Emory Upton. His first thoughts were directed toward refining tactics. The great lesson of the Civil War, he was convinced, was the unsuitability of the long, rigid line, and he believed that a new formal tactical system was needed. To employ three ranks, in the age of breech-loading, was no longer wise: one rank not only would suffice but would reduce casualties as well. American tactics should not thenceforth be based on the French system. Upton substituted "wheeling by fours"—the key to his drill—for the French facings and inversions that were necessary in three-rank tactics. Companies would be divided into groups of four men, and captains could form lines in any direction by ordering the "fours" forward, left, or right. This would evolve into subdividing companies into platoons and squads. On August 1, 1867, the War Department adopted Upton's system both for the army and for the militia.

The system made it easier to quickly extend a line of battle by throwing out more skirmishers, the greatest contribution of Upton's new scheme. Through this, Upton consciously aimed at facilitating adjustment to topographical variations. Upton prescribed new training techniques for skirmishers and conceived the method of fire and maneuver. A battalion would divide into two parts: one the fighting line, the other a reserve. The fighting line would also divide into two parts: one active as skirmishers, the other in support. Skirmishers would move forward by leaps and bounds, maintaining a constant harassing fire. Reserves would come up in column, following the advance of the skirmishers. When the skirmishers reached within about 150 yards of the position under attack, the reserves would be about 50 yards behind. One company of reserves would deploy from column into line and charge. If the attack faltered, the other company would do the same thing and thrust as far as it could beyond the first. The two charging companies would continue to advance by leaps and bounds until the position was taken.

In 1870 President Grant selected Upton to be commandant of cadets at West Point. Upton spent the next five years at the Academy, diligently reading and rewriting. In 1873 he published his revised *Infantry Tactics*. The system was also soon assimilated and applied to cavalry and artillery. Continuing to work on refinement, Upton published three subsequent editions during his lifetime. He never lost sight of his vision that it would be firepower, not the bayonet, and certainly not the saber, that would decide future battles.

Upton went on a world tour during 1875 and 1876 to study the world's major armies. Returning filled with ideas, he spent the next five years of his life—the last of his years as it turned out, for he committed suicide in 1881— dedicated to army reform. Upton published his second book in 1878, *The Armies of Asia and Europe*. He never ceased attempting to induce the United States Congress to adopt a scheme of reforms based on the Prussian model. He urged establishing advanced military schools, a comprehensive and improved system of efficiency reports for the ongoing evaluation of officer merit, compulsory retirement, and prerequisite examinations for promotion or appointment to the staff corps.

While Upton was not successful in selling what ultimately became his most favored idea—large-scale peacetime preparedness—Congress did respond favorably to many of his proposals. In 1870 Congress prohibited any officer on active service from holding any civil office. In 1878 Congress established firm guidelines concerning necessary educational processes for entering the officer corps. Legislation in 1862 and 1870 had provided for voluntary retirement or by compulsion at the discretion of the president; now in 1882 a law requiring mandatory retirement at the age of sixty-four was enacted.

Upton's magnum opus, *The Military Policy of the United States,* was not published until 1904, twenty-three years after his death; but it had long circulated in manuscript form and had been read by many influential officers. It was endorsed by Sherman, and it became something of a Bible for the Regular Army. Although the work was a somewhat twisted misuse of history—the attempt was made to demonstrate that all previous military policy in the nation had been too little, too late—Upton passionately asserted that much needless suffering had occurred, wars had been larger, longer, and more costly than necessary, and only luck had prevented much worse disasters. Upton wished to demonstrate that only a professional army—not civilians in arms—was capable of defending the nation. He had no objection to a militia as such; indeed, in his scheme a large militia would play an essential role. Militia, he asserted, *could* be effective against a regular enemy force but *only if* it was well led and adequately equipped and supported; and the key was that Upton wanted the reserve force to be under national, not state, control—and hence managed professionally.

So, while Upton failed during his lifetime to see all of his ideas implemented, he did achieve much success—and many more of his ideas were later adopted. The most immediate—and destined to be long-lived—institutional reforms brought about by Sherman and Upton were in military education. Quite significant was the Army Staff College at Fort Leavenworth, to which the Infantry and Cavalry school gave birth. Here at last in America was an elemental beginning for the formal training of higher staffs. Its dominating figure was Arthur L. Wagner, who taught there from 1886 to 1897 and subsequently became its commandant. Wagner, himself an exemplary military scholar, insisted on high standards of instruction and performance. His books, *Campaign of Koniggratz* and *Organization and Tactics,* were the best writings on military analysis done by an American between Upton's writings and World War I.

Conclusion

The work of Sherman and Upton in the 1870s and 1880s was carried on in the decades that followed by a second generation of reformers, especially Tasker H. Bliss, Arthur L. Wagner, Samuel M. B. Young, and William H. Carter. All were graduates of the Academy, and all had learned much from observing and studying foreign military institutions. The American version of military professionalism evolved as different from that of other countries in that it sprang entirely from the officers themselves; European military professionalism was more the spawning of sociopolitical forces from society at large.

By the later part of the nineteenth century, it had become certain that military professionalism had arrived to stay; and, while it would continue to evolve, it would surely never change dramatically into something *entirely* different. By definition, military professionalism is based on certain postulates concerning the human condition. Chief among these is that while permanent peace is to be devoutly desired and sought however practicable, future wars are inevitable. It is essential to prepare for them; and, in the modern industrial world, only a professional military structure can do this effectively.

Meanwhile, it is right to say that *some* of the lessons of the Civil War had *not* been learned (so, of course, neither had they been passed on) by those who participated in it. To a considerable and distorting extent those lessons were overshadowed by the overwhelming victory of Prussia over France in 1870. Certainly the story of World War I would have been different if the American Civil War—and not the short Franco-Prussian War—had been in the minds of the high commanders. But perhaps that great, bloody, and indecisively static conflict (like the Vietnam War would become in *its* aftermath) provided a necessary catalyst for some keen historical retrospection.

It is striking that the British theorist Basil Liddell Hart, in attempting to prescribe how a repetition of the bloody stalemate of the western front from 1914 to 1918 might be avoided in a future war, used Sherman's campaign of 1864 as a model of how commanders might overcome the primacy of the defense. Furthermore, in the years before World War II both Heinz Guderian (arguably "the father of blitzkrieg") and George S. Patton were influenced by Liddell Hart's interpretation of Sherman's campaign as the epitome of what he called "the indirect approach."

If it is true, as the Sandhurst professor William McElwee has written, that the lessons of the American Civil War were not to be put into practice with ruthless clarity and success until the battle of El Alamein in 1942, it is also worth noting that beginning in the mid-1930s Robert E. Lee's great biographer, Douglas Southall Freeman, was invited to make a series of speeches on the nature of leadership at the Army War College, and he continued to do so regularly until his death in 1953. During World War II more than one American general was known to be fond of reading Freeman's *Lee's Lieutenants: A Study in Command;* and Harry S. Truman much enjoyed T. Harry Williams's *Lincoln and His Generals*—even writing the professor an appreciative commentary. The lessons of history may not always be heeded, but they are *there,* to be heeded by those who will. The Civil War well may be forever a topic of both interest and importance.

SUGGESTED READINGS

The student's attention is called again to the works listed following the Prologue as well as those listed below:

Special Studies on Reconstruction

Army Generals and Reconstruction: Louisiana, 1862–1877, by Joseph G. Dawson III (Baton Rouge: Louisiana State University Press, 1982). Another of the thirty-six "Wee Harry's"—doctoral students of T. Harry Williams—Dawson does good work.

The Army in Texas during Reconstruction, by William L. Richter (College Station: Texas A&M University Press, 1987). Still another "Wee Harry," Richter resigned a college professorship with which he was frustrated, in somewhat of a colorful flourish, and moved to Tucson to make a living shoeing horses . . . and—the scholarly world rejoices—to write.

The United States Army and Reconstruction, 1865–1877, by James E. Sefton (Baton Rouge: Louisiana State University Press, 1967), pioneered the topic and tells much about the army's experiences. A separate study, however, for each state seems called for, and only a few have been completed.

The Impact and Relevance of the Civil War

The Art of War: Waterloo to Mons, by William McElwee (Bloomington: Indiana University Press, 1974), has a good brief discussion of the impact of the American Civil War on European military thought.

The Military Intellectuals in Britain, 1918–1939, by Robin Higham (New Brunswick: Rutgers University Press, 1966), provides insight on the larger and transcendent significance of Sherman's campaign.

The Military Legacy of the Civil War, by Jay Luvaas (Chicago: University of Chicago Press, 1959), is a very important and informative book and is probably ripe for revision.

On the Road to Total War: The American Civil War and the German Wars of Unification, 1861–1871, edited by Stig Förster and Jorg Nagler (Washington, D.C.: German Historical Institute, forthcoming). Some of the comparisons may seem a bit bizarre, but the papers were very interesting when read.

The American Experience

Crossing the Deadly Ground: United States Army Tactics, 1865–1899, by Perry D. Jamieson (Tuscaloosa and London: University of Alabama Press, 1994). No one is a keener student of tactics than Jamieson.

"Loyalty and Expertise: The Transformation of the Nineteenth-Century American General Staff and the Creation of the Modern Military Establishment," an unpublished Ph.D. dissertation by William R. Roberts (Johns Hopkins University, 1979), is available from University Microfilms, 300 North Zeeb Road, Ann Arbor, MI 48106. This interesting dissertation emphasizes the continuity of American military reform and shows that what is sometimes depicted as having been achieved suddenly in 1903 by Secretary of War Elihu Root actually closely resembled earlier staff-reform proposals.

Memoirs of General W. T. Sherman, by William Tecumseh Sherman, with notes by Charles Royster (Camp Hill, Pa.: Library of America, 1990). Sherman had a graceful way with words and was always entertaining.

Sheridan: The Life and Wars of General Phil Sheridan, by Roy Morris Jr. (New York: Random House, 1992), is a first-rate biography of the man destined to succeed Sherman as commanding general, by the able editor of the popular magazine *America's Civil War.*

Soldiers and Scholars: The U.S. Army and the Uses of Military History, 1865–1920, by Carol Reardon (Lawrence: University Press of Kansas, 1990).

Upton and the Army, by Stephen E. Ambrose (Baton Rouge: Louisiana State University Press, 1964), is a good and important book that will undoubtedly be fully superseded by the doctoral dissertation now being completed by David A. Fitzpatrick under the direction of John Shy at the University of Michigan.

The View from Officers' Row: Army Perceptions of Western Indians, by Sherry L. Smith (Tucson: University of Arizona Press, 1990).

The Franco-Prussian War

The Franco-Prussian War, by Michael Howard (New York: Dorset Press, 1961), is the singular classic on the topic.

Moltke: A Biographical and Critical Study, by William O'Connor Morris (New York: Haskel House, 1971).

Final Food for Thought

Douglas Southall Freeman on Leadership, edited (with commentary) by Stuart W. Smith (Shippensburg, Pa.: White Mane, 1993), is a wonderful and valuable book—a true treasure for both historians and students of leadership.

History of the United States Army, by Russell F. Weigley (New York: Macmillan, 1967), is a classic by a master of the genre.

The Search for Order, 1877–1920, by Robert H. Wiebe (New York: Hill and Wang, 1967). While not at all a military history, this book describes the rise of the concept of professionalism in other occupations in American society, and it delineates the army within the context of the times.

And Some Things Just for Fun

The Blue and Gray in Black and White, by Sparky Rucker and Rhonda Rucker (Chicago: Flying Fish Records, 1992). This compact disk, recorded by a wonderfully talented interracial couple, is the single best modern performance of Civil War–era music. And if you ain't heard it yet, you have a rare treat coming when you do.

The Guns of the South, by Harry Turtledove (New York: Ballantine Books, 1992). The picture on the cover says it all: a computer-enhanced portrait of Robert E. Lee holding an AK-47—guns supplied to the South by time-traveling South Africans. Despite the far-fetched premise, this is a great and insightful novel—really, it should be *must* reading for all truly devoted students of the war.

If the South Had Won the Civil War, by Mackinley Kantor (New York: Bantam, 1961). One of the funniest of all pieces of Civil War fiction, this one provides a few hours of high hilarity in fanciful pseudohistory, covering from the conclusion of the war to the time of the Centennial—when the separated countries reunited.

"That Was the War That Was," by Thomas L. Connelly (*The Journal of Mississippi History* 30 [1968]: 123–34), is the text of a hilarious speech delivered by Connelly at a state historical society convention.

Will Success Spoil Jeff Davis? by T. Lawrence Connelly (New York: McGraw Hill, 1963). The late quite-knowledgeable E. B. Long found this one "in bad taste," so sensitive readers be warned, but it is a very funny spoof on the Civil War Centennial, Round Tables, reenactors, and relic collectors.

GLOSSARY

Army, or Field army: A large, independent body of troops organized for combat, comprised of two or more corps and commanded by a general-grade officer (in the Union by a major general and in the Confederacy by a full general).

Battalion: A military unit of two to ten companies if infantry, or two to six batteries if artillery.

Battery: An artillery unit of men, equipment that possesses and services two to six cannons, and horses or mules.

Breastwork: Hastily arranged defensive protection. If strengthened and improved over time, they become fortifications.

Brevet: A system of honorary promotion, wherein an individual may be advanced in rank unofficially and allowed to receive the honors due the higher rank, including wearing the insignia, but does not (unless, in some circumstances, if he actively serves in a position calling for the higher rank) receive the higher pay that would have come if the promotion had been official and not brevet.

Brigade: A unit of troops, commanded usually by a brigadier general. In the Civil War, a brigade usually consisted of two to five regiments.

Cannon: A field gun, an artillery piece, designed to hurl projectiles at high velocities through maximal trajectories.

Carbine: A diminutive version of a larger prototype shoulder weapon, usually preferred for use by cavalrymen, but too light for the hard use and sometime close-quarter fighting done by infantrymen.

Coehorn: A type of mortar named for its Dutch inventor, Baron Menno van Coehoorn (who lived from 1641 to 1704). A small-sized mortar, it was usually mounted on a block of wood to which handles were attached, allowing portability.

Company: A unit of troops, usually commanded by a captain. In the Civil War, a company included approximately one hundred men.

Company-grade officers: Lieutenants and captains.

Concealment: A partial (or total) state of safety from visual observation by an enemy. Concealment does not ipso facto provide cover. (*See also* Cover.)

Cordon: Literally, it means "ribbon." A defensive array of troops and material arranged in such a manner as to attempt to hold and secure an extended front, or line.

Corps: A unit of troops commanded by a general-grade officer (usually in the Union army a major general and in the Confederate army a lieutenant general). In the Civil War, a corps usually consisted of two to five divisions (Confederate corps tended to be larger than Federal corps).

Cover: A partial (or total) state of enjoying physical protection from incoming enemy fire. (*See also* Concealment.)

Crest. *See* Topographical crest; Military crest.

Dead space: A part of an area over which an assault may be made, where geographic conditions (usually a physical dip in the ground) provide a measure of cover to the assaulting force. Thus, when in a defensive array, it is best to avoid having dead space close to one's front, whenever possible.

Division: A unit of troops commanded by a general-grade officer (usually a major general). In the Civil War, a brigade usually consisted of two to five brigades.

En cordon. *See* Cordon.

Enfilade, or Enfilade fire: A volume of fire from one gun (but usually from a mass of guns) wherein the long axis of the beaten zone corresponds with the long axis of the target area. A beaten zone always tends to be elliptical in shape, because more rounds will fall long or short than will fall wide in either direction. If, for example, a line of troops encountered incoming fire upon their position and that fire was coming from a direction whereby the majority of the bullets falling was mostly onto the same area through which the troops stretched, then the fire would be enfilade.

Field-grade officers: Majors and colonels.

Friction: A term used by the military theorist Karl von Clausewitz (who lived from 1780 to 1831) to name the collective things and incidents, foreseeable or unforeseeable, that can go wrong during a planned military operation or battle that would cause a military commander to either alter and refine the original plan or cancel and extricate, if possible.

Fundamental principles of war. *See* Principles of war.

G-1: Section of a general staff in charge of managing personnel procurement, assignment, and welfare.

G-2: Section of a general staff in charge of managing military intelligence and security.

G-3: Section of a general staff in charge of managing, planning, and operations.

G-4: Section of a general staff in charge of all logistical matters.

General-grade officers: Generals. In the Union army, they were identified by rank insignia of one, two, or three stars: brigadier general, major general, and lieutenant general. In the Confederate army, there were four grades of general, though all wore the same insignia: three stars surrounded by a wreath.

General staff: A group of officers and their assistants charged with providing needed and useful help and assistance to a military commander of general-grade rank. (*See also* G-1; G-2; G-3; G-4.)

Grenade: A hand-held, and hand-thrown, bomb.

Howitzer: A field gun with a medium-length tube (sometimes chambered inside the barrel), designed to hurl projectiles at medium-muzzle velocities through midranged trajectories. For example, it has higher-angled and shorter-range fire than a cannon but lesser-angled and longer-range fire than a mortar.

Logistics: The aspect of military art and science dealing with the procurement, maintenance, and transportation of military material, facilities, and personnel.

Military crest: The most advantageous high point on a hill or ridge, whereby maximally effective fire can be directed toward the front with a minimal amount of dead space.

Mines: Explosive devices (called torpedoes in the Civil War era) designed to be used either underwater to damage vessels or buried in sand or dirt and aimed at killing or wounding personnel.

Mortar: A relatively short-tubed field gun designed to hurl projectiles at low-muzzle velocities through extremely high trajectories (so as to fire over walls or other obstacles but at relatively short distances).

Operations: The act of placing and maneuvering troops toward and on a battlefield. Also includes logistics, planning, intelligence gathering, and security measures.

Principles of war: Fundamental rules that underlie wise and prudent exercise of military command. The United States currently inculcates nine principles of war: objective, offensive, mass, maneuver, unity of command, economy of force, security, simplicity, and surprise.

Redan: A small defensive work with two faces that form a salient angle that projects outward toward the enemy.

Redoubt: A small, enclosed defensive work; a secure place.

Regiment: A unit of troops, usually commanded by a colonel. In the Civil War, a regiment consisted of five to ten companies.

Rifling: Spiral grooves cut into the inside of a gun bore that cause a projectile to rotate about its long axis and travel through a longer and truer trajectory when fired.

Strategy: The science and art of employing the political, economic, psychological, and military forces and might of a nation, or group of nations, to afford the maximum support of adopted policies. The science and art of military command exercised to meet an enemy in combat under maximally advantageous conditions.

Tactics: The science and art of arranging and arraying troops in combat. The actual conduct of troops and the manner of using weaponry and equipment during a battle.

Topographical crest: The highest point on a hill or ridge. The topographical crest is almost never the same as the military crest.

Torpedoes: What Civil War–era military men called mines.

INDEX

Abatis, 216, 223. *See also* Fortifications
Aberdeen, Miss., 195
Abolition, 37, 154, 156
Airpower. *See* Balloons
Albuquerque, N.Mex., 62
Alexander, E. Porter, 108–9
Alexander, John H., 246
Allen's Farm, Battle of, 88
Alma, Battle of the, 17
Alsop's Farm, 212
Amelia Court House, Va., 237
American Revolution, 42, 228
Ammunition, 2, 12, 17, 37–40, 45, 94, 107, 134, 148, 159, 203, 232–33, 237, 255
Anaconda Plan, 32
Anderson, Ephraim, 134
Anderson, Richard, 116, 118–19
Anderson, Robert, 46–47
Andersonville, Ga., 162
Antietam, Battle of, 95–99, 106
Apache Canyon. *See* La Glorieta Pass, Battle of
Appomattox campaign, 237–38
Arkansas, 48, 64, 168
Armies, 46, 206
Armistead, Lewis A., 149
Army aviation. *See* Balloons
Army Corps of Engineers, 254
Army Medical Library, 255
Army of Northern Virginia, 92, 99, 120, 174, 211, 221; reorganized, 121, 150, 174; Appomattox campaign, 237
Army of Tennessee, 72–73, 100, 105, 132, 223, 231; Nashville campaign, 228
Army of the Cumberland, 103, 132, 169, 187, 210
Army of the Gulf, 131
Army of the James, 174, 217, 231
Army of the Ohio, 101, 210
Army of the Potomac, 55, 81, 89, 92, 106, 113–14, 118, 187, 206, 208, 216, 237
Army of the Tennessee, 189, 210
Army of Virginia, 91
Army Staff College at Fort Leavenworth, 259
Army War College, 260

Army Weather Service, 254
Arnold, James R., 207
Arsenals, 37–39
Artillery, 40–42, 198, 233, 255, 256, 258; First Bull Run, 50; Fort Henry, 67; Shiloh, 70–71; Malvern Hill, 88–90; reorganization of, in Army of Northern Virginia, 92–93; Second Bull Run, 93–94, 121; Harper's Ferry, 96; Fredericksburg, 108–9; Chancellorsville, 119, 121; Vicksburg, 129, 134; Gettysburg, 144–49; Battery Wagner, 159; Missionary Ridge, 190–91; Brice's Cross Roads, 201–5; Spotsylvania, 214; Bald Hill, 221; Rockfish Gap, 232; Franco-Prussian War, 251–53. *See also* Weaponry
Athens, Ala., 90
Atlanta, Ga., 170, 218, 220–24, 225
Atlanta campaign, 210–12, 214–15
Auerstadt, Battle of, 4
Austria, 146, 249
Austria-Hungary, 253
Averasborough, N.C., 235

Badges. *See* Divisional badges
Balaklava, Battle of, 18–19, 129
Bald Hill, Battle of, 221–23
Balloons, 56, 254
Baltimore and Ohio Railroad, 48, 164
Banks, Nathaniel P., 105, 131, 183, 206; Peninsula campaign, 82; Valley campaign, 84–85; Second Bull Run, 92; Chickasaw Bayou campaign, 128; Red River campaign, 199–200
Banks Ford, 111
Bastion, 217. *See also* Fortifications
Battery E, Massachusetts Artillery, 147
Battery Wagner, 159–60
Battle above the Clouds, 189
Bayonet, 44, 258; Chancellorsville, 119; Gettysburg, 145; Battery Wagner, 159; Franco-Prussian War, 251. *See also* Weaponry
Bazaine, Francois Achille, 251, 253

Beauregard, Pierre Gustave Toutant, 100, 152, 185; Mexican War, 15; Fort Sumter, 46–48; Shiloh, 69–70, 72
Beaver Dam Station, 210
Beech Grove, Battle of, 66
Bell, Tyree H., 203
Belmont, Mo., 61
Bentonville, Battle of, 235–36
Beringer, Richard E., 36, 239
Beverly Ford, Va., 141
Big Black River, Battle of, 133
Bismarck, Otto von, 249–50, 253–54
Black Hawk War, 64
Black Horse Cavalry, 50
Black Republicans, 29
Black troops, 156–61, 163, 180, 234, 246–47
Black Warrior River, 233
Bliss, Tasker H., 259
Blitzkrieg, 260
Blockade running, 39
Bloody Angle, 212, 213
Bloody Lane, 98
Blue and Gray Education Society, 214
Booneville, Miss., 201–2
Border states, 30
Bragg, Braxton, 100, 101–3, 168, 192; Second Seminole War, 11; Mexican War, 14–15; Stones River, 103–5; Tullahoma campaign, 131–32; after Stones River, 132; Chickamauga, 169–72, 187; Missionary Ridge, 190–92
Brandy Station, Battle of, 141, 161
Breastworks. See Fortifications
Breckinridge, John C., 103, 105
Brice's Cross Roads, Battle of, 136, 167, 200–205
Bridges, 97, 108. See also Pontoons
Brigade tactics, 44
Bristoe Station campaign, 186–87
Britain, 6, 17–20, 253; South expects aid from, 31, 38, 42; weapons from, 38, 166; Franco-Prussian War, 252
Brutality, 36–37
Buchanan, Franklin, 219
Buckner, Simon Boliver, 65, 67
Buell, Don Carlos, 64, 65, 68, 101–2, 103
Buena Vista, Battle of, 14
Buffalo, 247–48
Buford, John, 143
Bull Run, First Battle of, 10, 16–27, 48–52, 72, 162, 174
Bull Run, Second Battle of, 92–95, 140

Bummers, 227
Burgess, Lauren Cook, 135–37
Burnside, Ambrose E., 72, 106–12, 113–14, 156, 162, 170, 206, 209, 210; Second Bull Run campaign, 92; Antietam campaign, 95, 97–98; Fredericksburg, 107–11; Roanoke Island, 162; Department of the Ohio, 188
Burnside Bridge. See Bridges; Pontoons
Butler, Benjamin F., 39, 159, 163, 174, 183, 206–7, 217
Byers, Samuel H. M., 230–31

Cadets, 246. See also Schools; West Point
Calhoun, John C., 6, 9, 11–12
Campaigns. See specific names
Canby, Edward R. S., 62, 157, 246
Canister, 40, 94, 148. See also Ammunition
Cannon, 41–42, 67, 198. See also Double-barreled cannon; Weaponry
Canton, China, 42
Cape Fear River, 174, 231
Cape Hatteras, 57
Carbine, 39, 106–7, 141, 232–33. See also Weaponry
Cardigan, Earl of, 129
Carolinas, 228, 230–31
Carter, William H., 259
Cartridge. See Ammunition
Case shot, 40. See also Ammunition
Casey, Silas, 44
Cashier, Albert D. J., 135
Casualties. See Losses
Causes of war, 29
Cavalry, 39, 144, 231–33, 237, 248, 258; Balaklava, 19; Army of Northern Virginia, 92–93, 141; Chickasaw Bayou, 128; Brandy Station, 140–41; Chickamauga, 170; Brice's Cross Roads, 202–3; Spotsylvania, 212; Appomattox, 238; Franco-Prussian War, 251
Cedar Mountain, Battle of, 92
Celtic culture, 31
Cemetery Hill, 144
Cemetery Ridge, 144, 146–50
Cerro Gordo, Battle of, 15, 43, 53
Chamberlain, Joshua Lawrence, 145, 174
Chambersburg, Pa., 99, 143
Champion's Hill, Battle of, 133
Chancellorsville, campaign and Battle of, 113–21
Chantilly, Battle of, 95
Chapultepec, Battle of, 16, 147

Charleston, S.C., 174, 196–97
Charleston Harbor, 46
Chattanooga, Battle and siege of, 187–89
Chattanooga, Tenn., 100, 169–70, 172, 176, 187–89
Cheatham, Benjamin F., 172, 221, 223
Chesnut, Mary, 60
Chickamauga, campaign and Battle of, 125, 169–73, 176, 187
Chickasaw Bayou, campaign and Battle of, 127–29
Chippewa, Battle of, 7, 67
Citadel, 34, 46
City Point, Va., 43, 219–20
Civilians, 92, 236, 239–40; of Vicksburg, 137; Gettysburg campaign, 142; and black troops, 159; and Grant, 207; and Sherman's marches, 230
Clausewitz, Karl von, 5–6, 221
Coastal fortifications. See Fortifications
Coehorn, Baron Menno van, 41
Coehorn mortar. See Mortar; Weaponry
Cold Harbor, Battle of, 216
Colt, Samuel, 42
Colt Firearms Company, 38, 173
Columbia, S.C., 230–31
Columbus, Ga., 234–35
Column, 45
Combat power, 201
Combined arms, 167
Command and control, 34, 45, 70, 183
Committee on Conduct. See Joint Committee to Examine the Conduct of the War
Communications, 97, 100, 226
Company G, Ninety-fifth Illinois Infantry, 135–36
Confederate Secret Service Corps, 43, 219–20
Confederate States of America: formation, 29, 101; military mobilization, 31, 35; strategy, 31–32; Military Department System, 34, 152–53; Congress, 35, 48, 59; nationalism, 36, 239–40; factories, 39; experimentation, 41–43; Secret Service of, 43, 219–20; Provisional Government, 46–47; military establishment, 58–60, 87; naval strength, 130; response to black soldiers, 160–61; continuing viability, 164–76; builds submarines, 196–98; government flees Richmond, 237; capitulation, 239
Connelly, Thomas L., 47, 106, 152
Conscription, 31, 58, 156–57, 177
Containing force, 70

Contreras, Battle of, 16
Cooke, Philip St. George, 81, 246
Cooper, Samuel, 58, 64
Corbin's Bridge, 212
Cordon defense, 65–68
Corinth, Miss., 68, 71–72, 103
Corps organization, 71–73, 81–82, 92–93
Corregidor, 96
Couch, Darius N., 119
Courtney, Thomas E., 43
Cracker line, 188–89
Crater, Battle of the, 216
Crimean War, 9, 17–22, 31, 42, 49, 54
Crittenden, George B., 66
Crittenden, Thomas L., 170, 172
Crocker, Marcellus Monroe, 207
Cross Keys, Battle of, 85
Cuirassiers, 251
Cumberland River, 65–66, 229
Current, Richard N., 48
Custer, George A., 232, 248

Dahlgren gun, 198
Davenport, Va., 210
Davenport Ford, Va., 210
"Davids," 185–86
Davis, Jefferson: Mexican War, 12, 14–15; as secretary of war, 15, 54; commits CSA to war, 29; strategy, 31, 47; and coal-lump torpedo, 43; First Bull Run, 51; and McClellan, 54; military administration, 58–59; and A. S. Johnston, 64; and Polk, 65; errors in judgment, 79, 87; and Bragg, 100; as war leader, 152–54; Red River campaign, 199; and J. E. Johnston, 211, 220; and Sherman's march, 227; capture of, 235
Deavers, Bridget, 86–87
Decatur, Battle of, 221
Deer Creek expedition, 130
Defeat, 204
Defeatism, 239
Defense, 172–73, 212–13
"Defensive-offensive," 31–32, 149–50
Delafield, Richard, 54
Delafield Commission, 21, 54–55
Delaware, 30
Delvigne, Henri-Gustave, 2
Department No. 2, 64
Department of Alabama, Mississippi, and East Louisiana, 193
Department of the Cumberland, 188
Department of the Northwest, 95

Department of the Ohio, 188
Department of the Tennessee, 188
Devil's Den, 145–46
Disease, 11, 17, 20, 22, 90, 114
Divers, Bridget. See Deavers, Bridget
Divisional badges, 114
Division of the Potomac. See Army of the
    Potomac
Dix, John A., 162–63
Dix-Hill cartel, 162–63
Dominican Republic, 54
Double-barreled cannon, 41–42. See also
    Cannon; Weaponry
Double envelopment, 97
Draft. See Conscription
Dreyse, Nikolaus von, 249
Ducrot, Auguste Alexandre, 252
Duryee, Abram, 94–95

Eads Shipbuilding Company, 66
Early, Jubal, 218; Fredericksburg, 109;
    Chancellorsville campaign, 116–19;
    Gettysburg campaign, 143–44; Fisher's Hill,
    224; Rockfish Gap, 231–32
Earthworks, 217. See also Fortifications
Eaton, Clement, 153
Ebenezer Church, Battle of, 234
Ecole Militaire Superieure, 249
Ecole Polytechnique, 6
El Alamein, Battle of, 260
Elkhorn Tavern. See Pea Ridge, Battle of
Ellis, E. John, 103
Elyton, Ala., 233–34
Emancipation Proclamation, 156–57. See also
    Abolition
Enfilade fire, 94. See also Tactics
Engineers. See Army Corps of Engineers
England. See Britain
Enlisted personnel, 35–37
Entrenchments, 18, 21, 43–45, 121, 215;
    Shiloh, 69, 80; Antietam, 97–98; the
    Wilderness, 208–9; Spotsylvania, 214;
    North Anna, 215; Cold Harbor, 216;
    around Richmond, 216–17; Petersburg,
    216–17, 236; Nashville campaign, 229. See
    also Fortifications
Ericcson, John, 2, 57
Escott, Paul D., 36, 73
Ewell, Richard S., 121, 206; Valley campaign,
    85; Gettysburg, 143–44; Bristoe Station,
    186; the Wilderness, 208–9
Expansible army, 12

Ezra Church, Battle of, 221, 223

Fabian Strategy, 220. See also Strategy
Fair Oaks, Battle of, 86–87, 210
Falling Waters, W.Va., 150
Falmouth, Va., 111, 140
Farragut, David G., 131, 219
Far Western territory, 62, 64, 74
Fayetteville, N.C., 231, 235–36
Fayetteville Armory, 39
Fieldworks, 229. See also Fortifications
Fifth New York Zouaves, 94–95
Fifty-fourth Massachusetts (Colored)
    Infantry, 159–60
Firepower, 2, 255, 258. See also Weaponry
Fisher's Hill, Battle of, 224
Fishing Creek. See Beech Grove, Battle of
First Kansas Colored, 158
First South Carolina Volunteers, 158
Five Forks, Battle of, 237
Flags, 50
Floyd, John B., 65, 67
Flying battery, 109
Foote, Andrew H., 66
Foragers. See Bummers
Foreign observers, 176
Forrest, Nathan Bedford, 136, 166–68,
    175–76, 195–96, 200–205, 232–35, 238;
    Fort Donelson, 67; Holly Springs, 128;
    Fort Pillow, 160; Chickamauga, 171; Brice's
    Cross Roads, 200–205
Fort DeRussy, La., 199
Fort Donelson, 65–67, 73, 210
Fort Fisher, 174, 231
Fort Harrison, 217
Fort Henry, 65–67, 73
Fortifications, 18, 21, 80, 94, 121, 254; the
    Wilderness, 209–9; Sherman's use of, 215;
    at Petersburg, 216. See also Entrenchments
Fort Leavenworth, 255–56, 259
Fort Monroe, 256
Fort Morgan, 219
Fort Pemberton, 130
Fort Pillow, Tenn., 160
Fort Pulaski, 174
Forts: naming of, 217
Fort Steadman, 237
Fort Stevens, 218
Fort Sumter, 29, 46–48, 158, 238
Fort Vancouver, B.C., 54
Foster, Gaines M., 150
Foster, William Lovelace, 134

Fourteen Mile Creek, Miss., 132
France, 5–6, 17–18, 20, 31, 248–53, 260
Franco-Prussian War, 248–53, 260
Franklin, campaign and Battle of, 136
Franklin, William B., 107–8
Fraternization, 37
Frayser's Farm. *See* White Oak Swamp, Battle of
Fredericksburg, Va., 99, 106–12, 116, 118, 120, 140, 149
Frederick the Great, 152
Freeman, Douglas S., 260
Fremont, John C., 85–85, 158
French system, 257
Froeschwiller, Battle of, 250–51
Frontal battle, 229
Front Royal, Battle of, 85
Fulton, Robert, 2, 42
"Funnel effect," 129

Gaines, Edmund P., 10
Gatling gun, 39. *See also* Weaponry
Geary, John W., 188
Generalship, 106–12, 133, 174–76
General staff. *See* Staff
Geography, 151, 248–49
Geologic surveys, 254
Georgia, 218, 252
Germana Ford, 208
German American History Institute, 248
Germany, 248, 250, 252, 253
Gettysburg, 44, 125, 139–50, 165
Gettysburg National Military Park, 125
"Ghost Dance," 150
Glendale. *See* White Oak Swamp, Battle of
Gneisenau, August Wilhelm von, 5
Goen, C. C., 31
Gordon, John B., 208, 238
Grand Army of the Republic, 137
Grand Crimean Railway, 20
Grand Gulf, La., 131
Granger, Gordon, 172
Grant, Julia Dent, 128
Grant, Ulysses S., 61, 63, 68, 174, 206–8; strategy, 66–67, 121, 128, 132, 156, 183, 198, 200, 225, 227–28, 238; Forts Henry and Donelson, 67; promoted, 67–68, 192, 246; Shiloh, 68–71, 73; Vicksburg campaign and siege, 127, 130–35, 170; and prisoner exchange, 162–63; and Rosecrans, 170; Vicksburg campaign contrasted with Tullahoma campaign,

170; after Chickamauga, 188; Battle above the Clouds, 189; Missionary Ridge, 190–91; and Sheridan, 191; and Meade, 206; Spotsylvania, 212–14; and Upton, 213–14, 257–58; North Anna, 215; Cold Harbor, 216; Petersburg, 216–17, 237–38; City Point, 219; and Thomas, 229; orders Wilmington seized, 231; and Sheridan, 252; and Bismarck, 253–54; on slavery, 254
Gravelotte-St. Privat, Battle of, 251
Great Sioux Uprising, 95
Greeley, Horace, 110
Grierson, Benjamin H., 131
Groveton, Battle of, 93
Guderian, Heinz, 260
Guerilla warfare, 151, 164–69, 224, 238
Gunboats, 66, 198; Shiloh, 70; Vicksburg siege, 133; Red River campaign, 199–200; Mobile Bay, 219; Nashville campaign, 229
Guntown. *See* Brice's Cross Roads, Battle of

Halleck, Henry W., 8, 63–66, 71–72, 95, 246; Forts Henry and Donelson, 66–68; advances to Corinth, Miss., 71–72; and McClellan, 96; and Burnside, 111; and Rosecrans, 132; Gettysburg campaign, 142; and simultaneous advance, 155–56; stalemate in Virginia, 156; opposes siege of Richmond, 216; and taking of Atlanta, 224; and war policy, 227
Hamilton, Alexander, 6
Hampton Roads, Va., 57–58
Hancock, Winfield Scott, 120, 206, 208–9, 215, 246
Hardee, William J., 21, 44, 65; Army of Tennessee, 73; Kentucky campaign, 101–2; Stones River, 104; Atlanta campaign, 211, 221–22
Hard-war policy, 90–92, 125, 154, 192, 194, 224–27, 232, 252
Harker, Charles, 190–91
Harney, William S., 10
Harper's Ferry, 12, 37–39, 96
Hatcher's Run, Battle of, 236–37
Hatteras Inlet, 72
Heintzelman, Samuel P., 10–11, 81–82
Heliograph, 254
Hennessy, John, 93
Hesseltine, William B., 68
Heth, Henry, 143
Higginson, Thomas Wentworth, 158
Hill, Ambrose Powell, 121, 206, 212; Malvern Hill, 89; Second Bull Run, 92; Antietam, 98;

Fredericksburg, 109; Gettysburg campaign, 140, 143, 147; Bristoe Station campaign, 186–87; Wilderness campaign, 208–9

Hill, Daniel H., 86, 89, 162–63

Hill, Samuel S., 31

Hitchcock, Ethan Allan, 79

Hittle, J. D., 21

Hodgers, Jeannie. *See* Cashier, Albert D. J.

Holly Springs, Miss., 128

Hood, John B., 230; Gettysburg, 145, 226; Chickamauga, 171; Atlanta campaign, 211, 215, 221–23; Bald Hill, 221–23; after Atlanta falls, 224; attempts Tennessee invasion, 224; Nashville campaign, 228–30

Hooker, Joseph, 112, 113–15, 119, 142–43, 156, 209, 246; Second Seminole War, 11; Fredericksburg, 107–9; Chancellorsville, 113–20; Gettysburg, 139–42; around Chattanooga and Missionary Ridge, 187–90

"Hooker's Division," 115

"Hornet's Nest," 70–71, 121

Hospitals. *See* Medical care; Nursing

Hotchkiss, Jedediah, 139

Hough, Daniel, 48

Howard, Oliver O., 246; Chancellorsville campaign, 115, 117–19; Atlanta campaign, 223; Bentonville, 235

Howitzer, 40, 198. *See also* Weaponry

Huger, Benjamin, 89

Hunley, Horace L., 196–97

Hunt, Henry J., 88–90, 147

Hunter, David, 158, 216

Huntington, Samuel P., 3

Huntsville, Ala., 90

Hurlbut, Stephen A., 69

Imboden, John D., 150

Indiana, 165–66

Indians, 95, 248; Pea Ridge, 72

Indian Wars, 246–48, 254

Infantry and Cavalry School, 259

Inkerman, Battle of, 18–20

Insignia, 50

Intelligence, 83, 87–88, 116

Interior lines, 152; Antietam, 98

Ironclads, 56–58

Island No. 10, 61

Italy, 249, 253

Ivey's Farm, Miss., 195–96

Jackson, Miss., 132

Jackson, Thomas J. ("Stonewall"), 83, 85, 118, 143, 147; First Bull Run, 50–51; Valley campaign, 83–85; and McClellan, 84; Malvern Hill, 89; Second Bull Run, 92–94; Antietam, 96–97; Fredericksburg, 107, 109; Chancellorsville campaign, 116–18

Jackson, William H. ("Red"), 238

Jacksonian attitude, 9

James River, 58, 232

James River Canal, 232

Jamieson, Perry, 31, 44, 73

Jena, Battle of, 4

Jessup, Thomas S., 10

Johnson, Ludwell, 152

Johnston, Albert Sidney, 64–65, 69–70

Johnston, Joseph E., 87, 110, 168, 194, 209, 220–21, 231, 237, 238; Second Seminole War, 11; First Bull Run, 49; Peninsula campaign, 81, 83, 86–87; Vicksburg campaign, 131–33; Atlanta campaign, 210–11, 214–15; Bentonville, 235–36

Joint Committee to Examine the Conduct of the War, 80–81, 114

Jomini, Antoine Henri, Baron de, 6, 85

Jonesboro, Battle of, 223–24

"Jug-handle movement," 209

Julio, E. B. D. Fabrina, 117

Kearny, Philip, 95, 114

Kentucky, 30, 100–102, 105, 164–66

Kernstown, First Battle of, 84

Keyes, Erasmus D., 82, 86

Kirkland, Richard, 110

Kriegaskademie, 5

Ku Klux Klan, 247

La Glorieta Pass, Battle of, 62

Lane, Jim, 158, 159

Laurel Hill, Va., 212

Lawrence, Kans., 168

Leadership, 207, 239

Lee, Fitzhugh, 93, 161, 238

Lee, Robert E., 58–60, 87, 88, 99, 121, 183, 206, 209, 221, 238; Mexican War, 15–16; Malvern Hill, 89–90; Second Bull Run, 91–95; Antietam campaign, 96, 99; Fredericksburg, 99, 107–11; Maryland and Kentucky, 101–2; as general, 106, 120–21, 150, 152, 221, 260; Chancellorsville campaign, 115–21; Gettysburg campaign, 139–50, 151, 157; Bristoe Station campaign, 186–87; the Wilderness, 209; Spotsylvania, 212, 214; North Anna, 215; Petersburg, 216–17; Shenandoah valley, 217; Hatcher's Run, 237; after Petersburg, 237–38

Lee, Mrs. Robert E., 140

Lee, Stephen D., 194, 196, 239; Second Bull Run, 93–94, 121; Chickasaw Bayou campaign, 128–29; and Forest, 201; Nashville, 229–30

Leed's Foundry, 196

Leipzig, Battle of, 5

Liddell Hart, Basil, 260

Lincoln, Abraham, 29, 35, 56, 72, 162, 164, 218, 227, 238; strategy of, 32, 48, 52, 81, 90–92, 152, 154–56, 183, 198–99, 225, 238; Fort Sumter, 46, 48; military management of, 50–51, 53, 56, 79, 81–82, 95–96, 106–7, 111, 113–14, 132, 206, 216, 245; Antietam, 98–99; Gettysburg campaign, 141–42, 150

Line, 45, 257. *See also* Tactics

Line of communications, 96, 226

Little Bighorn, Battle of the, 248

Little Crow, 95

Little Round Top, 144–45

Livermore, Mary, 135

Logan, John, 207

Logan's Cross Roads. *See* Beech Grove, Battle of

Logistics: Kentucky campaign, 103; Vicksburg campaign, 132, 134; siege of Chattanooga, 188; and Forrest, 201; Appomattox campaign, 237; Indian Wars, 247–48

"Long Pull," 125, 151–63

Longstreet, James, 150, 206; Malvern Hill, 89; Second Bull Run, 92–94, 107–11; Chancellorsville campaign, 115–16; Gettysburg, 143–47; Chickamauga, 170–72; Wauhatchie Station, Tenn., 188; the Wilderness, 208–9; Spotsylvania, 212

Lookout Mountain, Tenn., 172

Loose-order formation, 45. *See also* Tactics

Losses: Contreras, 16; First Bull Run, 51; Shiloh, 71; Peninsula campaign, 87; Seven Days campaign and Malvern Hill, 90; Second Bull Run, 92–95; Antietam, 98; Perryville, 102; Stones River, 104–5; Fredericksburg, 110; Chancellorsville, 117–18, 120; Chickasaw Bayou, 129; Port Hudson, 131, 137–38; Raymond, 132; Tullahoma campaign, 132; Champion's Hill, 133; Vicksburg siege, 133–35; Brandy Station, 141; Gettysburg, 149–50, 176; Bristoe Station campaign, 187; Missionary Ridge, 192; Mansfield, 199–200; Brice's Cross Roads, 205; the Wilderness, 209; Nashville campaign, 214; Spotsylvania,

214; Cold Harbor, 216; prior to Petersburg siege, 216; Fort Harrison, 217; impact of, 218, 239; Wilson's Raid, 234–35; Bentonville operations, 236; Petersburg, 237; Franco-Prussian War, 251

Lost Cause, Myth of, 165

"Lost Order," 96–97

Lowe, Thaddeus S. C., 56

Lyon, Nathaniel, 52

Machine guns, 39–40. *See also* Weaponry

MacMahon, Marie Edme Patrice Maurice de, 250–51, 252

Macon, Ga., 235

Madison, James, 6

Magruder, John B., 82, 89

Mahan, Dennis Hart, 8, 59

Mahon, John K., 10

Mail, 100, 236

Malvern Hill, Battle of, 88–90

Manassas, campaigns and Battles of. *See* Bull Run

Manassas Gap Railroad, 49

Manassas Junction, Va., 95

Manchester, Tenn., 132

Mansfield, Battle of, 199–200

Maps, 34, 53, 88, 139

March to the Sea, 224–27

Marksmanship, 45. *See also* Weaponry

Marszalek, John F., 256

Marye's Heights, 108–10, 119–29

Maryland, 30, 96–99, 107

Massed firepower, 45, 70, 88–89, 94, 148

Maxwell, John, 220

McClean, Wilmer, 238

McClellan, George B., 114, 120, 147, 218; and Crimean War, 21; in western Virginia, 48; assessments of, 52–56, 64, 81, 83, 103; writes cavalry manual, 54; designs saddle, 54–55, 220; commands Army of the Potomac, 55; and airpower, 56; 83; Peninsula campaign, 81, 83; and Jackson, 84; and Lincoln, 84; Fair Oaks, 86–87; Seven Days, 87–90; and Pope, 91; Second Bull Run, 92–93; Antietam campaign, 95–99, 106; and soldiers, 103; and Burnside, 107; and simultaneous advance, 156; tactical failure of, 209, 216

McClernand, John A., 69, 133

McCook, Alexander, 172

McCulloch, Ben, 52

McDonald, Forest, 31

McDowell, Battle of, 84

McDowell, Irvin, 48–49, 53, 81, 84–85, 246

McElwee, William, 260

McEvoy, Ambrose, 42

McLaws, Lafayette, 116, 118–19

McLemore's Cove, Ga., 170

McMurry, Richard, 152, 222

McPherson, James B., 210–11, 221–22

McPherson Ridge, 143

Meade, George Gordon, 206, 213, 246; Second
    Seminole War, 11; Fredericksburg, 109;
    Chancellorsville, 115–16, 119; Gettysburg,
    142–44, 174; Bristoe Station campaign,
    186–87; the Wilderness, 208–9

Medal of Honor, 145

Medical care: significance of in warfare,
    17; surgeons, 44; at Fort Sumter, 47–48;
    during Vicksburg siege, 134; Army Medical
    Library, 255. *See also* Nursing; Disease

Memorandum of Military Policy, 51

Memphis, Tenn., 61

Memphis and Charleston Railroad, 72

Memphis and Ohio Railroad, 66–67, 195

Meridian campaign, 192–96

Metz, 251, 253

Mexican War, 8–9, 12–17, 43–44, 53, 59;
    impact of, 69, 82, 91, 113, 142, 147, 150;
    Scott's campaign to Mexico City, 83

Military Department System, 34, 152–53

Military districts, 247

Military Division of the Mississippi, 210

Military education, 236, 258, 259. *See also*
    Schools

Military establishment, 245, 254–55

Military prisons, 37, 160–63

Military professionalism: emergence of, 2–9,
    17; South appreciates, 33; assessed, 174–76;
    Grant injects new level of, 207; Wilson's
    Raid, 234; criteria for, 245–47; emergence
    of, 246–60; professional associations, 256

Military Service Institution of the United
    States, 256

Militia, 9, 11; Gettysburg campaign, 142;
    source for officers, 174–76; defends against
    Smith, 195–96; and Upton, 258–59

Miller, Dore, 135

Millikin's Bend, Battle of, 159

Mill Springs. *See* Beech Grove, Battle of

Mine Creek, Battle of, 224

Mines: use of, 42–43; in Vicksburg siege,
    42–43, 133–34; at Yorktown, and ethics
    debate, 82–83; in defense of Battery Wagner,

159; refinements of, 185–86; delivery of,
    by submarine, 197–98; Mobile Bay, 219;
    destroy supply depot, 220; Bentonville, 236

Mine sweepers, 83

Minié, Claude Etienne, 2

Minié ball, 2, 17, 38–39

Missionary Ridge, Battle of, 189–92, 252

Missionary Ridge, Tenn., 172

Mississippi militia, 195–96

Mississippi Mounted Volunteers, 12, 14

Mississippi River, 32, 61, 127, 129–38, 174

Missouri, 30, 52, 168

Missouri State Guard, 52

Mobile, Ala., 136, 196–97, 198, 200, 206, 219,
    238

Mobile Bay, Battle of, 219

Mobilization, 31, 35, 248

Model 1857 gun howitzer, 40, 148. *See also*
    Weaponry

Moltke, Helmuth von, 249, 251–52

Monroe, James, 7

Monterrey, Battle of, 16

Montevallo, Ala., 234

Montfordville, Battle of, 101

Montgomery, Ala., 234–35

Moorhead, James H., 31

Morale, 125, 151, 154, 156–57, 176, 239–40;
    and Brice's Cross Roads, 201, 218; and
    Sherman's March, 227; Nashville, 229; and
    mail, 236

Mordecai, Alfred, 54

Morgan, George W., 129

Morgan, John Hunt, 164–66, 219

Mormon War of 1858, 64

Morse, Samuel F. B., 2

Mortar, 41, 133–34. *See also* Weaponry

Mortar shells, 134. *See also* Ammunition

Morton, John C., 201, 204

Mosby, John S., 87–88, 168–69, 238

Motivation, 35–37, 139

Mount Pleasant, S.C., 197

"Mud March," 111–12, 120

"Mule Shoe," 212–13

Munfordville, Ky., 101

Murfreesboro. *See* Stones River, Battle of

Murray, Williamson, 151

Muskets, 12, 18, 38–39, 62

"Napoleon," 40, 148. *See also* Weaponry

Napoleon Bonaparte, 4–5, 7, 46

Napoleonic warfare, 5–6, 146–47, 150

Napoleon III, 40, 146, 251–53

Nashville, campaign and Battle of, 136, 228–30
Nashville and Chattanooga Railroad, 104, 188
Nationalism, 36, 239–40
Navy, Confederate, 130, 196–98
Navy, Union, 72, 198, 227; Peninsula campaign, 82–83, 88–90; Chickasaw Bayou and Vicksburg campaigns, 128–31, 134
New Bern, N.C., 72
New Orleans, La., 72, 99, 196
Newspapers, 49, 253
New York City, 157
Nightingale, Florence, 17
Ninth Ohio Regiment, 90
Nolan, Allan, 106
Norfolk, Va., 86
North Anna, Battle of the, 210, 215
North Carolina, 48, 107, 231. *See also* Carolinas
Nursing: significance of in warfare, 17; after Fort Sumter, 48; "Michigan Bridget," 86–87; in Vicksburg siege, 134. *See also* Medical care

Oak Hills. *See* Wilson's Creek, Battle of
Offensive-defensive strategy, 149. *See also* Strategy
Officers, 33
Ohio, 165–66
Okolona, Miss., 195
One Hundred Twenty-first New York Infantry, 212–13
Ord, Edward O. C., 11, 217, 246
Osceola, Chief, 10
Ox Hill. *See* Chantilly, Battle of

Palmetto Armory, 39
Paris, 253
Parole, 162–63
Parrott, Robert P., 40
Parrott guns, 41, 198
Partridge, Alden, 7
Patterson, Robert, 49
Patton, George S., 260
Peacetime, 246–48, 258
"Peach Orchard," 145
Peachtree Creek, Battle of, 221
Pea Ridge, Battle of, 72
Pelham, John, 109
Pemberton, John C., 11, 131–35
Peninsula campaign, 81–90
Pennsylvania, 142
Percussion cap. *See* Ammunition

Perryville, Battle of, 100–103
Petersburg, campaign and siege of, 216–17, 231, 236–37
Petersburg-Richmond Railroad, 207
Pettigrew, James J., 143, 147–48, 150, 175–76
Philippi, Battle of, 48
Phillips, Charles, 147
Photography, 17, 98
Pickett, George E., 144, 147–48, 150
Pickett's Charge, 146–50, 216
Pierce, Franklin, 15, 54
Pillow, Gideon J., 65, 67
Pinkerton, Allan, 83
Pittsburg Landing. *See* Shiloh, campaign and Battle of
Platoons, 257
Pleasant Grove. *See* Mansfield, Battle of
Pleasant Hill, La., 200
Pleasonton, Alfred, 140–41
Polk, James K., 13
Polk, Leonidas J., 72–73, 193–94; and Davis, 65; Kentucky campaign, 101–2; Chickamauga, 172; Atlanta campaign, 211–11
Political generals, 65, 207
Politics, 13–14, 34, 65, 151, 183, 198–99, 206–7, 216, 218, 239, 245
Pollard, Edward A., 15
Pontoons, 233; Fredericksburg, 108, 111–12, 140; Chattanooga, 188; Petersburg, 217. *See also* Bridges
Pope, John, 90–92, 95–96, 209, 246; Mexican War, 91; Army of Virginia, 91–95; Second Bull Run, 93–94
Porter, David D., 131, 199
Porter, Fitz John, 87–88, 94
Port Gibson, Miss., 131
Port Hudson, campaign and Battles of, 127, 130–31, 137–38, 159
Port Republic, Battle of, 85
Port Royal, S.C., 72, 174
Prairie Station, Miss., 195
Prentiss, Benjamin M., 69–70
Price, Sterling, 52, 103, 136, 224–25
Principles of war, 85–86, 95; at Antietam, 97; in western theater, 101; listed, 200–201; and Forrest, 200–205
Prisoners of war, 160–63
Prisons. *See* Military prisons
Professionalism. *See* Military professionalism
Propaganda, 151
Prostitution, 115

Prussia, 2–5, 248–53, 260
Prussian model, 258
Prussian system, 250
Pryor, Roger, 47–48
Psychological factors, 36–37, 43, 50–51, 82, 120, 125, 156–57, 160, 239–40; and Ewell, 143; Vicksburg siege, 134; and slavery, 154; and black troops, 157, 150; hard war, 225, 227, 230

Quaker guns, 82
Quantrill, William Clarke, 168

Race relations, 247
Racism, 36–37. *See also* Segregation; Black troops
Raglan, Fitzroy James Henry Somerset, First Baron, 17–19
Raiders, 164–69
Raids, 164–69, 196, 225
Railroads, 2, 20, 49–50, 66, 82, 88, 104, 127, 151, 164, 197, 207, 209; Baltimore and Ohio, 48; strategic redeployment, 49, 170; transcontinental span, 54; Corinth, 68; Memphis and Charleston, 72; after Shiloh, 73; Valley campaign, 85; Antietam campaign, 95; Kentucky campaign, 100; Vicksburg campaign, 132; Chickamauga campaign, 170–71; Chattanooga and Missionary Ridge, 187–88; and Sherman, 193; destroyed, 195; Brice's Cross Roads, 201; Atlanta campaign, 211, 215; and Army of the Potomac, 216; Petersburg, 217; and Sherman, 225–27, 232; and Sheridan, 231; Appomattox campaign, 237–38; military value of, 237–38, 246, 250, 252
Rains, Gabriel J., 11, 42–43, 82, 159
Rains fuse, 159
Ramage, James A., 165
Ranson, Thomas E. E., 207
Rapidan River, 115, 208
Rappahannock River, 107, 111, 115, 119, 139
Raymond, Battle of, 132
Reagan, John H., 139
Rebel Yell, 117
Reconstruction, 247, 254–56
Redans, 216. *See also* Fortifications
Redoubt, 229. *See also* Fortifications
Red River, 53, 129–30
Red River campaign, 136, 198–200
Regular Army, 11–12, 33–34, 35, 65, 212, 246–48, 255, 258–59; Second Seminole War, 10–11; Mexican War, 15; and McClellan,

55; and Buell, 64; Army of the Potomac, 81; and Terry, 174
Reinzi, Miss., 201
Religion, 13, 31, 156, 240
Rensselaer Polytechnic Institute, 8
Repeating weaponry, 39–40, 232–33. *See also* Weaponry
Revolvers, 62, 166, 233. *See also* Weaponry
Reynolds, John F., 118–19
Richmond, Va., 48, 141, 210, 211–12, 217, 236
Richmond and Danville Railroad, 237–38
Richmond and New York Railroad, 88
Richmond Armory, 39
Rifled artillery, 40. *See also* Weaponry
Rifles: evolving qualities of, 2, 9, 12, 14, 17–22, 37–39, 173, 251, 255; types of, 12, 14, 17–19, 21, 37–40, 166, 173, 255; Gettysburg, 145; defensive value, 154; as clubs, 203
Riply, Miss., 201
Riverine war, 66, 130
Roanoke Island, 72, 162
Roberts, Roy P., 4
Rockfish Gap, Va., 231–32
Rodman, Thomas J., 40
Rodman gun, 40
Rohrbach Bridge, 97. *See also* Bridges
Rolling Fork expedition, 130
Roon, Albrecht von, 249–50
Rosecrans, William S., 103, 156, 188, 246; Stones River, 103–5; Tullahoma campaign, 131–32; Chickamauga, 169–72; Chattanooga and Missionary Ridge, 187
Round Top, 144
Royal Military College, 6
Royster, Charles, 36, 255, 261
Rushes, 44. *See also* Tactics
Russell, William Howard: Crimean War, 17, 20; First Bull Run, 49; debacle of Sedan, 252
Russia, 5 17–21, 42, 54, 249, 252, 253

Sabers, 141, 233, 251, 258
Sabine Crossroads. *See* Mansfield, Battle of
Salt River, 102
San Augustin, Battle of, 16
Sandhurst, 260
Sanson, Emma, 166–67
Santa Anna, Antonio Lopez de, 14–16
Santa Fe, N.Mex., 62
Savage Station, Battle of, 88
Savannah, Ga., 227–28, 230
Savannah River, 227–28

Sayler's Creek, Battle of, 237–38
Scharnhorst, Gerhard Johann von, 5
Schofield, John M., 231, 246; Atlanta
  campaign, 210, 215, 223; Nashville
  campaign, 228–30; Bentonville, 235–36
School of Application for Infantry and
  Cavalry, 255–56
Schools, 4–7, 34, 46, 197, 234, 249, 255–56,
  258–60. *See also* West Point
Scorched-earth policy, 224. *See also* Hard-war
  policy
Scott, Winfield, 7, 10, 32, 34, 255; Mexican
  War, 13–17; and McClellan, 53, 55, 82; and
  R. E. Lee, 59; and Halleck, 64
Screw propeller, 57. *See also* Navy
Secession, 29
Second Seminole War, 8–11, 82, 113, 142
Second South Carolina Volunteers, 110
Secret Service. *See* Confederate Secret Service
  Corps
Sedan, debacle of, 252–53
Sedgwick, John, 118–19, 140, 206, 212
Segregation, 246–47. *See also* Racism
Selma, Ala., 232, 234–35
Seminole Wars: First and Third, 9. *See also*
  Second Seminole War
Sevastopol, 18–21
Seven Days campaign, 87–91, 215
Seven Pines, Battle of. *See* Fair Oaks, Battle of
Seventh Connecticut, 174
Sharpshooting, 39, 173, 188
Shaw, Robert Gould, 159–60
Shelby, Joseph O., 168
Shenandoah valley, 139, 216, 217, 219, 231–32
Sheridan, Philip H., 174, 191, 224, 237–38,
  246, 252, 253–54; Stones River, 104;
  Missionary Ridge, 190–92; and Grant,
  209–10; Shenandoah valley, 216, 219, 224,
  231–32; Petersburg, 237–38
Sherman, John, 192
Sherman, William T., 166–67, 174, 188,
  210, 225–26, 227, 238, 246, 254, 255–59;
  Second Seminole War, 11; First Bull
  Run, 50; Shiloh, 69; Chickasaw Bayou
  campaign, 128–29; Vicksburg, 131; at
  Missionary Ridge, 189–90; and Sheridan,
  191; Meridian campaign, 192–96; Atlanta
  campaign, 210–12, 214–15, 218, 221–24;
  March to the Sea, 224–27; march through
  the Carolinas, 230–31; Bentonville, 235–36;
  Franco-Prussian War, 252

Shiloh, campaign and Battle of, 68–73, 121,
  210
Ship Island, Miss., 72
Shotguns, 39, 62, 166. *See also* Weaponry
Sibley, Henry Hastings, 95
Sibley, Henry Hopkins, 62
Sickles, Daniel E., 117–19, 145
"Sickles' Salient," 145
Siege warfare, 18–22, 41, 82, 121
Sigel, Franz, 52, 206
Signal Corps, 254
Signaling, 50, 97. *See also* Communications
Simultaneous advance: North's ultimate
  strategy of, 51–52; refined, 155–56, 183;
  Meridian campaign, 196; and Grant, 200,
  225; and Lincoln, 225
Skelton, William R., 4
Skirmishers, 45, 173, 257
Slavery: as cause of Civil War, 29–30, 254;
  and racism, 36–37; and psychology and
  morale, 142, 154, 156–58; and captured
  black troops, 161; elimination of as war
  aim, 239, 254
Slaves, 195, 230, 234, 236, 247
Slocum, Henry W., 115–16, 118–19, 235–36
Smith, Edmund Kirby, of, 101, 168
Smith, John E., 207
Smith, Morgan L., 207
Smith, W. Sooy, 193–96
Snipers, 39, 173
Solferino, Battle of, 146
Somerset. *See* Beech Grove, Battle of
South Atlantic Blockading Squadron, 227
South Carolina, 46, 58, 174, 196–97, 230. *See
  also* Carolinas
South Mountain, Battle of, 96
Spiked helmet, 249
Spotsylvania, campaign and Battle of, 44,
  212–14
Sprichern, Battle of, 250
Springfield Armory, 38
Spring Hill Affair, 228
Spying, 83. *See also* Confederate Secret Service
  Corps; Pinkerton, Allan
Squads, 257
St. Augustine, Fla., 72
St. Paul, Minn., 54
Staff, 5–6, 34, 59, 79–80, 83, 87, 89, 206–7,
  248–51, 259
Stalemate, 79–80, 120, 156, 217, 238, 260
Staunton, Edwin M., 79, 81, 187–88
Staunton, Va., 231

Steam-powered vessels, 2, 151. *See also* Navy
Steele, Frederick, 131
Steele's Bayou expedition, 130
Steinmetz, Karl Friedrich von, 250
Stephenson, George, 2
Stevens, Isaak I., 95
Stewart, Alexander P., 221
Still, William, 36, 239
Stones River, Battle of, 102–5, 132
Strategic redeployment, 49, 187–89. *See also* Simultaneous advance
Strategy, 31–32, 34, 51, 155–56, 183
Streight, Abel D., 167
Stuart, James E. B., 99, 110–11, 210; Seven Days campaign, 87–88; Chancellorsville campaign, 115–18; Gettysburg campaign, 140–41, 143–44; Bristoe Station campaign, 186
Sturgis, Samuel, 91, 167, 201–5
Submarines, 196–98
Successive rushes, 44. *See also* Tactics
Sumner, Edwin V., 81, 97, 107–10
Sunken Road, 98. *See also* Entrenchments
Supply. *See* Logistics
Susquehanna River, 143

Tactics, 8, 43–45, 67, 134, 174, 204, 212–14, 255, 257–59; Chancellorsville, 117, 120; Chickasaw Bayou, 129; Brice's Cross Roads, 200–205; the Wilderness, 209; North Anna, 215; Franklin, 229
Taylor, Richard, 199–200
Taylor, Walter H., 236
Taylor, Zachary, 10, 13–15
Technology, 2–3, 8, 56–58, 151, 173, 185–86, 196, 251, 254–55. *See also* specific types
Telegraph, 2, 17, 20, 73, 100, 127–28, 187, 207, 246, 254
Telephone, 254
Tennessee, 30, 48, 100–101, 105, 166–67, 196, 224, 252
Tennessee River, 65, 67
Tents, 18
Terry, Alfred H., 174–75, 231, 246
Texas, 53–54, 62, 64, 131
Thayer, John Milton, 129
Thayer, Sylvanus, 7–9
Thermoplyae, Battle of, 128
Third Louisiana Redan, 133
Thirty-fifth Mississippi Infantry, 134
Thirty-fifth Ohio Regiment, 90
Thirty-third U.S. Colored Infantry, 158

Thomas, George H., 174, 188, 231, 246; Second Seminole War, 11; Beech Grove, 65–66; Stones River, 104; Chickamauga, 171–73; Missionary Ridge, 189–90; Atlanta campaign, 210; Nashville campaign, 228–30
Tishomingo Creek, Battle of. *See* Brice's Cross Roads
Todd's Tavern, Va., 212
Tolstoy, Count Lev Nikolaevich, 21
Topographical Engineers, 142
Torpedoes. *See* Mines
Totleben, E. I., 18
Training, 35, 55, 58, 114, 225–26, 232, 257–59. *See also* Schools; West Point
Treaty of Frankfurt, 253
Treaty of Guadalupe Hidalgo, 16
Trench warfare, 216. *See also* Siege warfare
Tullahoma campaign, 131–32, 170
Turkey, 17–18
Turning movement, 53, 59, 101, 154
Tuscaloosa, Ala., 234
Twentieth Maine Regiment, 145
Twenty-first Ohio Volunteer Infantry, 173
Twiggs, David E., 34

U.S. Army: evolution of, 11–12, 34, 48; 1861 organization of, 81, 93, 95; 1863 troops in, 164; post–Civil War work of, 246–48, 255; French influence, 249; in peacetime, 254–55. *See also* Regular Army
U.S. Army Ordnance Department, 12
U.S. Congress, 51, 258
U.S. Constitution, 245
U.S. Military Academy. *See* West Point
U.S. Sanitary Commission, 135
U.S. War Department, 257
Uniforms, 50
Upton, Emory, 35, 212–14, 232–34, 257–59
Urbana Plan, 82

Valley campaign, 83–85
Valverde, N.Mex., Battle of, 62
Vandiver, Frank E., 225
Van Dorn, Earl, 64, 103, 128
Vauban, Sebastien Le Prestre de, 21–22
Vera Cruz, 82
Veterans, 150, 167. *See also* Grand Army of the Republic; Lost Cause, Myth of
Vicksburg campaign and siege of, 125, 127–38, 165, 207
Vicksburg National Military Park, 125, 136
Vietnam War, 260
Vincent, Strong, 145

Virginia, 42, 48, 50, 219–20; and Lee, 106; stalemate in, 156; and Mosby, 168; and Early, 218; and Sheridan, 252
Virginia Central Railroad, 232
Virginia Military Institute, 34
Volunteers, 31, 34, 46, 51, 55, 58, 67, 95, 110; as officers, 174–76

Wade, Jennie, 150
Wagner, Arthur L., 259
Wakeman, Sarah Rosetta, 136
Wallace, Lew, 69–70
Wallace, William H. L., 69
War Board, 79–80, 87
Warfare, 121; evolution of, 3, 22, 56–60, 73, 120, 172–73, 201–5, 245, 249–54; Napoleonic, 6, 150, 172–73
War of 1812, 6, 157
Warren, Gouverneur K., 145, 206, 208–9
Wars of German Unification, 248–53
Washington, D.C., 81, 95, 107, 143, 218
Washington, George, 59–61, 81
Washington Monument, 254
Washington Navy Yard, 196
Watkins, Sam, 229
Wauhatchie Station, Tenn., 188–89
Weaponry: evolution of, 2, 9, 12, 14, 17–21, 31, 37–43, 56, 106–7, 141, 173, 225, 232–34; Valverde, 62; Fort Henry, 67; tactics modified by, 121, 212; Gettysburg, 148; types preferred by raiders, 166; Chickamauga, 173; naval guns, 198; Wilson's Raid, 232–33; Wars of German Unification, 249–53; Army experiments, 255; and Upton, 258. *See also* specific types
Weather, 67, 254; Shiloh, 69; Fair Oaks, 86; Kentucky campaign, 101; Perryville, 102; Stones River, 104; Mud March, 111–12; Tullahoma campaign, 132; Gettysburg campaign, 142; Brice's Cross Roads, 201; Spotsylvania, 214; Nashville campaign, 229–30
Weed, Stephen H., 145
Weldon Railroad, 216
Western Department, 63–64, 100

Western theater, 61, 63–65, 79, 156
West Point, 6–8, 11, 33–34, 40, 63–65, 74, 76, 83, 91, 113, 206, 209–10, 212, 232, 246–47, 256–58
West Port, Battle of, 224
West Virginia, 30, 58
Wheeler, Joseph, 168, 211, 221–22
White Oak Swamp, Battle of, 88
Whitney, Eli, Jr., 12
Wig Wag. *See* Signaling
Wilderness, campaign and Battle of the, 115–16, 208–9, 211
William I, King, 249, 252
Williams, T. Harry, 23, 47, 53–54
Wilmington, N.C., 219, 231
Wilson, James Harrison, 232–35
Wilson's Creek, Battle of, 52
Wilson's Raid, 232–35
Winchester, First Battle of, 85
Winchester, Va., 231
Women, 166–67, 239; as nurses, 17, 48; in combat, 86–87, 135–37; Vicksburg, 135–37; Gettysburg, 150
Wood, Thomas J., 171
Wood Lake, Battle of, 95
Wool, John E., 34
World War I, 260
World War II, 87, 96, 245, 260
Worth, William Jenkins, 10, 16
Wounded Knee, Battle of, 248

Xerxes, 250

Yazoo Pass expedition, 130
Yazoo River, 127–30, 133
Yellow Tavern, Va., 210
Yorktown, 82–83
Young, Charles, 246
Young, John Russell, 253–54
Young, Samuel M. B., 259
Young's Point, Miss., 131

Zollicoffer, Felix K., 65–66
Zouaves, 94

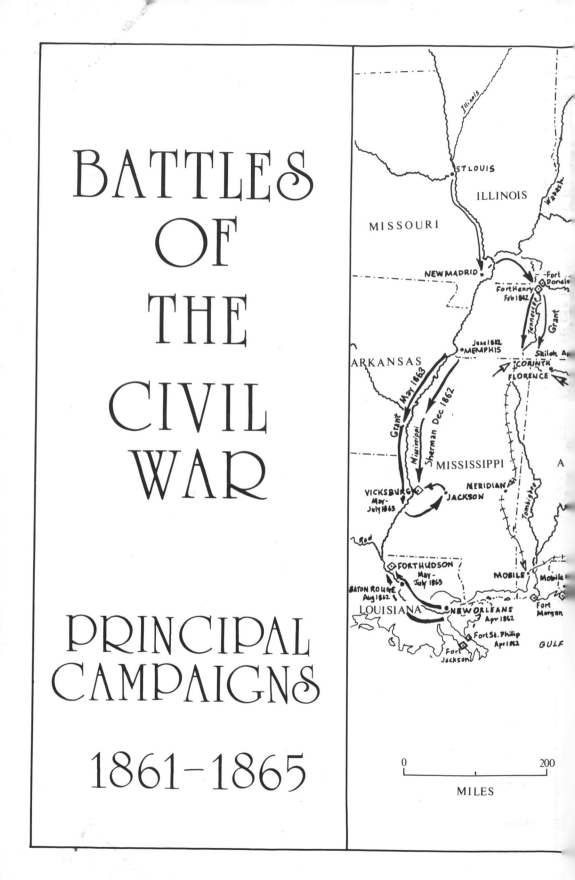

BATTLES
OF
THE
CIVIL
WAR

PRINCIPAL
CAMPAIGNS

1861–1865